FIRST CORINTHIANS
A FAITH COMMUNITY COMMENTARY

FIRST CORINTHIANS
A FAITH COMMUNITY
COMMENTARY

BY
GRAYDON F. SNYDER

MERCER UNIVERSITY PRESS
1992

ISBN 0-86554-393-3

BS
2675.3
.S59
1992

First Corinthians. A Faith Community Commentary.
Copyright ©1992
Mercer University Press
Macon, Georgia 31207 USA
All rights reserved
Printed in the United States of America

The paper used in this publication meets
the minimum requirements of American National Standard
for Information Sciences—Permanence of Paper
for Printed Library Materials, ANSI Z39.48–1984.

Library of Congress Cataloging-in-Publication Data

Snyder, Graydon F., 1930–

First Corinthians. A faith community commentary.
ix+267 pp. 6x9" (15x23 cm.).
Includes bibliographical references and index.
ISBN 0-86554-393-3 (alk. paper).
1. Bible. N.T. Corinthians, 1st—Commentaries. I. Title.
BS2675.3.S59   1991   91-35595
227'.207—dc20   CIP

CONTENTS

PREFACE

There are not many biblical commentaries written by scholars from the Radical Reformation churches. Yet the hermeneutic does differ from mainline interpretations. It comes to the Bible with particular faith experiences: a moral earnestness; a vital sense of community; a deep sense of the nearness of the Reign of God; a joy in family life; a loyalty to one's faith network; a refusal to use force; a life-style based on consensus and equality; and a love for Jesus who seeks all to be his disciples. When the Bible is read from this hermeneutical stance it can be quite different than when it is read from the more individualistic, sometimes academic exegesis of Western Christianity.

I have also come to the conviction that a community close to the original community can perceive things not apparent to a different type of social structure. I agree with those who say the early church was a close community with a fairly high sense of personal individuation. Coming from a similar modern community, though the historical circumstances are vastly different, makes it possible for us to empathize with the material in a manner not available to everyone.

For these reasons I find it a real privilege to share this particular reading of Paul's epistle with other readers. Very likely Paul's letter to the Christians at Corinth best exhibits the characteristics I have named above, and therefore makes most evident the distinctiveness of a free-church reading of the text.

When the text is read in the faith community, it is understood in terms of the whole people of God. Therefore each section of 1 Corinthians has been read in light of its biblical context. And the text is always read for direction in faith and practice. For each section there is a short reflection on present-day implications.

Many persons have helped me prepare this volume. I think primarily of the dozens of students at Bethany Theological Seminary and Chicago Theological Seminary who have dialogued with me regarding almost every verse. Recently some students and friends took the time to read this manuscript and make helpful suggestions. I thank especially George Cairns, Carolyn Thompson, and George Thomas. I had special assistance from colleagues Estella Horning, David Garber, and Howard Charles. Finally, I deeply appreciate the support shown by the staff at Chicago Theological Seminary: Linda Parrish, Rosalynn Russell, and Max Havlick.

—*Graydon F. Snyder*
Chicago Theological Seminary

*To a modern cross-cultural,
    multiracial inner-city church,
    First Church of the Brethren, Chicago,
    where, for the past forty years,
I have learned the meaning of membership
in the body of Christ.*

*Far be it from me to glory
except in the cross
of our Lord Jesus Christ,
by which the world has been crucified to me,
and I to the world.*
—GALATIANS 6:14

ABBREVIATIONS

TEXTS AND VERSIONS

Grk Greek New Testament (Nestle-Aland 26th ed.; UBS 3rd ed.)

ASV American Standard Version (OT + NT/1901
 = The Standard American Edition of the Revised Version)

ERV (English) Revised Version (NT/1881, OT/1885, Ap/1889)

CPV Cotton Patch Version (portions, 1968, 1969)

NASV New American Standard Version (NT/1963, OT/1971)
NASB NAS Bible = alternate and usual title for NASV

NIV New International Version (NT/1973, OT/1978)

NRSV New Revised Standard Version (OT + NT + Ap/1990, c1989)

RSV Revised Standard Version (NT/1946, ²1971, OT/1952, Ap/
 1957 + 1977)

INTRODUCTION

CORINTH

The great city of Corinth lies on an isthmus between the mainland of Greece and a peninsula called the Peloponnese/Peloponnesus. To the north of the isthmus lies a body of water, called the Gulf of Corinth, leading to the Ionian and Adriatic Seas. To the south the Saronic Gulf leads to the Aegean Sea. Because sailors of antiquity preferred to hug the coastlands rather than sail the open seas, Corinth handled much of the traffic between Greece and Asia Minor, on the one hand, and Italy, on the other. Boats loaded and unloaded at the southern harbor called Cenchreae, the town from which Paul embarked when he left Corinth for Ephesus (Acts 18:18). On the north side of the isthmus they used the harbor called Lechaeum. As the place where the transfer of goods occurred, Corinth by necessity became an international port city.

From the very beginning, then, Corinth was a multiracial, croscultural city. How could such a variety of people be included in one community of faith? The letter to the Corinthians is replete with problems created by cultural differences—eating meat offered to idols, the function of common religious meals, appropriate clothing for men and women during worship, and the ordering of worship itself.

Because of its favorable location Corinth has been inhabited since the fourth millenium BCE. Early during the first millennium BCE it became a Greek power until conflicts with Rome caused its destruction in 146 BCE. Just before his death in 44 BCE, Julius Caesar reestablished it as a Roman colony (*Colonia Laus Julia Corinthiensis*). This city, which Paul visited, would have been populated by Romans, Greeks, and Jews. As indicated, the combination of a multiethnic population and transient business gave Corinth a certain flavor well known among the Greeks.

Among the many ancient writers who provide us information about Corinth, the geographer Strabo may be the most helpful. In his *Geography* 8.6.20c (written about 7 BCE), he calls Corinth a "city of love" that attracted many because of its famous temple of Aphrodite. According to Strabo, this temple—located on a high hill called Acrocorinth (or "acropolis—high city—of Corinth"), to the south of the city—owned more than a thousand slaves and prostitutes. This may have been. But the archaeological remains on Acrocorinth do not substantiate the presence of such a large establishment. Regardless of the cause, Corinth's notoriety was widespread. The dramatist Aristophanes (450–385 BCE) coined the term *korinthiazesthai,* one who acts like a Corinthian, or fornicator. Paul surely alluded to the presence of loose sexual practices in Corinth when he said membership in the faith community did not allow intercourse with other communities (6:15-20).

Every other year Corinth was the home of the famous Isthmian games, second only to the Olympic games. The games also brought many people to the city and must have required constant preparation. Some have suggested Paul could flourish as a tentmaker in Corinth because of so many transients. In any case Paul spoke directly of the games in 9:24-27 when he compared the discipline of the Christian life with the discipline necessary to run in the games.

The games may have influenced Paul and the Corinthian Christians in yet another way. The Isthmian games apparently were conducted for both men and women. According to an inscription a certain Hermesianax congratulated his daughters—Tryphosa, Hedea, and Dionysia—for winning the 200 meter race at various times.[1] In Jewish circles women did not participate equally in synagogue worship, yet Paul speaks of equal participation at Corinth (11:5). Does this practice reflect Gentile churches in general, or was Corinth, accustomed to equal participation of women in public matters, an exception?

The Corinth rebuilt by Rome has been largely excavated. From the north, one approaches the city by the road from Lechaeum. The road—twenty to twenty-five feet wide—was lined with sidewalks and columns. At the juncture of the road and the main square was found a fragment of an inscription on a now-broken marble slab that reads

---

[1] Jerome Murphy-O'Connor, *St. Paul's Corinth: Texts and Archaeology* (Wilmington DE: Michael Glazier, 1983) 16.

...ΓΩΓΗΕΒΡ... .² That block of stone must have identified the building called ΣΥΝΑ]ΓΩΓΗΕΒΡ[ΑΙΩΝ ("Synagogue of the Hebrews"), a likely successor to the synagogue where Paul first preached (Acts 18:4).

As one enters the main square or *agora* at Corinth, the *bema,* or public rostrum, dominates the scene. It was here that Paul was brought to judgment (tribunal in Acts 18:12-17). The most imposing remain, though, is the sixth-century BCE temple of Apollo with seven of its original thirty-eight columns still standing. The *agora* itself was lined with shops. Though the issue of meat offered to idols still remains a mystery to us, we can be sure the kind of meat shop, or *makellon,* mentioned by Paul in 10:25 was located somewhere in the *agora.* At least one such inscription for a shop has been found nearby.

There are no signs of an early Christian community. We are not surprised. The first churches consistently met in houses. Until the year 300 we know of no buildings first built as churches.³

We have surely uncovered many house-churches in cities like Corinth, Ephesus, Pompeii, Ostia, Rome, and Philippi, but we have no means of identifying them. Surely Aquila and Priscilla owned such a house in Corinth (Acts 18:3; see 1 Cor. 16:19 and Romans 16:3-5), and we can suppose the same is true of Stephanas (1 Cor. 1:16; 16:15). Among the inscriptions found in Corinth one may refer to an early convert, Erastus (Rom. 16:23). As Paul sends his greetings from Corinth to Rome, he identifies Erastus as the city treasurer. A piece of pavement between the *agora* and the theatre bears an inscription which could be translated "Erastus in return for his aedileship laid (this pavement) at his own expense."⁴ Though an aedile was more the commissioner of public works than a city treasurer, many have supposed this is the same Erastus mentioned by Paul.

We also know there was a house-church at Cenchreae. In his letter to the church at Rome, written from Corinth, Paul commends to them Phoebe, a minister (*diakonos*) of the church in the harbor town of Cenchreae (Rom. 16:1-2).

²Murphy-O'Connor, *St. Paul's Corinth,* 78.
³Graydon F. Snyder, *Ante Pacem: Archaeological Evidence of Church Life Before Constantine* (Macon GA: Mercer University Press, 1985; rpt. 1991) 75.
⁴Murphy-O'Connor, *St. Paul's Corinth,* 37.

PAUL

The Apostle Paul has to be one of the most complex persons ever to cross the pages of Christian history. The author of 2 Peter acknowledged this complexity with his admission that the ignorant and unstable can find in Paul most anything they please. According to Luke even the Roman proconsul, Festus, could not understand him. Festus claimed Paul's great learning had made him crazy (Acts 26:24).

Some Christian groups have tended to avoid Paul. The figure of Jesus fits better their understanding of trust, community, and radical discipleship. But Christians who take seriously the close nature of the faith community, who seek reconciliation for all persons, who believe in a future without prejudice, abuse, and violence—such Christians will understand Paul and his Jesus Christ. It is well, then, for adherents of Jesus-centered churches, from their particular perspective, to read this Paul, who is called the "first Christian" by some because of the centrality of the Christ in his letters.

Paul was born and raised in Tarsus, the capital of the Roman province of Cilicia, located just a few miles from the coast in southeast Asia Minor. The city was an ancient (neolithic) site, prominent because of its location in a fertile plain near the Mediterranean Sea. During the Roman period it was known as an intellectual center. At the time of Paul it was surely populated by Greeks, Romans, and Jews, though practically nothing is known of the Jewish colony there.

We can be sure Paul grew up in a multicultural environment well known for its cultural and intellectual life. It may be Paul was educated in such a Hellenistic milieu, but if the Jewish population was of any significant size, Paul would also have been trained in the synagogue. His letters do reflect a good command of the Greek language, the use of Greek epistolary form, and some Greek rhetorical style. He must have learned his Greek style in Tarsus. On the other hand, Paul's use of the Hebrew Bible, his method of argument, and his vocabulary point to a rabbinical style of education (Phil. 3:5). In addition to his Jewish education at Tarsus, Paul was sent to Jerusalem to study under the famous Gamaliel (Acts 22:3), a liberalizing student of the teacher Hillel.

We can only suppose Paul came from a fairly well-to-do family which had the resources to support such a remarkable education. In any case the result was astounding. In Paul we had a Jew who knew the Hebrew Bible and rabbinic thought as well as anyone. We had a Greek who could communicate throughout the Mediterranean world, even to the Greek academy (Acts 17:16-34). He spoke Greek and Hebrew (Aramaic?) fluently (Acts 21:37-22:2). He confounded his opponents by appearing to be Greek (Acts 21:37), appearing to be Hebrew (Acts 22:2), and, when necessary, identifying himself as a Roman citizen (Acts 16:37)—another sign of the prominence of his family in Tarsus. As Paul himself told the Corinthians, he was all things to all people (1 Cor. 9:22).

Paul was in Jerusalem when Christianity began. We cannot be sure he ever knew Jesus, though some read 2 Cor. 5:16 that way. We cannot fully comprehend why Paul and other Jews so violently opposed the new faith. What was at stake? Few people have been killed simply because their ideas were different (see Matt. 26:65-66). The Jews themselves presented Jesus as a threat to the *pax romana,* the military peace created by the Romans (Luke 23:2). It seems likely the Jews, and perhaps the Romans, saw in Jesus a (Zealot-like) revolutionary leader who would lead some Palestinians in an insurrection against the power of Rome. The ruling Jews did not want their rapproachment with Rome disrupted. Apparently Jesus was killed as a messianic pretender in order to save the Jewish-Roman coalition (John 11:50). Presumably some of the disciples, like Peter, Simon the Zealot, James and John (the sons of thunder), and particularly Judas Iscariot ("knife-man"?) could not themselves see that Jesus avoided the violence of the revolutionaries. Jesus did speak of the imminence of the coming kingdom, but he did not advocate a violent takeover.

Did the Jewish Sanhedrin (ruling body) see in the first Christian movement a continuing threat to the peace of Palestine? Did they see in the Way (Acts 22:4) a threat to the worldwide Jewish community? Did apocalyptic Judaism (Christianity, Zealots, Qumran community) thoroughly disrupt the Jewish worldview? The answer to all of the above may be yes. We do know that Jerusalem leaders intended to stamp out the new movement and later Paul himself was opposed by Jews wherever he went.

Jesus was likely crucified during the Passover of the year 33 (presumably the 15th of Nisan, or 3 April). Most readers allow about a year and a half for the new community to develop and for the persecution to gain momentum. During that time the Jerusalem community met for worship and the breaking of bread (Acts 2:43-47). Eventually they elected deacons, Jews of the diaspora, to help with the details of community activities. The outspoken Stephen, one of those elected (Acts

6:1-5), came into violent conflict with other diaspora groups (Acts 6:9). As a result Stephen was stoned. For the first time in the New Testament we meet Saul, a consenting bystander at the martyrdom (Acts 7:58; 8:1). From that time on, Saul/Paul (Acts 13:9) persecuted the new faith community. He even sought for the opportunity to ferret out any believers who might reside in Damascus (Acts 9:1-2).

On the way to Damascus he had an encounter with Jesus the Lord, an encounter he variously calls a resurrection appearance (1 Cor. 15:8; 9:1), a revelation (Gal. 1:16), or a vision (2 Cor. 12:1-2). Blinded by the experience, he was led to Damascus (Acts 9:1-9) and lodged in an apartment on the street called Straight. Here occurred the most important conversion in the history of Christianity. An incredibly brave disciple named Ananias was chosen to visit his lethal opponent, Saul. The reluctant Ananias made the visit and laid hands on the blind Paul. When Paul could see and understand, Ananias baptized him and broke bread with him. Paul had entered the new community of faith! Some time after this conversion, perhaps during October 34, Paul was forced to leave Damascus by night, hidden in a basket (Acts 9:25).

Because of the conflicts between Acts and Paul's own account in his letters, the story of Paul becomes confusing from this time until he appears in Corinth about seventeen years later. According to his own account he went away for three years and then went up to Jerusalem for a visit with Peter (Gal. 1:18). It was fourteen years before he returned to Jerusalem (Gal. 2:1-2) for what we have come to call the Apostolic Council (Acts 15). If we follow this outline, then Paul must have made his first missionary journey through Asia Minor during the years 43–45 (Acts 13-14). In 46 he started his second journey, but was called to cross over into Macedonia while in Troas, the far-western end of Asia Minor (Acts 16:9-10). So the official beginning of Christianity in Europe was with Paul's foray into Greece, first at Neapolis, then Philippi, Thessalonica, and Athens (Acts 16:11-17:15). Churches were formed in Philippi and Thessalonica.

Paul arrived in Corinth early in the year 50. We can be fairly sure of this date because, while in Corinth, he had an encounter with the new proconsul Gallio (Acts 18:12-17). Gallio did not become proconsul until 51 and likely did not arrive before the middle of that year. When Paul first arrived at Corinth he was welcomed by Priscilla and Aquila, who had just arrived from Italy. Most readers suppose Priscilla and Aquila left Italy because of the decree of the Roman Emperor Claudius which exiled some Jews. According to the historian Suetonius, Claudius exiled the Jews because of riots *impulsore chresto,* "instigated by Chrestus" (*Vita Claudii,* 25.4). If the "Chrestus" is a reference to Christ, then we know Christianity had reached the large Jewish population in Rome. Because of the conflicts, Claudius forced some of the principals to leave. It seems best to place that edict in early 49. That means Aquila and Priscilla arrived in Corinth just before Paul, but not soon enough to have founded a local house church.

Sometime during the years 50–51 Paul received a communication from the new church in Thessalonica. The church there was having difficulties with Paul's preaching about the endtime. It did not seem right to them for some to die and not participate in the promised endtime. But they were taking the Jewish sense of the old and new age in a chronological way.[5] Paul's response to the Thessalonians was his first-known letter—perhaps even the first document of the New Testament.[6] He had to remind them that hope in the coming new age included the living and the dead (1 Thess. 4:13-18). Other than that, the letter does not reflect the kind of faith we find in the Corinthian correspondence or in Romans and Galatians.

In 1 Thessalonians Paul speaks of Jesus as the Lord of the endtime. Apocalyptic Jews (see summary essay, 238) believed the present age would pass away and a new age would come. In this kind of framework Jesus would be the one who brought in the new age. We see the same pattern evident when Jesus told the high priest he would "see the Son of man sitting at the right hand of Power, and coming with the clouds of heaven" (Mk. 14:62 ASV). By the time Paul wrote Corinthians he had shifted that framework to the present time. Jesus on the cross was the end of the old age and the resurrection of Jesus marked the beginning of the new. In this way the death and resurrection of Jesus became the paradigm or pattern for the Christian faith. That is why we sometimes speak of Paul as the "first Christian." It was he who articulated the death and resurrection of Jesus as the heart of our faith.

The application of Jewish endtime thinking to the death and resurrection of Jesus (the Christ) caused a major change from the Jewish understanding of life. The endtime is not something toward which

---

[5]Graydon F. Snyder, "The Literalization of the Apocalyptic Form in the New Testament Church," *Biblical Research* 14 (1969): 5-18.

[6]Robert Jewett, *A Chronology of Paul's Life* (Philadelphia: Fortress Press, 1979) 103.

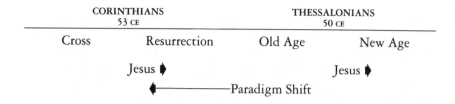

CORINTHIANS 53 CE		THESSALONIANS 50 CE	
Cross	Resurrection	Old Age	New Age
	Jesus ▶		Jesus ▶
	◀————————Paradigm Shift		

Christians live, but, because of our intense hope and expectation, is already partially present. We speak of such a change as a paradigm shift. The shift was from a Jewish apocalyptic hope in the coming new age to a Christian faith in the presence of the resurrection community. In that sense 1 Corinthians marks the literary beginning of Christianity.

It was only later that Paul spoke more sharply to the Jews (and countless others living under the law) about trying to earn a right relationship with God by doing things that made them acceptable. He tried to show that people who lived by rules or for causes could not earn God's favor. Like life, trust is a gift. Paul insisted that we are justified by faith only—that is, God wants our trust, not our accomplishments (Rom 1:17). This insight has guided the Christian church through many conflicts. It was the slogan of the Reformation and still characterizes many Protestant groups. Romans, the letter that insists on faith alone, was written in late 56 or early 57.

Returning to the stay at Corinth, Paul wrote to the Thessalonians in 50. After about eighteen months (Acts 18:11) Paul sailed with Aquila and Priscilla for Syria. At this time he must have returned first to Jerusalem for the Apostolic Council described in Acts 15 and Galatians 2:1-10. Following the agreement with the Jerusalem church he started yet another journey to the area of Ephesus and Asia Minor. Paul spent most of the years 53 and 54 in Ephesus. It was during that time that he wrote the Corinthian correspondence. We now turn to that special, complex history.

THE CORINTHIAN CORRESPONDENCE

The two letters we call 1 and 2 Corinthians have a very complex history. John Hurd has described the history as a series of exchanges between Paul and the Corinthian church.[7] We might outline that process in this way.

---

[7]John C. Hurd, *The Origin of 1 Corinthians* (New York: Seabury Press; London: S.P.C.K., 1965; updated rpt., Macon GA: Mercer University Press, 1983).

1. The preaching of Paul at Corinth
2. The first or previous letter from Paul (1 Cor. 5:9; 2 Cor. 6:14–7:1?)
3. A letter from a Corinthian house-church
4. Paul's response to the letter (1 Cor. 7-16)
5. News from Chloe's people (1 Cor. 1:11)
6. Paul's response to the news (1 Cor. 1-6)
7. Paul's second visit to Corinth (2 Cor. 2:1; 12:14; 13:1)
8. Paul's angry letter (2 Cor. 10–13; see 2 Cor. 2:3-11; 7:8)
9. The successful visit of Titus (2 Cor. 7:6-7)
10. Paul's joyful letter (2 Cor. 1:1–6:13 and 7:2–9:15)

THE PREACHING OF PAUL AT CORINTH

Everyone, especially a public speaker, knows how easily listeners can misunderstand. Even within a family the simplest communication can go astray. How much more room for error when there are cultural differences or more than one language. Would a Canadian and an American understand the succession to King David in the same way? Because he constantly spoke in multicultural situations, Paul was bound to be misunderstood. New Christians at Thessalonica took Paul's preaching about the endtime in a chronological way. Paul said things at Corinth that he held to be true, but which clearly were not understood as Paul had intended. Paul surely preached about Jesus as the Christ, the power of the cross, the passing old age, the coming and present new age, and life in the new age. We cannot be sure how well Paul communicated the heart of his faith. We do know some things were important to Paul, but led to false assumptions at Corinth. Paul said "all things are lawful" (6:12; 10:23) and he meant it. But he did not mean you could or should do things which would destroy the *koinonia* (Greek term for community and community participation). Paul said all Christians "possess knowledge" (8:1), but he did not mean that believers could flaunt that knowledge in front of uncertain sisters and brothers. He said it was "better for a man not to touch a woman at all than to create dissension in the faith community" (see commentary on 7:1), but he didn't mean Christians should avoid sexual relationships. Throughout the Corinthian correspondence we need to be aware that Paul will defend what he has said to them, but often needs to explain what he meant.

THE FIRST OR PREVIOUS LETTER FROM PAUL

We do not have any written correspondence from the Corinthians to Paul, except as reflected in Paul's quotations. We do not possess everything Paul wrote to the Corinthians, and probably we do not have the letters in the order they were written. This can add to our confusion as we read the documents called 1 and 2 Corinthians. Paul speaks of a previous letter (5:9). He says he advised them not to associate with immoral people, but they had apparently misunderstood. He says he meant the immoral *who consider themselves sisters or brothers,* not immoral people in general.

We could assume the previous letter has been lost. But readers have long noted the presence of a misplaced fragment in 2 Corinthians. Readers of modern translations of the New Testament will notice that 2 Corinthians 6:14–7:1 is set apart from the rest of the book. Obviously the fragment interrupts the flow of the letter. In 6:13 Paul asks the Corinthians to widen their hearts, while in 7:2 he asks them to open their hearts to him. The fragment 6:14–7:1 simply has no place in the sequence. The misplaced verses speak of being mismated with unbelievers or of the presence of unbelievers in the faith community.

Little wonder then that readers suspect 2 Corinthians 6:14–7:1 must be a part of the body of the so-called previous letter. Why was it written? Actually it does not seem like Paul to write so harshly about being mismated with unbelievers or associating with immoral people. Indeed, Paul spoke positively about the relationship of the believer to the unbelieving spouse (1 Cor. 7:12-16). Some suppose Paul wrote this rather stringent letter after attending the Jerusalem Council (during the year 51). Since there is nothing in Acts 15 or Galatians 2 about mixed marriages, this argument does not seem convincing. Despite the general belief that part of the previous letter of 1 Cor. 5:9 can be found in 2 Cor. 6:14–7:1, we might do better to say that a later church leader felt the need for a letter about mixed marriages and saw in 1 Cor. 5:9 the occasion to compose a harsh letter (2 Cor. 6:14–7:1) in the name of Paul.

Some readers believe the problems in 1 Corinthians 5 and 6 were actually part of the previous letter. The issues of incest (5:1-5) and prostitution (6:12-20) might have specifically caused such a letter, but we do better to read those sections as examples of excessive spiritualism. Presumably we do not possess the previous letter.

A LETTER FROM A CORINTHIAN HOUSE CHURCH

Apparently unrelated to Paul's previous letter, some of the Christians at Corinth encountered conflicting opinions about life in the new age. So they wrote a letter to Paul in which they expressed their questions. From Paul's style here and elsewhere (1 Thess. 5:1) we know that the recurring Greek phrase *peri de,* usually translated in 1 Corinthians as "now" or "now concerning," refers to questions put by the Corinthians. Those questions begin with the problem of second marriage and sexuality in 7:1; then continue with the issue of first marriage in 7:25; the eating of meat offered to idols in 8:1; the function of spiritual gifts in 12:1; the collection for the saints in Jerusalem in 16:1; and a request for a visit from Apollos in 16:12.

The nature of these questions, especially the first four, point to conflicts regarding asceticism (marriage and sex in chapter 7); autonomous freedom (meat offered to idols in chapters 8–11); and charismatic worship (spiritual gifts in chapters 12–15). Because of the radical spiritual nature of these questions, we suspect the letter, with its questions, came from a particular group in Corinth, the segment we have called the Christ house-church.

PAUL'S RESPONSE TO THE LETTER

As we have seen, Paul apparently begins in 1 Cor. 7:1 to answer the letter from the Corinthians. For the most part Paul needs to clarify misunderstandings which have arisen from his preaching and teaching. In 7:1-24 he restated his position on remarriage; in 7:25-40 he answered their question about first marriages. In chapters 8–11 he defended his statement on freedom—"all things are lawful"—but insisted that association with any other community can compromise one's life in Christ. In chapters 12–15 he describes the ordering, by love, of gifts of the Spirit, even the gift of resurrection. In a final section he answers their questions about the collection (16:1-11), and a visit from the other "pastor," Apollos (16:12).

NEWS FROM CHLOE'S PEOPLE

A close reading of 1 Corinthians reveals there were at least two messages from the Corinthian Christians. One, a letter asking Paul to answer some nagging questions, and the other, an oral communication from his friend Chloe. In 1:11 Paul mentions a report from "Chloe's people," that there was quarreling among the sisters and brothers at

Corinth. This information caused the writing of chapters 1–6.

We cannot identify Chloe. We do know there were several wealthy women who became attached to Pauline Christianity. We hear of Lydia, a seller of purple (Acts 16:14), and Phoebe of Cenchreae, who helped many (Rom. 16:1-2). Such women likely were first attracted to Judaism, but could not become Jews on their own. For women who had no male counterpart, Christianity offered a way to embrace Judaism. It may be safe to conjecture that Chloe was such a wealthy woman whose business included a branch office in Ephesus. The report received in Ephesus (16:8) by Paul may well have been carried through Chloe's business network.

PAUL'S RESPONSE TO THE NEWS

As the letter begins it clearly deals with the issue of divisions among the house-churches. Some adhere to Paul, some to Peter, some to Apollos, and now a group to Christ (1:12). In chapters 1–4 Paul tries to show that leadership based on the cross of Christ does not lead to veneration. Quite the contrary: genuine leadership still suffers the conflict between the two ages. A true leader lives in the old age with all of its problems, yet exhibits the life and faith of the new age. Paul could describe that conflict with incredible poignancy (4:8-13).

Chapters 5 and 6 illustrate the nature of the conflict between the two ages. The Christ church may believe they live in the new age, but actually their spiritual pride has let them condone a marital situation acceptable to neither Jews nor Greeks (5:1-2). They are so filled with spiritual pride they even try to avoid anyone not patently of the new age (5:9-11). On the other hand, some in the Corinthian church still allow the old age to rule in their lives. How could they let the courts of Corinth decide on legal quarrels between them? How could the courts of this age enable members of the faith community to love each other? Chapters 5 and 6, then, illustrate the continuing, constant conflict between the ages, a conflict which does not allow any to think of themselves as already "in" the new age. Quarrels, pride and position belong to the old age.

Since Paul had already written chapters 7–16, he added the first six chapters and sent the entire letter to the Christians at Corinth. With some possible exceptions (see commentary on 14:34-36), the letter sent by Paul is the one we call First Corinthians. Paul's colleague, Timothy, either carried the letter or was to arrive about the same time (4:17;

16:10-11). He would have clarified Paul's response.

PAUL'S SECOND VISIT TO CORINTH

After a stay in Ephesus Paul once again returned to Macedonia, thence to "Greece" (Achaia) and Corinth (Acts 20:1-6). That three-month visit to Corinth is well known. The letter to the Romans was written from Corinth about the year 56 and the greetings of Romans 16 come from the Christians at Corinth (Rom. 16:23).

Less obvious is the visit Paul made to Corinth from Ephesus before his recorded return to Macedonia. In the so-called angry letter of 2 Corinthians 10–13, Paul mentions his coming visit as a "third time" (2 Cor. 12:14; 13:1). In fact he refers to his most-recent unpleasant visit as his second (13:2). Apparently Paul's major letter (1 Corinthians) did not succeed in quieting the quarrels or settling the disputes. Paul felt it necessary to make a personal visit in order to put everything in order.

Paul's second visit was a disaster. He came away accused of vacillation (2 Cor. 1:17), considered inferior to the real apostles (2 Cor. 12:11), lacking skill in public presentations (2 Cor. 11:6), generally weak in presence (2 Cor. 13:1-4; 10:1,9), and possibly possessing a debilitating illness (2 Cor. 12:7, the "thorn in the flesh"). One suspects Paul was unable to deal with rising local leadership (2 Cor. 2:5), so he returned to Ephesus angry and defeated.

PAUL'S ANGRY LETTER

Upon returning to Ephesus Paul penned an angry, aggressive letter, which we have identified as 2 Corinthians 10–13. The letter lacks a greeting and thanksgiving, but does begin with the *parakalo* or request section (2 Cor. 10:1). Paul feels compelled in this letter to defend his apostleship. As in 1 Corinthians 4:8-13, Paul stresses the plight of an apostle caught between the two ages. Reluctantly he "boasts" of his suffering for the sake of the new age (11:21b-33), so that the power of Christ could be seen in his weakness (12:9-10).

THE SUCCESSFUL VISIT OF TITUS

After the dismal second visit and Paul's angry response (2 Cor. 2:2-11; 7:8), Titus paid a visit to the recalcitrant Corinthians. We do not know what happened during that visit. We do know that Timothy and Titus had pastoral skills which perhaps Paul lacked. In a recommendation Paul speaks highly of Titus his coworker (2 Cor. 8:16-24). Titus did accomplish what Paul had not (2 Cor. 7:13-16). The quarrels subsided and the Christians at Corinth were reconciled to Paul (2 Cor. 7:6-7).

PAUL'S JOYFUL LETTER

In response to the joyful news from Titus, Paul wrote a loving, happy letter which we identify as 2 Corinthians 1:1–6:13 and 7:2–9:15. Paul rejoices in the reconciliation that occurred and the way God works in these earthen vessels of ours. In the midst of this he pens one of the greatest sections of the Bible, the description of reconciliation as God standing with us in the midst of our brokenness (2 Cor. 5:1-21).

Second Corinthians, then, consists of no less than three letters: the previous one, the angry one, and the joyful one. It may be that chapters 8 and 9 are also a separate letter in which Paul addresses the matter of the contribution to the saints and commends Titus.

OUTLINE OF FIRST CORINTHIANS

1:1–4:21 Divisions in the Church at Corinth

    1:1-3   The Opening

    1:4-9   The Thanksgiving

    1:10-17   The Divisions at Corinth

          1:10   Paul's request (*parakalo* sentence)

          1:11   The news that initiated the letter

          1:12-13   The divisions in Corinth

          1:14-17   Paul denies responsibility for any house church

    1:18-2:5 The Foolishness of the Cross

          1:18-21   The power of the cross makes wisdom seem foolish

          1:22-25   The weakness of the cross satisfies no one

          1:26-31   An analogy of the cross in the church at Corinth

          2:1-5   An analogy of the cross in Paul's preaching

    2:6-16   The Mind of Christ

          2:6-9   God's wisdom is not understood by this age

          2:10-13   The Spirit imparts divine wisdom

          2:14-16   Those led by the Spirit know the mind of Christ

    3:1-23   The Function of Leadership

          3:1-4   Divisions indicate the Corinthians are *sarkikoi*

          3:5-9   God alone gives growth

          3:10-15   Christ alone is the building's foundation

          3:16-17   The community of faith is that building, God's temple

          3:18-23   For the Christian there are no human limitations

    4:1-21   On Being Fools for Christ

          4:1-5   Leaders are servants and stewards

          4:6-7   Analogies of leadership applied

          4:8-13   The end time is not yet

          4:14-21   There is power in the kingdom of God

5:1–6:20 Two Case Studies at Corinth

    5:1-13   Spiritual Arrogance Can Blind the Faith Community

          5:1-5   One member is not living in the new age

          5:6-8   An analogy: old leaven destroys the new lump

          5:9-13   On living in the old age, while being in the new

    6:1-11   The Old Cannot Inherit the New

          6:1-4   Those of the new age will judge the old age

FIRST CORINTHIANS 1:1–4:21
DIVISIONS IN THE CHURCH AT CORINTH

INTRODUCTION

As in all the major cities of the Roman Empire, the church of Corinth was made up of several distinct units called house churches (see summary essay, 248). Although Paul does not greet each group separately, as in Philemon 2, nor does he give directions for the reading of his letter in other house churches, as in Colossians 4:15-16, we know nevertheless that such groups did indeed exist (16:19). Often the letters of the New Testament deal with tensions within or between the house churches that are receiving the letter. For example, in Romans 14 we note conflicts between the so-called strong and weak, much like what we see in 1 Corinthians 8. Some of the conflicts recorded in the Corinthian correspondence must have existed within the congregation, namely, the question of dress, or the problem with the Lord's Supper (chapter 11). It also seems very likely some of the conflicts had occurred between house churches themselves. This may be the particular characteristic of the Corinthian situation: that some of the conflicts existed between the distinct congregations.

The section 1:1–4:21 deals with the apparent conflict between the house churches. Chapters 5–6 illustrate the problems of living between the times, while chapters 7–16 reflect also inner congregational conflicts between men and women, rich and poor, Jew and Gentile. In fact, in chapters 7–16 Paul does not sense the divisions nearly as sharply as they are seen in chapters 1–4 (11:18-19). For these reasons, it seems highly probable chapters 7–16 were written before chapters 1–6 (see above, 13).

As indicated in the introduction (see p. 11), Paul must have written chapters 7–16 in response to a letter from some Christians at Corinth. After completing that letter he then received news of a more serious situation: conflicts between the house churches themselves. Very likely it was Chloe's people (see summary essay, 248) who had brought this news (1:11). Paul responds with several attacks on the problem: (1) the divisions have no basis in fact; (2) the foolishness of the cross renders human divisions meaningless; and (3) leaders are present more to serve a function than to create a following.

• OUTLINE •

1:1-3 The Opening
1:4-9 Thanksgiving
1:10-17 Parties at Corinth
1:18–2:5 The Foolishness of the Cross
2:6-16 Knowing the Mind of Christ
3:1-23 The Function of Leaders
4:1-21 On Being Fools for Christ

THE OPENING 1:1-3

Greek letters at the time of Paul opened much as this letter (see summary essay, 241-42): the name of the sender, the name of the receiver and a greeting. The authors of ancient letters often dictated to a scribe. We know Paul followed that practice (Rom. 16:22; 2 Thess. 3:17). It seems likely Paul dictated this letter to Sosthenes and then signed it at 16:21. The opening and the thanksgiving are both formal elements of a letter, so further study may not shed much light on the actual intent of the letter itself. We can only note with interest that certain elements have become formalized. Paul considers himself an apostle, though we know from 2 Corinthians 10–13 that not everyone connected with the Corinthian mission agreed with him (see summary essay, 222). It is true that Paul was not an apostle in the same sense as those who had been with Jesus from the beginning and had witnessed the resurrection (Acts 1:21-26). But Paul was confident of his call and his mission to the Gentiles (see esp. 2 Cor. 5:20).

Jesus here is designated formally as the Christ (see summary essay, 229). As will be seen in this chapter, Jesus did not satisfy the Jewish insistence for a sign of his messiahship. The cross contradicted the Jewish hopes for a triumphant messianic figure. Then how did Jesus so quickly become known as Jesus the Messiah? For the Pauline churches, at least, Jesus became the person who signaled the coming of the kingdom (1 Thess. 1:9-10). That person could be known as the Christ.

Yet another formal designation occurs in the phrase "church of God" (see summary essay, 231). Paul does not understand the church as something other than the people of God (Israel) chosen to serve as a blessing to all the nations (Gen. 12:1-3). Consequently, he has not yet made a distinction between church and synagogue. The *ekklesia* (Greek for "assembly of those called out") of this letter corresponds in function to the *qahal* (assembly) of the Hebrew Bible. That identity of function becomes evident in the formal term "saints" (see summary essay, 232) which Paul used consistently to describe the members of the churches of God. It picks up the sense of a special people, set aside (holy) and called out for God's ultimate purposes (Ex. 19:6).

The greeting of a Greek letter normally involved some form of the word *charis* (grace) as a wish to the reader. Paul invents for his letters a combination of the Greek greeting with the universal Hebrew greeting, *shalom,* translated by him as *eirene* in Greek. This hybrid combination of grace and peace points clearly to the multilingual and multicultural nature of the Pauline congregations.

THE THANKSGIVING 1:4-9

Another formal element of the Greek letter is the thanksgiving. The writer of the letter gives thanks to his deity for the health and good fortune of the recipient. In early Christian letters the word God was used in place of Hellenistic deities such as Serapis.[1] Paul follows the custom of his time by placing a thanksgiving after the greeting. Only in the letter to the Galatians was Paul so anxious to make his point that he failed to include the normal thanksgiving (or blessing as in 2 Corinthians and Ephesians).

Despite the formal nature of this thanksgiving, the content does point to the heart of Paul's faith: Christians are those who are awaiting the endtime revelation of our Lord Jesus Christ and who are receiving from God those spiritual gifts required to sustain them until that end time (v.7). The theme will be repeated quite often.

---

[1]Snyder, *Ante Pacem,* 149, 169

THE DIVISIONS AT CORINTH 1:10-17

PREVIEW

Paul moves immediately to the problem. The various house churches at Corinth have attached themselves to famous persons in the early Church. These attachments have led to, or reflect, a developing animosity or competition between the groups. It is not certain that the four groups are indeed house churches in Corinth. It is easier, however, to think of them as house churches than as amorphous networks which never met as congregations. Even more difficult to determine is the nature of the quarrel.

Whether or not it is appropriate, the way we read the nature of the quarrel at Corinth also determines how we will read the rest of the letter. It has been widely assumed that the quarrel arose between Jews and Gentiles.[2] Throughout Paul's mission trips apparently some type of Jewish-Christian missionary opposed him (Gal. 3:1-5, 5:12; 2 Cor. 11:1-6, 22). It is argued then that the two opposing parties at Corinth are the Pauline (Gentile) and the Petrine (Jewish). It is the same conflict as seen in Galatians 2. Furthermore it is argued that Paul's message should be understood as a conflict between Jewish law and Christian freedom, Jewish contract and Christian grace.

As one looks at the conflicts found in Corinth: a man living with his stepmother, settling disputes in the secular court, marrying a second time, abstaining from sexual relationships, women failing to cover their hair, eating meat offered to idols, and speaking in tongues, it would be difficult to say these are Jewish-Gentile problems. From this list it would appear that the conflict has arisen between those who are above the law and those who feel caught in the web of this age. Three of the house churches have named themselves after three prominent leaders: Peter, Paul, and Apollos. But a fourth group has risen above the law to enter into spiritual perfection. This group has called itself the Christ house church, that is, the true group. The conflict at Corinth

---

[2]Ferdinand Christian Baur, "Die Christuspartei in der korinthischen Gemeinde, der Gegensatz des petrinischen und paulinischen Christenthums in der ltesten Kirche," *Tübinger Zeitschrift für Theologie* (1831): 61-206. For the critique see Johannes Munck, *Paulus und die Heilsgeschichte* (Kōbenhavn: Munksgaard, 1954) 127-61; ET, *Paul and the Salvation of Mankind* (Richmond VA: John Knox Press, 1959).

is more than a Jewish-Gentile problem. It has developed between the regular house churches and the so-called "true believers" or, as we call them, "gnostics" (see summary essay, 245). Gnostics were persons who believed they had been granted full spiritual knowledge.

• OUTLINE •

1:10 Paul's request
1:11 The news that initiated the letter
1:12-13 The divisions in Corinth
1:14-17 Paul denies responsibility for any house church

EXPLANATORY NOTES

1:10 In the Greek letter form the writer states the purpose of the letter with the term "I beseech" or "I exhort" (*parakalo*). Paul's purpose for these first four chapters is to encourage the Corinthians to say the same thing (agree with one another, NIV) and be united in mind and perception. One must be careful here. Paul seldom recommends unanimity as a means of solving conflicts. More often than not he calls for love and understanding (Romans 14; 1 Cor. 13:13). There are not splits in the church at Corinth, only dissensions. Paul does not ask for either theological or even behavioral oneness. Paul uses the Greek term *phronein* to mean active mutuality in the faith community (Rom. 12:16). Those who think and act on their own "think too highly of themselves." The dissension at Corinth was a problem of *huperphronēma* (Rom. 12:3), that is, acting and thinking without the Spirit (Rom 8:27). Paul only asks that they speak and act as a community of faith in which love, understanding, and forgiveness are operative (note "this mind" in Phil. 2:5).[3] Were this not true the paradigm (an event or narrative which defines a group) of the cross (1:11–2:5) would have no meaning.

1:11 The news regarding trouble in Corinth came by means of Chloe's people (household, NIV). In a linear or hierarchical system news travels officially up and down lines of authority. In a family or community system news travels by networking (see summary essay, 236). Within the networking society it is amazing how quickly information could be

---

[3]Virginia Wiles, unpublished paper, Society of Biblical Literature, 1990.

passed throughout the Roman Empire.[4] Presumably Chloe's people in Ephesus were a branch of her business in Corinth. So the news of the divisions reached Paul before he could reply to their more formal letter of inquiry.

We know nothing more about Chloe than that she had connections in both Corinth and Ephesus. Apparently the new community of faith attracted many women of means.[5] Sometimes those who listened to Paul were primarily women (Acts 16:13-15). The Jewish faith must have attracted many thoughtful women, persons who could not become Jews because they were widows or because their husbands would not become Jews. Very likely Chloe was one of these former "God-fearers."[6]

1:12-13 Paul names the four house churches involved in the conflict. Two are named after leaders of the Corinthian church: Apollos and Paul. Little is known of Apollos except that he hailed from Alexandria, was learned in the Hebrew Bible (in its Greek version), was instructed in the Christian faith by Priscilla and Aquila, and followed Paul as the pastor of the Corinthian church (see Acts 18:24-28). There is no reason to suppose that Peter had ever visited Corinth. Paul never mentions him as a past personal influence at Corinth, nor does he indicate any quarrel with Peter such as we find in Galatians 2. Presumably one house church simply took on the name of a famous Christian leader. Clearly the appellation "Christ church" has scandalized Paul. The term "Christ" should designate the total. How could one house church dare call itself by the name that belongs to all? That could only mean Christ is divided.

1:14-17 Though Paul was most troubled by the formation of a Christ party, nevertheless he took steps to deny any reason for the formation of a Paul party (see summary essay, 252). He had not been responsible for forming any of the distinct congregations, that is, he had not baptized anyone into a local community of faith (see summary essay, 225).

---

[4]Elizabeth Clark, "Elite Networks and Heresy Accusations: Towards a Social Description of the Origenist Controversy," unpublished paper, Society of Biblical Literature 1984 (SBL Abstracts 1984, 168).

[5]Stevan L. Davies, *The Revolt of the Widows: The Social World of the Apocryphal Acts* (Carbondale: Southern Illinois University Press, 1980).

[6]Kenan T. Erim, *Aphrodisias: City of Venus Aphrodite* (New York: Facts on File Publications, 1986) 131.

Then in a rather humorous way he recalls that indeed he had baptized a few. Baptism was, for Paul, a dying with Christ and a resurrection into his body, the community of faith (Romans 6:1-14). Paul knows no baptism for personal salvation. Baptism joins one to the community of the faithful. Consequently, had he baptized anyone it would have necessarily been in the context of a house church. He tried to deny, without much success, that he had baptized anyone into a congregation which could bear his name. The three persons mentioned by Paul are known only briefly elsewhere: Crispus had been the ruler of the synagogue in Corinth (Acts 18:8); Gaius owned one of the homes in Corinth where a house church met (Romans 16:23); Stephanus and his household were the first converts in Achaia (1 Cor. 16:15-17).

In v. 17 Paul makes a distinction which can be found throughout the early church. Itinerant evangelists, prophets, and teachers did not form local congregations. They called out leaders and preached to people in general, but they did not create congregations, that is, they did not baptize. It was local leadership, such as elders and deacons, who were responsible for the distinct local groups within a larger locale. Itinerant leaders continued to visit local churches through the second century. In the second-century Christian document called the Didache they were strongly warned not to stay more than three days in the same place. Paul did not baptize, nor did he preach with eloquent wisdom, a term in Greek which probably referred to Greek rhetorical technique and skill (rightly "cleverness of speech," NASB). He insisted on presenting the Gospel in such a way that the communication was congruent with the message (cross of Christ) itself. With this transition, Paul then shifts to the foolishness of the cross and why he came in weakness (2:1-5).

THE TEXT IN ITS BIBLICAL CONTEXT

In the history of the people of God prior to the New Testament period, theological pluralism or diversity seldom became a cause for divisions. Within a familial structure plurality normally can be accepted, even welcomed. Much more threatening is behavioral diversity. In the Hebrew Bible one thinks of inhospitable behavior exhibited by the men of Gibeah (Judges 19); the sin of David with Bathsheba (2 Samuel 11); or Ahab's deception of Naboth (1 Kings 21). All were punished severely, sometimes even terminally. No such counterpart exists for theological diversity. Quite the contrary, within the same canon exist documents as diverse as Numbers and Leviticus, Malachi and Job,

Judges and Ezekiel. Ultimate divisions were avoided by being inclusive, developing consensus, or using the "lot" in the face of potentially divisive decisions.

It may be that this passage marks the first time the people of God have been threatened by theological schism. (It should be noted that Jewish theological self regulation first began at Jamnia about 100 C.E.). Here, as often later, the conflict was not caused by diversity, but by a sense of rectitude on the part of one group. This sense of certainty, of being right, marks the destruction of the family system. Paul, from his Jewish background, was not prepared for the intense Hellenistic sense of individuality. Here, as in Romans, he needs to articulate for non-Jews how people may act together as a primary community without destroying their deep individual convictions.

THE TEXT IN THE LIFE OF THE CHURCH

Historically heresy seldom derives from error or variation from a standard norm. So-called heretics normally can quote chapter and verse for their peculiar belief system, just as the Christ congregation in Corinth could correctly quote Paul's words, yet miss his intent. Heresy occurs when a person or group of persons suppose their particular grasp on the truth, however imperfect or limited, actually reflects the only truth. Through the ages, as the church has so often faced that rigorous sense of rectitude, there has been little to do but enter into schism. For that reason Christendom has been fractured by denominationalism.

Congregational type churches have acted more like families, as the people of God in the Hebrew Bible. Theological plurality has not been as much a problem as alienating behavior, a behavior which has developed a sense of uncompromising rectitude on the part of some people. Because of this unexpected acculturation, some congregations find themselves in seemingly unresolvable conflict. As they reflect on what has happened, they often speak of losing those qualities of family which allowed them to deal with diversity. With the church at Corinth they find themselves in a conflict they cannot resolve, and with Paul they will once more need to learn what it means to be a community of faith, "saying the same thing" even in plurality.

THE FOOLISHNESS OF THE CROSS 1:18–2:5

PREVIEW

In order to convey to the Corinthian church, and especially the Christ congregation, the manner in which a community of faith operates, Paul presents three observations: our faith paradigm is one of self-giving on the cross; leadership roles are merely functions in the divine process; we are living in anticipation of the endtime. This justly famous section of 1 Corinthians states Paul's theology of the cross for the first time (assuming the only prior letter is 1 Thessalonians). For Paul the cross is a sign of God's use of what is weak, marginal, and even disorderly for the purposes of salvation. There is practically no emphasis in this first Pauline *theologia crucis* (theology of the cross) on what God did in Jesus Christ (as in 2 Cor. 5:21 or Romans 5:9). Paul is not working on the saving effect of the cross, but on the perception that God works through what is weak or foolish in our eyes. The cross signifies the essential way God deals with humanity.

Since the cross marks a primary truth of life, it is available only to those who can perceive that truth. It is available only to those who know they are weak, marginal, lost, and perishing. In fact, to state it even stronger, the cross only has meaning if one already is experiencing the redeeming action of God. Therein lies the scandal of the cross. Only when one has experienced the redeeming act of God does the cross seem wise. Otherwise, from the human perspective it can only appear to be folly. Paul notes that it surely appears folly to the educators (vv. 19-21). Then changing the tack of his argument he observes that to the Jew the cross is a scandal, while to the Greek it must be foolishness (vv. 22-24). In this argument he lumps the Greeks with the educated.

For the Jews a cross does not signify what they expected of the Messiah. They had expected a triumphal figure with some triumphant event, i.e., some initial victory over the Romans. Dying as a criminal at the hands of the very Romans he should have conquered can hardly serve as the sign of a Messiah.

Paul then shifts to an analogy of faith (Romans 12:6). As so often in his letters, and presumably his preaching, he attaches the significance of the cross to their own experience. That is, they were once a marginal people, but now have become God's chosen people (vv. 26-31). Ending the section with a personal analogy, he recalls the time he first met the Corinthian Christians, how he appeared weak and lacking in any formal persuasive ability (Greek rhetoric?). He appeared this way because he had resolved that they should learn of the cross in a way congruent with that cross itself. So he came to them in weakness.

• OUTLINE •

1:18-21 The power of the cross makes wisdom seem foolish

1:22-25 The weakness of the cross satisfies no one

1:26-31 An analogy of the cross in the church at Corinth

2:1-5 An analogy of the cross in Paul's preaching

EXPLANATORY NOTES

1:18-21 Paul's initial response to the divisions at Corinth seems at first glance rather oblique. The folly of the cross hardly seems an appropriate response to their conflicts. Granted the indirect nature of the argument, nevertheless the point is critical. In order for a conflict to occur there must be some persons who know they are right and are willing to use power and persuasion to assert that rectitude. Even though they are in the process of destroying themselves in conflict (perishing, NRSV), they cannot understand the cross the power and wisdom of God's weakness. In their struggle for power they can hardly accept a paradigm of self-giving.

Paul's faith was rooted deeply in experience. Though he could pen lofty abstractions, those theological affirmations could always be stated in experiential language. In v. 18 he states the meaning of the cross pointblank. If one is experiencing loneliness and has a sense of perishing then one only understands the language of self-defense (flesh in Pauline language), language of increased order (wisdom in Paul's language), or violence towards those who threaten (wrath or vengeance). It is only as one is experiencing the redemptive action of the redeeming community that one can perceive the power of the cross.

Paul then makes two subpoints regarding the cross. First, God has always confounded the wise of the world by working through the weak and the foolish (vv. 19-21). Quoting Isaiah 29:14 he notes that God, as recorded in the Hebrew Bible, used the marginal people of life (youngest son, rejected, woman, poor) to achieve the divine purposes. This has not been an accident. It is a part of the wisdom of God itself (see summary essay, 261), that we cannot know God through our own intelligence (v. 21). The best of human wisdom has never been able to know God. If that were not true what we call God would simply be the distillation of the best of human thinking. If God were nothing but the best of human wisdom, rather than the Holy Other, then there would be no functional covenant with God, no genuine dialogue, no possibility for growth (i.e., no outside critique). In God's wisdom God cannot be known by human wisdom. Rather God and God's way can only be known through revelation, the folly of preaching the good news a genuine dialogue between the human and the divine.

1:22-25 Secondly, the power of the cross cannot be discerned by either of the two major world views known to Paul (vv.22-25). Paul has already noted that human wisdom cannot know God, and neither can Greek (Gentile) wisdom perceive the power of the cross. It appears as foolishness to them. Wisdom in the Greek world deals primarily with universal order. For the Greeks, perfect order would be an ultimate expression of wisdom. The cross, and its paradigm of self-giving even to death, could not possibly lead to good order. Therefore Greeks could not understand the power of the cross.

Jews, on the other hand, looked less to wisdom and more to signals of divine favor and direction. Jews sought a sign. The problem of a sign plagued the early relationship of nascent Christianity with Judaism. In the Synoptic Gospels Jesus constantly struggled with Jews who wanted signs (Matt. 12:38-39; Mk. 8:12). In the Gospel of John, Jesus did do signs but they are not seen or correctly perceived (John 4:48; 6:30). For Paul the cross is a sign which cannot be assimilated by the Jews. They expected a sign which demonstrated God's victory. If the cross were really a sign, as the Christians claimed, then it became a hindrance to their accepting Jesus as the Christ. Paul spoke of this hindrance as a stumbling block. The stumbling block, or *skandalon* in Greek, was a cornerstone used to build cut stone edifices. It stuck out at the corner, so that workers constantly had to avoid it or stumble over it. The cross caused Jews to "trip" in their expectation of a Messiah.

One ought not suppose that the cross was weak or chaotic. It was the power of God. Indeed Christ was the wisdom of God. That is, the cross had its own interior strength and Christ had his own interior wisdom. Wisdom of God (see summary essay, 261) was a way of expressing the kind of order which characterized the Jewish understanding of God, in its personal, relational sense. Wisdom is closely associated with God in Proverbs 8:22-31 and is said to be express deity in Wisdom of Solomon 7:25-26. Paul identifies (Jesus) Christ with that personified wisdom. Christ as wisdom does bring a sense of community peace and order not easily understood by those who think perfect order requires structural perfection. Christ on the cross is that foolishness and weakness of God which is wiser and stronger than the human counterpart.

1:26-31 Paul does not leave the experience of the cross simply in implied examples from the Hebrew Bible. In demonstrating how God works through the weak of the world, he uses the experience of the Corinthians as newborn Christians. They were not powerful, yet they have become the very people of God. The intent of the passage lies in the analogy, and that should not be forgotten. Yet the passage has been used constantly to analyze the sociological makeup of this early Pauline church (see summary essay, 231). Radical sociologists claim the early church was composed of socially and politically marginal people who sought a more central position in the Greco-Roman society.[7] That theory fits well with the substance of this passage and with the thesis of this passage. That is, God works the divine purpose with those who are weak in the eyes of this world.

But a prosopography (study of biographies) of the Corinthian church does not support such a radical position. Aquila and Prisca owned a house where one congregation met (16:19). So did Gaius, who may have been the "bishop" (host) of Corinth (Romans 16:23). Crispus, past ruler of the synagogue, and Erastus, city treasurer, were members of the church at Corinth. People with proper Roman names were deeply involved in the church: Tertius (Romans 16:22); Lucius (Romans 16:21); Quartus (Romans 16:23). At the same time, it must be admitted there are clearly marginal persons in the church. Fortunatus (16:17) possesses a virtue name which indicates slave origin. And the conflict over the Lord's supper arose between the wealthy and the poor (slaves?). Paul's opening comments (the "not many") probably reflect the truth. Some were

---

[7]For the debate, see Gerd Theissen, *The Social Setting of Pauline Christianity: Essays on Corinth* (Philadelphia: Fortress, 1982) 69-119; Wayne A. Meeks, *The First Urban Christians: The Social World of the Apostle Paul* (New Haven CT: Yale University Press, 1983) 51-73.

wealthy, some were of noble birth, some were well educated, but, on the whole, the church represented a cross section of Corinthian society. That society contained many slaves and poor. His point is that God did not choose the powerful, noble born, and educated to lead the others. Consequently they can understand the power of weakness as shown in the cross.

One of the parallel phrases of this great passage deserves special attention. Paul said God had chosen the low and despised things (v. 28), and then parenthetically, apparently in apposition, he speaks of them as the *ta me onta*, the things that are not, in order to nullify the *ta onta*, the things that are. These Greek terms are technical terms for being and nonbeing. But in the thought world of Paul, as a Jew, nonbeing was not a reasonable possibility. In a covenant world view people and things can be false or alienated, but not nonexistent. Even in the creation narrative, the world was created from chaos, rather than "nothing" or nonbeing. In Romans 4:17 Paul speaks of God calling into *onta* (being) the *ta me onta* (the things that did not exist). The immediate context in Romans deals with giving life to the dead. Paul must have known he was using a technical philosophical term, even though many of his readers would not have. Or perhaps he did mean for the Greek reader to catch the nuance. But the "nonbeing" of Corinth were those once dead to God, but now alive. They stand in contrast to those who thought they were something.

In v. 30 Paul summarizes the way in which Christ as wisdom creates order. It is not by hierarchy or class. Rather it is by the development of the new faith community. The community is created by the rightwising activity of God in Christ. Though not explicit here, Paul must think of the cross as that rightwising activity. When people are then justified (accepted by God and the faith community) they are called out (see commentary on 1:2) for God's purpose (sanctified). The purpose of that call is ultimate endtime inclusion of all people. So we who are called cannot boast in ourselves, but only in the Lord who has created the faith community.

2:1-5 In a more personal analogy, or, perhaps, even apology, Paul explains why he came to the Corinthians with such weakness. As in 1:17 he makes it clear that people should not be persuaded to believe in the cross because of eloquent speech. Rather, the cross of Christ should be placed before the nonbeliever in a way which itself demonstrates the nature of the cross. Then in a nearly unbelievable demonstration of vulnerability, Paul reminds them of his own weakness, trembling, and poor speech habits. Yet, and now the analogy is both clear and complete, from this weakness came the power of God which has transformed them.

One doubts that Paul's weakness was a deliberate style for the sake of the Corinthians. Apparently his poor speaking ability stood in sharp contrast to his facile "pen." Or, at least, his opponents at Corinth used that weakness as a pretext for doubting the authenticity of his apostleship (2 Cor. 10:10). On the other hand, there were special circumstances. Paul had just come to Corinth from a rather dismal failure in Athens. He had displayed his rhetorical skill before some Athenians. The reception was cool (Acts 17:32). Perhaps he resolved that next time (Corinth) the message and the means of communication would match. In any case he affirms once more that the use of weakness for power was demonstrated on the cross by Jesus the Christ who, therefore, is the wisdom of God.

THE TEXT IN ITS BIBLICAL CONTEXT

First of all this passage sums up the difference between the early Christian and the Jewish understanding of the Hebrew Bible. The Hebrew Bible closes with a sense of impending victory over the foes of the Jews. The Lord will defeat all those who wage war against Jerusalem (Zech. 14). Soon the kingdom of the saints of the Most High will replace the great universal empires (Daniel 7). In sharp contrast we find New Testament writers reinterpreting the Hebrew Scriptures in terms of the death of Jesus. The Ethiopian eunuch is shown that Jesus was the suffering servant of Isaiah 53 (Acts 8:26-40). On the way to Emmaus followers of Jesus learn that the Hebrew Bible pointed to a Messiah who would suffer and die (Lk. 24:27). Jesus himself reinterpreted the Jewish messianic expectation by saying the Son of Man must suffer many things (Mk. 8:31). Paul summarizes that understanding of the faith in this passage on the cross. Often surprising us with the unexpected, God works through the marginal and the weak.

The earliest understanding of the cross actually portrayed Jesus dying on a tree (Acts 5:30; 10:39; 13:29; Gal. 3:13; 1 Peter 2:24). Quoting Deuteronomy 21:23 the early Christians thought of Jesus as one from God who identified with us even to the point of suffering with us under our (God's) law.[8] Jesus became a criminal (curse, Gal. 3:13; sin, 2 Cor. 5:21). In covenant theology (see summary essay, 235) the most powerful means of reconciliation is to identify with the alienated person (2 Cor. 5:21). God did just that on the cross and thereby granted covenant where alienation had existed. In this first known and written reflection on the meaning of the cross, Paul turns the point slightly. Speaking, presumably, to those who had the temerity to make something of themselves, Paul responds that the wisdom of God, shown on the cross, works in quite another way: power is expressed in weakness (see summary essay, 261). Here the cross is more a heuristic (learning) device than a proclamation of the good news.

The analogies used by Paul, though directly applicable to the Corinthians, are deeply rooted in biblical tradition. It was said of the first Jews that they too were marginal. "My father was a wandering Aramean" (Deut. 26:5) was a theological confession which intended to say that the original "Jews" had no characteristics which made them appealing or valuable to God. It was God who made of them a people and a faith community (Ex. 19:4-6). Again we must be careful not to suppose the people who became Jews were riffraff. Abraham and Sarah, Isaac and Rebecca could hardly have been poor.

But one cannot enter a mutually submissive covenant relationship if one supposes she or he possesses a characteristic which impels the other to make the covenant. Covenants are made in gratitude for the care, love, and grace which makes such a relationship possible. So it was in the early church. The first Christians were nobodies (1 Pet. 2:10), just as "not many" of the Corinthian Christians were well born. Paul is dealing with a theological necessity, not necessarily a sociological fact. It is expressed here because there are some Corinthians who think sufficiently highly of themselves to cause divisions.

Likewise Paul's personal analogy has deep roots in biblical tradition. Just as Paul came to the Corinthians in weakness and trembling, so also Moses claimed lack of eloquence (Ex. 4:10); Isaiah had unclean lips (Isa. 6:5); and Jeremiah was too young for public speaking (Jer. 1:6). God's spokesperson, like the people themselves, dare not have characteristics which compel her or his selection. The power of the speaker is a gift of God (Matt. 10:19).

---

[8]John Dominic Crossan, *The Cross That Spoke* (San Francisco: Harper & Row, 1988).

THE TEXT IN THE LIFE OF THE CHURCH

As 1:10-17 speaks to us sharply about the divisions among us, so also 1:18–2:5 speaks to us sharply about our self-perception. Perhaps with all good intentions the 20th century church has busied itself with snatching souls from the burning embers. As the Jews of the postexilic period expected the world to come to Jerusalem, the present church has supposed that salvation is an acceptance of a Jesus Christ clothed in the garb of Western culture. All nations eventually will come and receive a blessing from the Christian civilization. Like the Christ party we have a triumphant view of the present time. In order to do this we must have assumed we are "something," and we must assume little is to be gained in genuine covenant with others. Both are serious errors.

The most serious problem of triumphalism in the churches arises in so-called foreign missions. Some Christian missionaries have traveled the earth to persuade people to leave their indigenous belief system and life-style in order to become Western style Christians. Eventually people in the Third World have severely protested this patronizing missionary attitude. They have insisted that the task of evangelism must be mutual and reciprocal, that is, the West is as non-Christian as any others, and that evangelism is a two-way street. For this reason many Third World churches have declared a moratorium on Western missionaries. The paradigm of relationship between Christian groups must be the cross, a symbol of self-giving and mutuality with full sharing in each other's social context.

At the same time, there is more in this passage than service. Genuine mutuality recognizes the equal gift of all partners. Many Western Christians understand service, but often do not understand mutuality, because a person trained for service often fails to give and receive on an equal basis. But the deep meaning of the cross in everyday life is that power derives from weakness. God does work through and speak through the poor and the marginal. The churches should proclaim the Gospel and serve those in need, but recognize that God is speaking to them also through the recipients. Only in this way can we hear what God is doing in our time.[9]

However the Gospel may be presented, it needs to be congruent with the cross. If the Gospel persuades through eloquent wisdom, superior

---

[9]Richard L. Rubenstein, *Morality and Eros* (New York: McGraw Hill, 1970) 52.

standard of living, greater technology, or promise of wealth, then it will be a short-lived Gospel. The Gospel is powerful when it demonstrates identity with the people in their context rather than hints of a "superior life-style."

THE MIND OF CHRIST 2:6-16

PREVIEW

In a powerful passage on the cross (1:18–2:5) Paul has chastised the divisive Corinthians for depending on their wisdom rather than God's. But Paul does not really wish to say the cross lacks its own interior wisdom. So in this section he explores the nature of that wisdom. To be sure God's wisdom, as expressed in the cross, does not correspond to the wisdom of this age. Still, one of the gifts of God to the Christian is a wisdom that helps us understand the progression and meaning of history. That wisdom does see order in life, but not as others understand it. If the world had understood, it would not have acted as it did toward Jesus (2:6-9).

But the wisdom of God consists of much more than understanding. The wisdom of God comes to us through the Spirit of God (2:10-13). That Spirit creates among Christians an order which is in touch with ultimate reality, the very depth of God. Even though nonbelievers cannot recognize the order of the Spirit, believers can (and therefore ought not act as if they did not). Knowing the gift of the Spirit is to know the mind of Christ (2:14-16).

• OUTLINE •

2:6-9 God's wisdom is not understood by this age
2:10-13 The Spirit imparts divine wisdom
2:14-16 Those led by the Spirit know the mind of Christ

EXPLANATORY NOTES

2:6-9 Paul was unwilling to say that the cross and the Christian faith were without their own wisdom, so he does claim a wisdom for the mature Christians. That he speaks of the wisdom in a *musterion,* a mystery (see summary essay, 261), does not mean wisdom is a secret *gnosis* (knowledge). The theme suggested in vv. 7-8 is an ancient thread in the Hebrew Bible. In the wisdom section of Genesis (approximately chapters 37–47) Joseph is granted an understanding of history which eludes the "ruler of this age," Pharaoh. In a similar section of Daniel (chapters 1-6), Daniel can understand dreams which none of the king's wisemen can fathom. It is said of Daniel that he has been given the ability to understand mysteries (Hebrew *razim*). Although this gift of understanding mysteries was only granted to special wise persons in the Hebrew Bible, Paul says such wisdom is available to all mature Christians. That wisdom is no less than an understanding of the divine order, an understanding of the process of history. The cross has become a way of understanding life.

When the cross can be seen in this light, obviously the rulers of this age (see summary essay, 246) ought not to have crucified the Lord of glory (see summary essay, 244). Paul does not say specifically why they should not have. Had they understood the cross, they also would have understood the mystery and would have acted quite differently. Or, had they understood the cross, they would have refused to take part in their own defeat. In either case the rulers of this age are shown to be what they are: agents of the divine power (Rom. 13:1) no longer in touch with God's ultimate purpose. By crucifying the Lord of glory they lost their right to govern the new age (see 6:1-11). To confirm the nature of God's wisdom to those who love him, Paul offers a considerably reworked version of Isaiah 64:4.

2:10-13 The wisdom of God comes to the Christian through the activity of the Spirit of God. For Paul a primary function of the Spirit (see summary essay, 256) is to create an order within community, an order which enhances the community. The Spirit can create order where it does not exist (Gen. 1:2). It can pull together disparate communities for a common purpose (Judges 3:10). It spoke to the prophets of Israel and Judah regarding national decisions (1 Kgs. 22:24). The Spirit creates those gifts which are necessary for the functioning of a community (see chapter 12). While other functions of the Spirit can be discerned in the New Testament, Paul often understands the function of the Spirit to create the order of the community. In this way a hierarchy (authority expressed through superordinate and subordinate offices) has been avoided (see summary essay, 223).

In an unusual statement Paul makes the Spirit the sole medium of revelation. Only the Spirit can be in touch with the depth of that ultimate reality, God. Restating 1:21, Paul insists that human wisdom cannot discern that ultimate reality. Rather, any direct human way of knowing God comes through the Spirit. Even in the human relationship one communes with others through the Spirit, that is, the interconnectedness of one personality with another or others (see especially 5:4). The presence of the Spirit of God creates the community of faith in which the divine revelation (dialogue) can be received. Paul understands that he can convey to the faith community this wisdom taught by the Spirit (v. 13), though only to those who are "spiritual" (spiritual truths to those who possess the Spirit, RSV; to those who are spiritual, Grk.).

2:14-16 Paul continues his assertion that the wisdom of God can be imparted only to the *pneumatikos* person(s). The English translation "possessed by the Spirit" does a kindness to Paul. Actually, Paul consistently uses a distinction common to the gnostics of the time. He can divide people into categories of perception: *sarkikos,* those who are materialistic and understand nothing of spiritual things (3:3); *psuchikos,* those who are neither materialistic nor spiritual (therefore the translations "natural" [NIV] or "without the Spirit" [NASB], "unspiritual," [NRSV], 2:14); and the *pneumatikos,* those who discern spiritual things (2:15). If these were levels of life chosen by persons, or even gifts of God (suggested by the NRSV in v. 12), then the implication would not be so difficult. But in gnostic thought these are created categories over which the individual has no control. One assumes Paul did not intend these rigid gnostic classifications as genetic, but as levels of participation in the faith community.

Is this indeed the beginning of the Christ party at Corinth? Have all the *pneumatikoi* gathered together in one house church? In any case Paul reiterates the beginning sentence of this section (2:6): only the mature or spiritual can assimilate the wisdom of God. And, since the spiritual person has received the Spirit, a Spirit that knows the very depths of God, that person cannot be critiqued by the *psuchikoi* or the *sarkikoi.* Paul quotes Isa. 40:13, now applied to Jesus Christ, as a buttress for his argument. Then with incredible audacity he claims he and the "mature" have the mind of Christ, that is, they know the mystery.

THE TEXT IN ITS BIBLICAL CONTEXT

We have already seen how the wisdom of God here depends on an understanding of wisdom in earlier Jewish writings. In such wisdom literature an understanding of life and history is revealed by God to the wise person. If they will listen, the rulers of this age may learn from the revelation of God as granted to the Jewish faithful. Now we see that the same mystery has been granted to the mature Christian. Yet other threads converge. The Christian wisdom is based on the cross, that is, power and order derive from weakness and what appears to be foolishness. This thread weaves in and out of the biblical narrative, from the youngest sons Jacob, Gideon, and David, to the suffering servant of Isaiah 53. Paul has combined the Hebrew sense of revealed mystery with the belief that God works through the weak person or the unexpected event. This kind of faith would be possible only if Paul had a strong sense of the endtime. It is the wisdom of God which points to the coming life of the kingdom. God uses the weak (the cross) as a means of reaching that endtime. Consequently the cross seldom appears useful or pragmatic to those who must build for the present (the rulers of this age).

There are several understandings of spirit in the New Testament (see summary essay, 256). Occasionally one sees the spirit of the good impulse, a spirit which dwells in a person to guide him or her in the appropriate direction (2 Tim. 1:7). Though seldom seen in the New Testament, this use of spirit occurs frequently in intertestamental literature and in postapostolic writings.

In Luke-Acts we see another use: the Spirit is the one who empowers persons for mission (Acts 13:2). In the Johannine material the Spirit comes as the powerful presence (glory) of God (John 14:16-17) to continue the effect of the word become flesh (John 1:14). For Paul the Spirit works out the purpose of God in this world and therefore often expresses more the ordering power of God for the community of faith. The presence of this ordering power as it enhances the purpose of God is called revelation (*apokalupsis*). When the faith community gathers for worship, for study, for action, for organization, there the Spirit is present creating the divine order (5:4).

THE TEXT IN THE LIFE OF THE CHURCH

In this passage we come to the heart of the faith community's attitude toward the state. Though the state carries out a function of order, that order has been based on human wisdom: pragmatic and present oriented. The faith community understands the cross as the focal point of the wisdom of God. The cross points to a divine order (the kingdom of God) which is coming, though not yet present. So though it may seem foolish now, the faith community lives according to the endtime expectation. Frequently that kind of life and faith carries with it a cross—a seemingly contradictory sign of the presence of God. When the faith community lives according to this wisdom of God it deprives the state of its ultimate power, for the state shows to all that it does not understand the ultimate good for all people: the kingdom of God.

The people of the faith community know this wisdom as they meet together to wait for the Spirit of God to guide them. Revelation then is not locked into a writing (the Bible) or into a personal experience. Rather, revelation occurs when the community of faith meets around the word of God to receive its Spirit-led direction.

THE FUNCTION OF LEADERSHIP 3:1-23

PREVIEW

Paul ties together his two arguments: the Corinthian Christians are not sufficiently mature to understand the wisdom of God (solid food) and their quarreling proves it. Naming the house churches after Paul or Apollos was childish in the first place. Leaders are not heroes, but simply instruments of God in the process of Christian development. To show this Paul uses two analogies of growth: the planting of a field and the construction of a building (see summary essay, 220). He uses the two analogies in different ways, however. In regard to the field, he and Apollos planted and watered, but God caused the growth (3:5-9). Apollos and Paul, along with the church at Corinth, would together share in the joy of the harvest. But in the building analogy each builder is given skill to build on the foundation which is Jesus Christ (3:10-15). When the building goes through testing, then the work of the builder will be self-evident and appropriate compensation will be made. The two analogies are appropriate here because the meaning (tenor) of each points to the congregation.

The building analogy was well known in the ancient world. Perhaps its very familiarity triggered in Paul a thought on the temple. Or perhaps he feared the church at Corinth would miss the obvious inference. So he reminds them that they are that building, actually the temple of God itself (3:16-17). In a final statement he returns to the opening thesis: the very presence of divisions indicates they are following the wisdom of this age rather than the wisdom of God.

• OUTLINE •

3:1-4 Divisions indicate the Corinthians are *sarkikoi*

3:5-9 God alone gives growth

3:10-15 Christ alone is the building's foundation

3:16-17 The community of faith is that building, God's temple

3:18-23 For the Christian there are no human limitations

EXPLANATORY NOTES

3:1-4 Once more Paul makes the distinction between the spiritual, *pneumatikoi,* and the worldly, *sarkikoi.* As *sarkikoi* (people of the flesh, NRSV; men of flesh, RSV, NIV; worldly, NASB) the Corinthians could not receive the full truth of the Gospel. Furthermore, attacking their divisiveness, Paul claims the presence of strife proves they are still *sarkikoi* (ordinary men, RSV; mere men, NIV, NASB). Fortunately, Paul avoids the gnostic trap (see explanatory notes for 2:14-16) by explaining how Christians may move from being *sarkikoi* to being *pneumatikoi,* from ordinary people to mature Christians. At first the "babes in Christ" received milk and then gradually moved to "solid food."

Paul was fond of the analogy of human development to describe faith development. In chapter 13 he will speak of the Christian as one who moves from babyhood to endtime adulthood (see explanatory notes for 13:11). In Galatians 4:1-7 he describes the movement from non-Christian to Christian as the development from babies to adopted "children." In Ephesians 4:13-14 Paul exhorts the readers to reach mature adulthood so that they will no longer be tossed about like babies in the winds of false teaching. Little wonder that Paul compares his role as missionary with that of a nurse, gentle with the babies (1 Thess. 2:7).[10]

The two primary "nurses" for the Corinthians were Paul and Apollos. It is to these two that the Corinthian Christians have given allegiance by forming house churches around each. There is here no mention of Peter as such a primary leader. Very likely the spiritual group, the

---

[10]Abraham J. Malherbe, " 'Gentle as a Nurse': The Cynic Background to I Thess ii," *Novum Testamentum* 12 (1970): 203-17; and *Paul and the Thessalonians* (Philadelphia: Fortress Press, 1987) 52-60.

Christ house church, had no need for such childish allegiances.

3:5-9 Paul shifts now to two analogies of growth: a field and a building. While the analogy of human growth dealt primarily with personal formation, these two are congregational in nature. The field, or more particularly the vineyard, was a longstanding analogy for the people of God. The prophet Isaiah used a contemporary love song about a vinekeeper's care for his vineyard as an analogy of God's care for and development of Israel (Isa. 5:1-7). Jesus frequently used the field or vineyard in his parables. The parable of the owner who eventually sent his son to the vineyard reflects the same use of field for Israel (Matt. 21:33-41). Surely the parable of the wheat and the tares implies the analogy of field as the people of God (Matt. 13:24-30).

Paul uses the field as a means of clarifying the interrelationship between himself and the subsequent leader, Apollos. Paul planted and Apollos watered, that is, both were involved in the formation of the church. But formation techniques never automatically produce results. Whatever growth occurred came from God. That is, the developmental process is a God function, not a human technique. Humans can only assist. Consequently, there is no reason to elevate the founder of a church (Paul) above a later leader (Apollos). Nor is there any reason for either to be elevated beyond human capability. Neither could guarantee a satisfactory developmental process. They were only coworkers under God.

3:10-15 The use of a building to describe a community was also well known. The author of 1 Peter (1 Peter 2:4-8) used material from Isaiah 28:16 and Psalm 118:22 to construct a building analogy in which Jesus Christ was the cornerstone rejected by the builders (leaders of the people). In a speech by the apostle Peter, Luke uses the same analogy (Acts 4:11). Even more informative is the attachment of the building analogy to the field or vineyard analogy in Mark 12:1-11, Matthew 21:33-42 and Luke 20:9-18. Obviously these two analogies, rooted deeply in the Hebrew Bible, were very important, as a pair, to the early Christians. Eventually the building illustration became a favorite for postapostolic writers (Shepherd of Hermas, *Vision* 3).

The analogy of the building does not express the same attitude as that of the field. As with the field, Paul acknowledges he founded the church at Corinth and that another (Apollos) is nurturing it. The field illustration stresses the grace of God in granting growth, while the building stresses the necessity of Jesus Christ as the foundation. If anyone uses another foundation, the whole building will be burned up on the day of testing. The analogy of the field stresses the action of God who produces the results of the growth process. The analogy of the building stresses appropriate and skilled building on the basis of the one correct foundation. The minister or leader of the congregation must be skilled as a builder. Paul speaks of himself as a wise architect (v. 10), one trained in the skill of building a congregation. The grace of God comes more in giving the skill to Paul (v. 10, gift; commission, RSV; grace, NIV, NASB) than it does in producing the results.

The Day of v. 13 has a technical meaning (as indicated in the NRSV and NASB). It refers to the Day of the Lord (see summary essay, 237) so often mentioned in the prophetic literature of the Hebrew Bible. That Day refers, in Jewish thought, to the endtime. Without making it strictly chronological, the Day will be the time when God's promise has been realized. Of course that should be a day of great rejoicing, but the prophets spoke of it as a day of wrath and judgment. The Jews had violated the covenant and, therefore, would no longer be reckoned as children of the promise (Hosea 11:1-7). The Jews would do well not to anticipate the coming Day, for it would be darkness for them, not light (Amos 5:18).

Nevertheless, through the centuries anticipation of the coming Day of the Lord remained essential to the Jewish people, for they believed more in a kingdom coming in history than an ideal world in heaven. All decisions, all endeavors must pass the test of that coming Day. Paul, perhaps more than any other person in the New Testament, lived in keen anticipation of the coming Day. The work of ministry must be ultimate, that is, it must be acceptable at the endtime. For Paul only that church and ministry based on Jesus Christ (and the cross!) will endure the tests of history.

In vv. 14-15 Paul offers a rather strange disclaimer, not unlike the picture of the prophet as a watchman in Ezekiel 33:7-9. As the watchman must speak the word of the Lord whether successful or not, so, for Paul, the minister must build whether or not the "building" finally stands. Do we see here a shadow of doubt in Paul, a cry that he must do what he is doing regardless of the consequences?

3:16-17 Though with the building analogy Paul tries to establish the centrality of Jesus Christ as the foundation, he shifts temporarily to the logical extension of his thought: the faith community has now replaced the Jewish temple. Only briefly mentioned here and in 6:19, the movement from Jewish temple to Christian faith community became an absolute necessity for the first Christians. In the Hebrew Bible the people of God centered in the temple at Jerusalem, where the Lord was sitting mighty and lifted up, that is, as the king of the people (Isa. 6:1). We do have some intimations of dissatisfaction with spatial limitations of the temple. The oftquoted Isaiah 28:16 indicates the temple cornerstone has more to do with the covenant among the people (justice and righteousness) than with a prime cut stone. And the all-important Isaiah 66:1 chastises the peoples for limiting the Lord's kingly throne to a place in Jerusalem:

> Heaven is my throne
> and the earth is my footstool.

Following this critique of the temple in the Hebrew Bible, the early Christians spoke of God's presence in terms of the Spirit acting among the community of believers wherever they may be. Jesus promised to be where two or three were gathered (Matt. 18:20). The first martyr for the new faith, Stephen, lost his life because of his attack on the temple and its limitations (Acts 7:48). Jesus, in the Gospel of John, insisted that his body would replace the temple (John 2:19-22), and the day was at hand when God would no longer be limited to the temple in Jerusalem. True worshipers will worship in the Spirit (John 4:19-24). And above all the author of Hebrews sees in Jesus Christ the fulfillment of temple practice, so that the temple has been rendered unnecessary (Hebrews 8:13). Paul uses this primary understanding of the Spirit working in the community to say that divisions in the body rip apart the presence of God in the world. Making a somewhat legal threat, Paul claims God will destroy anyone who destroys that divine presence.

3:18-23 Paul returns to his main theme: just as God's wisdom seems foolish to humans, so human wisdom appears folly in the light of God's purpose. But this time, as he deflates the importance of himself and Apollos as leaders, he returns also to the Cephas or Peter group. Peter had had no connection with the Corinthian church. The group named after him was simply honoring the famous spokesperson of the Twelve. In language which foreshadows the great affirmation of Romans 8:38-39, Paul denies the possibility that human groupings could limit the Christian—nor could historical existence (the world), nor the concerns of life (life), nor the separation of death (death), nor life in its present disunity (things present), nor life in its future conclusion (things about to be). The person in Christ has no such limitations. At that point Paul has sharp words for the Christ group. There are no boundaries for the faithful precisely because they are all of Christ, and Christ is from the universal, God. How could there be a Christ party, a Christ house church?

THE TEXT IN ITS BIBLICAL CONTEXT

Images of leadership in the Bible almost invariably refer to guidance in the process of growth. The two images used here: a vinedresser or farmer, and a builder, stress the skills of nurture and development. Paul also used another popular comparison when he spoke of himself as a parent (3:2). In fact, the image of process was implied by his decision to feed them milk rather than solid food. We could add to these three well-known examples yet another: that of a shepherd (John 10:1-18; 1 Peter 5:1-5). Even more pointedly in Hebrews the leaders of the people have been precisely those who guided the people on their faith journey (Heb. 11). For human leadership of the people of God, images of power and authority are consistently lacking (though those issues are always present; see 5:4, and summary essay, 220). Images like owner and owned, master and slave, king and subjects, even teacher and student, are remarkably absent. Paul uses this point to show the foolishness of divisions in the church along lines of authority, or the futility of attachment to leadership figures.

Though planting and conceiving are critical in the growth process, Paul stresses more the end of development than the beginning. He understands himself as a responsible worker for God, as one who works on an assigned task, the results of which are in the hands of God. Most of the materials of the Bible are oriented toward the endtime, that is, toward results. For example, one can tell a proper prophet by results (Jer. 28:9). Under stress Paul places his own call under the scrutiny of results (2 Cor. 10-13). [11] Leaders are to be followed because they have properly matured, that is, their faith has produced fruit (Heb. 13:7; 1 Tim. 3:1-13). In the Bible leadership seldom depends on the right start. From the biblical perspective the result depends more on the action of God

---

[11] Bengt Holmberg, *Paul and Power: The Structure of Authority in the Primitive Church as Reflected in the Pauline Epistles* (Philadelphia: Fortress Press, 1980).

in the process than it does on the faithfulness of humans to the right beginning. In fact, the biblical narrative oftens exults in the inappropriate beginning of the leader. Leadership depends more on the Hebraic sense of wise maturation than it does on the hellenistic sense of reproducing or maintaining the original qualities of authority.

The analogy of the building does introduce, however, the necessity of a correct start. One builds on the foundation of Jesus Christ. While Paul meant to say, by the simile, that none of the first leaders can be considered a founder of the church, the analogy was later taken in quite a different sense. In the early church the building analogy was a favorite. As the church universal became more and more divided, authors spoke of the true church as that which built on Jesus and the apostles. Each successive generation became a new course of stones in the growing building. By this analogy it was thought one could determine which church genuinely goes back to the original (Shepherd of Hermas 89). By the same standard the building analogy could be used for reformation of the church—to show that the building no longer corresponds to the foundation. For that reason some reformers made 3:11 their slogan.

THE TEXT IN THE LIFE OF THE CHURCH

When the church becomes divided it seems only natural to suppose it lacks strong, authoritative leadership. People need authoritative leadership for at least two reasons. For people who work every day at a business or craft, or any kind of daily labor, there is little time for reflection. They need trustworthy leadership which can give them specific direction. Additionally, people who live in what we call the social matrix (as opposed to those who live a more transient, translocal life) feel a deep need for the kind of direction which holds together family and community. Since much of their time is spent earning a living it is only reasonable for them to seek out persons who can offer clear direction. For these two reasons people seek strong leadership: to express clear direction and to resolve family and community conflicts.

The problem has always been with us. It occurred in the Corinthian church. Someone gained enough power to thwart Paul's second visit (2 Cor. 2:5-9; 7:5-13). That created a crisis in leadership at Corinth. But we also live in a time when powerful leaders can easily enter the dynamics of a local community. By means of the media, television and radio personalities with strong authority can offer their power to local people. Consequently the temptation to accept strong authority seems stronger and divisiveness more prevalent. To shift toward authoritative leadership may create stability and unity, but at the cost of vision and growth. Paul almost shouted to the Corinthians: Do not limit yourselves in Christ. No human is ultimate; no authority final; all leadership must contribute to the developmental pattern of life (note Eph. 4:11-16).

ON BEING FOOLS FOR CHRIST 4:1-21

PREVIEW

In this final section of Paul's response to the issue of divisions, he summarizes the first three chapters. In 4:1-5 he reiterates the functions of leaders in the church; they are stewards of the mysteries. Guardians are to be faithful in their service, but only when the mystery (endtime) has been revealed will it be possible to judge the leader's work. According to vv. 6-7 he has applied these teachings to himself and Apollos for two reasons: that they can see how Scripture applies to their life, and that there is no reason for one leader to be elevated above another. After all, life is a gift. But, according to vv. 8-13, some Corinthians seem to have forgotten the gift of Christ. They considered themselves wealthy and complete without that redemptive action of God still visible in the apostles. Paul has tried to instruct the Corinthians according to his analogies of leadership, that is, as a parent. But if it is authority they wish, then he can also bear a rod (4:14-21).

• OUTLINE •

4:1-5 Leaders are Servants and Stewards
4:6-7 Analogies of Leadership Applied
4:8-13 The End Time is Not Yet
4:14-21 There is Power in the Kingdom of God

EXPLANATORY NOTES

4:1-5 Paul applies his arguments now to himself as an apostle. His apostleship does not lie in his authority nor even in his divine call. He wishes the Corinthians to consider him an administrator for Jesus Christ and a steward of the mysteries of God. The term translated servant in v. 1 refers more to a subordinate administrator. The translation servant (only here and John 18:36, RSV) dares not convey the sense of slave (*dou-*

los). When Paul works with the congregation, he is acting as a skilled subordinate in the service of Jesus Christ. It is not his responsibility to establish and keep a certain doctrinal stance or a defined style of life. Rather, he is charged to be a steward of the mystery (see 2:7). In New Testament language an *oikonomos* serves as a manager of the household. Among the steward's responsibilities were financial management (see Luke 16:1-8). Paul was not responsible for the money so much as to hold in trust that wisdom of God which made life meaningful.

In vv. 3-5 Paul once more appears defensive (see 3:14-15). How they or any human court judge him is the least of his concerns. Clearly Paul feels under attack, likely coming from the same person mentioned in 2 Corinthians (2:5-11 and 7:12). But as the analogies indicate, "the proof is in the pudding": God will assess his work in the endtime.

4:6-7 The prior analogies are now applied to the leadership question at Corinth. Though the intent of v. 6 is fairly clear, the translation is not. The word translated "apply" would normally mean transform (Phil. 3:21), or even disguise (2 Cor. 11:12-15). The use here of the Greek term *metaschematizo* helps us understand Paul's use of Scripture. Even though there is very little reflection within the New Testament on a style of interpretation itself, when there is one expects the root word *hermeneuo* to be used. On the road to Emmaus (Lk. 24) Jesus interpreted (*diermeneuo*) the entire Hebrew Bible to the two disciples.

Paul uses the words from the root of *hermeneuo* for the interpreting of tongues (12:10, 30; 14:5, 13, 26, 27, 28). In a technical situation the author of 2 Peter says Scripture is not a matter of one's own interpretation (*epilusis*, enlightenment). Paul's use of *metaschematizo* implies a certain style of using the Hebrew Bible. Paul transfers the meaning of a passage, or collection of passages, to a present situation. The Hebrew Bible relates analogously to the present day; or, the Hebrew Bible contains analogies for the church at Corinth.[12] True to his understanding of the Law, Paul does not use the Hebrew Bible as a source of rules or directives (only 3:17 states a *lex talionis* [law of retaliation] based on divine vengeance). But he does claim to be a steward of the mysteries.

The translation of v. 6 becomes more complicated if 6b contains a slogan. There are many slogans in 1 Corinthians (see summary essay,

---

[12]Richard B. Hays, *Echoes of Scripture in the Letters of Paul* (New Haven CT: Yale University Press, 1989) 184.

241). The origin of most of them has been difficult to determine. Frequently, though, the source will be important for understanding the letter. Some of the slogans are

> All things are lawful for me. (6:12; 10:23)
> It is well for a man not to touch a woman. (7:1)
> All of us possess knowledge. (8:1)
> An idol has no real existence. (8:4)
> There is no God but one. (8:4)

It is probable these slogans originated in the preaching of Paul, but they have been misapplied by particular groups at Corinth. Some can be identified. The Christ house church surely utilized the slogans "All of us possess knowledge (*gnosis*)" and "All things are lawful." The slogan in 6b is best translated by the NASB and NIV: "Do not go beyond what is written." Apparently some group or groups at Corinth were concerned that the emerging Christianity not move beyond the limits of the Hebrew Bible. It might be impossible to discern whether this group was still Jewish in its religious expression or whether it was simply conservative toward tradition. We do know that attempts to identify the opponents of Paul as traditional Jews have invariably met with difficulty.

One group does not wish to go beyond the Scriptures, and another group, the Christ house church, says all things are lawful. Paul cannot take sides with either, yet wishes to offend neither. Since, in the context of chapter 3 he has chastised the Cephas, Paul, and Apollos groups for immature attachment to leadership, it seems most likely one or all of them has countered the freewheeling Christ group with the traditionalist slogan of v. 6b. It is to them, the three groups, that he addresses the remarks of v. 6. He has used the analogies from the Hebrew Bible in order to demonstrate the proper use of the Scriptures. Paraphrased he says: You want to stick with the Bible? Then apply these truths to yourself! And the truth is: there is no reason for any one of us to be elevated above another. But then his mind shifts. There is nothing exceptional about Paul, Cephas, or Apollos, or any one of the Corinthians, nothing that would demand adulation or excessive loyalty. For that matter there is nothing exceptional about the Christ party either. So he turns, so to speak, and asks them (the Christ party) what they have that they did not receive as a gift (repeating the theme of 1:26-29). What do they have about which they can boast (see summary essay, 246)? With that he pens a devastating attack on the Christ house church, the most sarcastic verses of the New Testament.

4:8-13 The Christ group thinks it has reached the endtime; if so, it reached it too soon. The church always lives between the old age and the age to come, the present life and the life to come, the fact of redemption without the perfection of salvation, the already but not yet. That gap cannot be closed, indeed dare not be closed. From the Jewish (and hence Christian) perspective life moves from promise to fulfillment. The people of God live in the promise (Gal. 3:29; 4:28) as they move toward and anticipate the fulfillment of that promise. Moving towards and anticipating the fulfillment (endtime) greatly alters our present life, as this letter abundantly demonstrates. But the church has not yet reached the end. To pretend it has destroys the servant nature of the people of God, that is, it obliterates the meaning of the cross. The people of God are facilitators of the endtime, not owners of it. The Christ house church has a prematurely realized endtime. In an extraordinarily powerful passage Paul makes this point scathingly clear to the Christ group.

Picking up some of their claims, he states with feigned amazement, "already you have been satiated." The metaphor does not refer to faith "fulfillment," but the loss of that creative tension caused by yearning for the endtime. They no longer hunger and thirst after the kingdom. They have been filled up (the tense of the Greek verb is perfect and therefore underlines the "already") and now are satisfied. In the next simile, referring to the spiritual knowledge (*gnosis*) of 1:5, Paul says they are already rich. They have no need of God to enrich them, or of Paul to share the mystery, for they already have *gnosis* "piled sky-high" (4:8, CPV). Since they have lost the tension between already and not yet, and have possession of full knowledge, he cynically supposes they must already be kings in the kingdom of God. They have reached the endtime and rule in it. And most sarcastically of all, he wishes this were true, so they could come to him, the apostle Paul, and offer him a place in that very kingdom he first preached to them!

If they are living between the times, between promise and fulfillment, then the world should be able to see the results of the conflict right at the front ranks of God's people. So Paul reflects with them how the life of the apostles demonstrates the "not yet" nature of Christian life (v. 9). He uses a startling illustration to make the point. The analogy surely must be the cruel games of the Roman Empire, specifically the procession which preceded the fights. In such games the official priests came first, then various dignitaries, and finally the criminals or gladiators—those condemned to die. The apostles (and therefore all Christians?—see below, 52) do not march with the priests at the beginning of the parade. Their role is not triumphal or celebrative. Rather, they belong with the criminal, the riffraff, the condemned. Yet there is more here than first meets the eye. Yes, they take a place with the outcasts rather than the victorious, but the outcasts have a very important function. The gladiatorial games probably originated with Etruscans, who believed that the shed blood of the fighters fed the souls of the prior dead. The fights had a serious significance: they kept "alive" the souls of previous generations. To be last in the procession, among those condemned to death, was significant. The apostles (and Christians?) were performing, even in their sufferings, a redemptive act for others. The nature of this redemptive act becomes clear in v. 13.

Still reflecting on the gladiatorial games, Paul says the apostles are a spectacle (*theatron*, v.9) for everyone to see. Paul mentions three groups which will see this "theater": the *kosmos*, the *angeloi*, and *anthropoi*. *Kosmos* in Paul may refer to the world in the same sense as "this age" stands overagainst the "age to come" (5:10; 7:31). But generally it is the world (and its people) as we know it—neither evil nor redeemed (14:10; Rom. 1:8).

The *angeloi* (angels) present much more difficulty (see summary essay, 255). An angel normally is a messenger. In the New Testament it usually refers to a messenger from God (transliterated "angel" in most translations), though the word *angelos* must sometimes be understood as a messenger from humans (Lk. 7:24; 9:52).

But not even all divine messengers, angels, have the same function. In the Hebrew Bible the throne of God was surrounded by "sons of God" who had various functions in the "divine state." Among these functions was the responsibility for human corporate institutions, primarily the nations (Deut. 32:8, RSV). That is, God rules the universal corporate life, but there are lesser corporate structures, such as nations. These also are a part of God's rule. Only in this way can we understand Romans 13:1-7. During the intertestamental period these "sons of God" were known by other names, such as spirits (1 Pet. 3:19) or angels. Paul sometimes uses the term angel in this way (6:3; 11:10; perhaps Gal. 3:19). So here Paul means the apostles have appeared before the nations (especially Rome).

The third category is simply the general word, *anthropos* (see summary essay, 220), for humankind. So Paul speaks in descending order of the apostles appearing before the world (to make sure descending order is conveyed, the NIV "whole universe" would be a better translation), before nations and before humanity in general.

Continuing the theme of apostolic (Christian) life between the times, Paul builds a set of contrasts between himself and the Christ house church. In the first contrast (v. 10) they are wise and he is a fool (*moros*). Paul has already spoken ironically of human wisdom as foolishness and divine foolishness as wisdom (see 1:18-21). Here he identifies the Christ house church as people who believe they have the wisdom of God, yet he, their teacher, knows God's wisdom takes the form of foolishness in his life. Even though the term "fool" has highly derogatory connotations (Mt. 5:22; Lk. 11:40; 12:20), Paul consistently uses it with theological irony (also 3:18; 2 Cor. 11:16, 17, 19, 21; 12:6, 11). Historically the Pauline slogan "fools for Christ" has been one of the most powerful parabolic expressions of Christian life between the times (see summary essay, 261).

In the second contrast the Christ group is strong while he is weak. Paul has already made the same ironic contrast between weak and strong as he did between wise and foolish. The weakness of God is stronger than the strength of humans (1:25). And he has identified all Christians as weak in comparison with those who think they are strong (1:27). Again he censures the Christ group for so quickly assuming they already live in the endtime, for thinking they are the strong in the Lord. One wonders how consistently Paul used the terms "strong" and "weak" in the Corinthian correspondence. Are the weak of 8:7-13, those whose consciences are damaged by eating meat offered to idols, the same weak as here? Surely the strong, who say all things are lawful (10:23), must include the Christ group. Are the weak those who know the end has not yet come, and therefore recognize a need for order?

In a third ironic contrast he speaks of the Christ group as glorious or splendid, a condition of the endtime (Eph. 5:27), while Paul lives without honor (see summary essay, 246). Following these sarcastic contrasts Paul lists some characteristics of living before the endtime (vv. 11-12a). The conditions—hungry, thirsty, naked (or poorly clothed), beat up, without a home, and self supporting—all sound like the condition of "the least" in Matthew 25. "The least" there, however, were the marginal people, while Paul here speaks of everyone's life in the service of God.

In vv. 12b-13a Paul speaks finally of how the apostle, or Christian, faces a hostile world. It sounds much like an exposition of the "turn the other cheek" passage in the Sermon on the Mount (Mt. 5:39-42). Paul not only refuses to retaliate, he gives something in return. Under attack he blesses, he refuses to strike back (submits), and he comforts. Paul does not develop an ethic of nonviolence, even though he clearly will refer to the Sermon on the Mount as an ethic for Christians (Rom. 12:9-21). As the next half verse indicates Paul is more concerned with reconciliation than with nonretaliation.

In v. 13b Paul makes it quite evident why the apostles and other Christians can be found in difficult and painful circumstances. Lacking are Stoic (ethical repression of emotions) or heroic (discipleship at any cost) motifs. Paul says they have become the scum (refuse, RSV; rubbish, NRSV) of the world, the offscouring (dregs, NASB, NRSV; refuse, NIV) of all things, even until now. As can be seen from the variety of translations, both terms (*perikatharma* and *peripsema*) refer to the act of scouring (the term dregs, as "the poorest part of anything," misses the critical point).

The two terms occur only here in the New Testament, but have become unusually powerful metaphors for the church and its mission between the times (after the call, but before the consummation). If one were to extend Paul's metaphor, it might be clearer. The Christ group would be a clean sink, thought to be already in the endtime; the church of Luke-Acts might be soap, called to transform (cleanse) the world. But the presence of the Pauline church indicates the cleansing has already occurred. The church is the goop or scum left over after the cleansing. The church does not represent the marginal element of society (the dregs), but, like the self-giving of God on the cross, represents a church which gives itself for the world. The appearance of the church as offscouring indicates that cleansing action has occurred. The church is not that which is cleansed, nor does it have the power of cleaning. God is the cleaner and the church is God's agent in the process. The faith community both functions for redemption and parabolically demonstrates God's action of cleansing. The two metaphors here parallel closely the liturgical metaphor "living sacrifice" in Romans 12:1.[13]

---

[13] J. N. Bremer, "Scapegoat Rituals in Ancient Greece," *Harvard Studies in Classical Philology* 87 (1983): 299-320.

4:14-21 As a personality Paul must have been extraordinarily complex. That complexity is nowhere more self-evident than in this short passage. Having described himself as weak, compared to the strong at Corinth, and having used the metaphor of offscouring to describe the apostles, now he indicates without much finesse and subtlety that he can force them to "get their act together." After insisting that leaders are not to be emulated or honored, he reminds them that only he, Paul, can be considered their father (see summary essay, 252).

Paul claimed he was not trying to shame (see summary essay, 248) the Corinthians, but was only acting as their father. No matter how many "legal guardians" they would have, there was only one real father, or founder. By denigrating Apollos to legal guardian (the term *paidagogos* may also refer to one who has custody over a child, Gal. 3:24-25), and elevating himself as their only father, he appears to reinforce the divisions which already had surfaced at Corinth. He strives to avoid that by noting his fatherhood was a gift in the gospel, not a choice on his part. Nevertheless as their father he asks them, in v. 16, to imitate him (see summary essay, 252).

The "imitation of Paul" has produced problems for many Christians, especially those who hold dearly the imitation of Jesus. Though Jesus calls for discipleship, he does not call for imitation of himself (e.g., Mark 8:34). Jesus admonishes people to hear his words (Matt. 7:24) and urges listeners to be as mature in the dealing with others as is God (Matt. 5:48). Later in this letter Paul will ask the Corinthians to imitate him as he does Christ (11:1) But more often he simply asks people to imitate him (11:1; 1 Thess. 1:6; 2 Thess. 3:7, 9; Phil. 3:17). He also asked the Thessalonians to imitate the Judean churches (1 Thess. 2:14) and the Ephesians to imitate God (5:1). The "imitation of Paul," however, need not disturb those who would follow the footsteps of Jesus (1 Pet. 2:21). Invariably Paul asks the faith community to imitate him in his stance toward the endtime. In 4:16, speaking directly to the Christ party, he asks them to live between the times as does he. At this point we realize the apostolic life applies also to the faith community (see explanatory notes on v. 9), that Paul only stands in the front line of a march which includes all Christians.

In order to remind them of their position before the endtime Paul has sent Timothy for further instruction (v. 17), though apparently he has not yet arrived (16:10). Paul himself also plans to return even though his opponents have spread the rumor that he has no intention of coming back. Presumably the same opponents also accused him of speaking out of both sides of his mouth (the Yes and No of 2 Cor. 1:15-22). But, says Paul, that is just so much talk. The kingdom of God deals with power not talk, and Paul can come to them with power if that is needed (see the same threat in 2 Cor. 13:1-4).

THE TEXT IN ITS BIBLICAL CONTEXT

The people of God have always been plagued by the problem of a prematurely realized endtime. In simpler times, when people are moving toward the fulfillment of a promise, they grumble because the goal has not yet been realized. The problem is one of instant eschatological (referring to endtime) gratification. While on the forty-year march in the desert, the Hebrew people, whose goal was the Promised Land, constantly murmured against Moses (Num. 11:1-6; 14:1-35). They either wished to arrive immediately, or they wished to return to Egypt. Finally God determined none of them would enter the Promised Land (Num. 14:26-35). It is striking that in the Gospel of John the Jews also murmured even when the end was present in Jesus (the real bread from heaven, John 6:41-42).

In more complex situations, when security seems within reach, the people of God have sought wealth, possessions, families, property, power, and divine favor, rather than continue the process of blessing the world (Gen. 12:1-3). The classical prophets saw the problem. They chastised those who were at ease in Zion (Amos 6:1), those who no longer functioned as the servants of Yahweh (Micah 6:8). Jesus made the same critique of those who stored up treasures for themselves (Matt. 6:19-21) or were anxious about this world rather than the kingdom and its righteousness (6:25-33). In the face of such a diversion from God's promise the people of God are asked to "repent" or turn around and once more serve the Lord (Hosea 14:1).

Sometimes the people of God grumbled because the promise had not yet been fulfilled. Sometimes the people of God lived as if the promise were fulfilled, when, in fact, there are many who had not received the blessing.

The problem of the Christ group at Corinth was more complex, however. Before the Exile the Jewish people had failed to respond to the prophetic call for repentance. Judea was overrun by the Babylonians and the people taken into captivity. In despair Jewish prophets doubted whether the people of God could ever bring the promise to fulfillment.

They spoke of an end to this age and the age of fulfillment as a gift of God. We call this type of Jewish prophetic thinking "apocalypticism" (see summary essay, 237). It formed the basis for much of the faith found in the earliest Christians. Jesus Christ on the cross brought an end to this age (10:11; Rom. 10:4), and by his resurrection brought people into the new age (Rom. 8:11).

The Apostle Paul took this message to the Gentile world. He was totally unaware of the traps which might lie in wait for Hellenistic Christians who heard the good news of life in a new age. He did not expect the Christ party to enter into the new age, the time of fulfillment, without awareness that they were still living between the resurrection and the end (see explanatory notes for 15:12). Most of the problems mentioned in 1 Corinthians revolve around this dilemma: the new Christians at Corinth did not understand Paul's Jewish apocalypticism. In this letter we can see Paul insist that the end is not yet, but simultaneously urge his readers to be done with their past life under the old order.

THE TEXT IN THE LIFE OF THE CHURCH

Members of the present-day faith community find themselves caught in the dynamics of this powerful passage. On the one hand, historically many Christians have inadvertently identified with the Christ group. Though often far from the spiritual arrogance that marked the first gnostic faith community, we have sometimes practiced a life of spiritual exactitude which assumes the end has been reached. At those times we claim a superior Christian life-style, separate from the world and other Christians. We fail to take responsibility for the condition of a world still between the times, and we ignore the plight of marginal people.

On the other hand, few know better than the faith community the cost of living between the times. Having left behind the "old age" they find themselves caught between the call to live in the kingdom and the power of a world not willing to see the vision of peace, of justice, and of equality. The church is called to keep before it the vision of a world in which there is no longer a qualitative difference between insider and outsider, employer and employee, male and female (Gal. 3:28). Those who try to live, parabolically, according to this vision will, with the apostle Paul, appear like fools to the world, the governments, and all people. The trap is painful, but all Christians, like the first Corinthian communities of faith, are called to live between the times.

FIRST CORINTHIANS 5:1–6:20
TWO CASE STUDIES AT CORINTH

INTRODUCTION

In these chapters Paul deals with two problems in the Corinthian church. As a section the two chapters are sufficiently unique to puzzle the person who reads the letter as a whole. We have already seen that chapters 1–4 were written in response to information from Chloe's people. They had told Paul about the quarrels between the house churches. The first four chapters speak only to that issue of divisions. Chapters 7 to 15 deal specifically with questions raised by a letter from the church at Corinth, questions which have seemingly little to do with the divisions. Chapter 7 begins specifically with the phrase "Now concerning the things about which you wrote." The phrase "now concerning" is repeated at each change of subject (7:25; 8:1; 12:1; 16:1, 12). If chapters 1–4 respond to the issue of divisions and 7–15 are a reply to the letter, then what are 5 and 6?

Since chapters 5 and 6 deal with specific problems apparently unrelated to the divisions, it has been assumed these two issues were carried to Paul by another oral report—just like Chloe's (1:11). Paul first responded to this second oral report before moving on to the concerns formally raised by the letter from Corinth.

But there is a catch. Chapters 7–15 deal with congregational issues. With the possible exception of remarriage in chapter 7, there is no discussion of immorality in that section. Nevertheless, readers frequently suppose Paul wrote to the Christians at Corinth in order to warn them of immorality. That opinion could only come from reading 5:1-8 and 6:12-20. In other words, the only seeming discussions of immorality in 1 Corinthians occur in these two chapters.

But are they really discussions of immorality? Chapter 5:1-8 has more to do with the Christ house church living above the law than it does with a gross sexual sin. The discussion of prostitution in 6:12-20 refers more to betrayal of the faith community than it does to brothers visiting the temple brothel. If this be true chapters 5 and 6 actually continue the discussion of chapters 1-4. Chapter 5 is addressed to the Christ house church. It is a specific demonstration (case study) that their living in the endtime has already backfired. Chapter 6 is addressed more to the other three groups. It shows them (by means of a second case study) that their secular practicality has kept them from living in the endtime.

If chapters 5 and 6 are examples or case studies coming out of the argument in chapters 1–4, then there is little reason to suppose chapters 5–15 were written as one unit. Either chapters 5–6 were written to illustrate chapters 1–4 and therefore belong with them, or they were written in response to some information which is neither from Chloe or the letter. In the latter case they serve as a bridge between the discussion about divisions and the specific questions which begin in chapter 7. In either case chapters 5 and 6, like chapters 1–4, probably were written after chapters 7–15 had been penned.

Chapter 5 was written primarily for the benefit of the Christ house church (see explanatory note on 1:12). In 5:1-5 Paul accuses them of living so intensely in the endtime that they have ignored a case of immorality right in their congregation. He asks them to take formal congregational action. In vv. 6-8, noting that their spiritual self-confidence has led them astray, he reflects on the Jewish festival of unleavened bread as an analogy of community disintegration from within.

By this time Paul recognizes how his words could be misinterpreted. So in vv. 9-13 he protects himself. To be sure, he had written in a previous letter (see introduction above, 10) that they should not associate with immoral people. But he had not meant they should leave the real world (and live only in the endtime; v. 10; see summary essay, 237). Rather he had meant they need to be careful about accepting people in the congregation who have not really experienced a change (v. 11).

In chapter 6 Paul does a complete turn. Speaking now to the other house churches, he admonishes them for allowing authorities of this age to make judgments about those living in the age to come. How could they possibly use the local judicial system (6:1-8)? After all, the unrighteous cannot inherit the kingdom of God, not unless they too are changed as the Corinthian Christians were changed (vv. 9-11).

Bringing the argument of chapters 1–6 to a close, Paul shifts to body language in such a way that both concerns are caught up. In 6:12-14 he quotes the Christ party slogan—"All things are lawful"—but reminds them that only the faith community, the body of Christ, will last forever. Using the same metaphor (see summary essay, 227) he tells the others that joining themselves to structures outside the body of Christ (the old age) will prostitute the body. Individual Christians are members of the body of Christ, the new temple, and they dare not betray that fact by forming other loyalties and commitments. Finally Paul's message is only one: Christians live in an endtime community. By their actions or by their commitments they can destroy or damage their own relationship to the body of Christ.

Understood this way, the passage progresses in the following manner.

5:1-13 Spiritual arrogance can blind the faith community
6:1-11 This age cannot inherit the age to come
6:12-20 Formation of the body of Christ is ultimate

SPIRITUAL ARROGANCE 5:1-13

PREVIEW

This chapter follows the critique of the Christ group in chapters 1–4. In 4:8-13 Paul had accused the Christ house church of entering the endtime too quickly. Now he deals with a problem they have created by their spiritual arrogance. In 5:1-5 he speaks of the specific case: one of the house church members is living with his stepmother. Apparently the Christ house church had accepted a member whose spiritual knowledge was exceptional, but whose lifestyle created serious difficulties. Paul insists they take care of the matter. By comparing their situation with the Feast of Unleavened Bread (and the Christian Easter), he shows them, in vv. 6-8, that even one person living in the old age can destroy the faith community of the new age. Yet he has already learned that his Jewish endtime thinking can be easily misunderstood. So he tries to make it perfectly clear. In vv. 9-13, referring back to his wrongly interpreted previous letter, he says entering the new age does not mean leaving this world and its problems. It does mean a newness of life which excludes behavior that belongs in the old age.

• OUTLINE •

5:1-5 One member is not living in the new age
5:6-8 An analogy: old leaven destroys the new lump
5:9-13 On living in the old age, while being in the new

EXPLANATORY NOTES

5:1-5 Everyone knows there is a member of the church at Corinth who is living with his stepmother, namely, a woman who had been married to his father but who was not his mother. We can be fairly sure the member belongs to the Christ house church. In the first place the house church is arrogant about the matter. This fits the sarcastic attack on the Christ group found in 4:8-13 and even repeats the words of 4:18-19 (puffed up or arrogant). In the Corinthian church only the Christ house church would have considered itself above the reproach of law and social custom. Furthermore, the Christ house church did not simply overlook the situation. They had proudly included the man in their fellowship because, in their opinion, he was acting under the leadership of the Holy Spirit (see explanatory notes on v.4). It is difficult to determine now whether Paul was really concerned about the morality issue or whether he simply wished to use this situation as a case study for the Christ house church. As it stands the instance was surely very exceptional, not a burning ethical issue of the time, and only marginally a moral issue. Marrying one's stepmother was forbidden by the Jewish Holiness Code (Lev. 18:8). It occurs in a list of twelve prohibitions which define the boundaries of incest (mother, aunt, wife's sister and the like; Lev. 20:11). Presumably, in dealing with the issue of incest, we are defining morality, but it was a political issue when Absalom went in to his father's concubines (2 Sam. 16:20-23), or Adonijah asked for Abishag the Shunammite (1 Kings 2:22). Paul called it an immorality (*porneia*), but he did not press that accusation. For example, he says nothing about the disposition of the woman involved.

It is equally difficult to know what the Hellenistic Corinthian Christians felt about the situation. Paul says even the Gentiles do not countenance such behavior (note, e.g., Euripides' *Hippolytus*). There is evidence that Roman law did consider marriage to a stepmother or stepson incestuous, so Paul could have been justified in his statement. Nevertheless, Paul probably overstated the case. The situation was not sufficiently serious to appear in the letter from the Corinthians (i.e., not mentioned in chapters 7–15). "Spirit" or no "spirit," one can hardly believe the Christ house church would have ignored a grossly immoral situation. Paul was using the case of a man living with his stepmother to puncture the "puffed up" balloon of the Christ house church.

Paul calls the case an immorality (*porneia*). The word *porneia* cannot be easily translated. It may mean sexual relationship between persons not married (and translated fornication or unchastity), or sexual relationship by married persons outside the marriage bond (translated immorality), or sexual relationship for profit (translated prostitution). One cannot always easily decide what an author meant. In a severe list like 1 Timothy 1:9-10, surely the immoral man (*pornos*) uses sex for profit ("pimp" in English). The presence of *pornoi*, the immoral ones, in the rapacious lists of 5:9-11 and 6:9-10 make it likely these too were persons involved in selling sex. The claim by the Jews that they were not born of *porneia* (John 8:41) must refer to illicit sexual relationships and perhaps even prostitution. The Jews said they had one Father.

Since adultery is mentioned specifically in the lists of Matthew 15:19 and Mark 7:21-22, one must suppose *porneia* there refers more to indiscriminate sexual relationships, or fornication. On the other hand, the decree of the Jerusalem council (Acts 15:20, 29) called on Gentiles to abstain from the unfaithfulness of idolatry and the unfaithfulness of *porneia*, in this case illicit sexual relationships by persons already married. There is no simple way to translate *porneia*, yet the interpretation of *porneia* will be critical for our interpretation of several passages in 1 Corinthians (see explanatory notes for 5:9-11; 6:9-10, 15-20; 7:2; 10:8).

In this passage we assume the phrase "to have a woman" means married rather than "living together" (7:2, 29; also "to have a man," John 4:18). Since the man of 5:1 has been married to his stepmother, *porneia* must have yet another nuance of meaning—an illicit marriage, that is, incest.

Though the Christ house church has been puffed up (arrogant, NRSV), this case ought rather to make them mourn. Mourning normally signifies the grief that accompanies a loss (Matt. 9:15; Rev. 18:7), but it can also refer to contrition. Concerned about violence and conflict, James says people should draw near to God (James 4:8) and let their laughter turn to mourning (James 4:9). The situation in the Christ house church called for contrition and repentance—mourning. And they should cast out the one who has done this.

Now Paul pursues how this should be done. Though absent in the body, Paul says he is present in the spirit. In Greek letter writing, the author had various ways of expressing contact with and presence among the readers. We have already seen how Paul made his presence felt at Corinth by sending Timothy (see explanatory notes on 4:14-19). Here he uses a typical phrase (formula) to express his presence with them. The same phrase occurs in Colossians 2:5, though there he speaks of being absent in the *sarx* (flesh) rather than *soma* (body). A standard phrase or formula (see summary essay, 241) normally conveys a set meaning to the reader.

Having expressed his presence with the faith community, Paul stated with striking authority that he had already made his decision (see summary essay, 223). The key issue for this passage, and, perhaps even for all of chapters 5 and 6, lies in the disposition of the phrase "in the name of the Lord Jesus." Many translations take it with the following phrase, "when you are assembled."

> I have already judged the man who has done this thing. When you come together in the name of the Lord. . . . (Cf. NASB, NIV, NEB.)

Since Paul seldom places such a clause in front of the main sentence, several recent translations prefer to put the phrase with "I have judged."

> I have already pronounced judgment in the name of the Lord Jesus on the man who has done such a thing. (5:3b-4a, RSV, NRSV)

What then was done "in the name of the Lord"? In terms of the Greek construction and Paul's use of the language there is no compelling linguistic reason to take "in the name of the Lord" with anything that follows. That means we should translate it either "I have already pronounced judgment in the name of the Lord on the man who has done this thing," or exactly as the Greek order dictates: "I have already passed judgment on the man who has done such a thing in the name of the Lord Jesus" (NRSV footnote).

The natural order of the verse has been avoided because translators have assumed Paul was dealing sternly with an offensive immoral situation. Once it is seen that Paul primarily used the instance as a warning to the Christ house church, then the natural translation becomes not only possible, but desirable. The spiritual arrogance of the Christ group became evident when they allowed an immoral or inappropriate situation to occur precisely because they were, in their minds, free in the name of the Lord Jesus.[1]

In v. 4 Paul asks them to gather again as a faith community. But this time they should meet with the spirit of Paul and with the power of God. Spirit normally refers to that power or energy which works among persons (see summary essay, 256). Seldom in the New Testament does spirit refer to a part of a person. It means here that the intention or disposition of Paul should be present at the meeting. We noticed it as a disposition of gentleness in 4:21 (compare Gal. 6:1). Paul's attitude, to be imitated by all Christians, was, as we have seen (see explanatory notes of 4:16), an awareness that we live between the times. At the same time, the faith community meets, as it should, with the power of Lord Jesus (see summary essay, 223). The Christian community does not lack power. It is the community of the Lord of life and the endtime. It has the power to make life decisions (Matt. 18:18-20).

Paul has already determined (v. 3) that this man should be delivered to Satan. The term Satan is a Hebrew term meaning "prosecuting attorney" (see summary essay, 255). That meaning can still be discerned in the Hebrew Bible (Zech. 3:1-2; Job 2:1-6). Because the prosecuting attorney takes responsibility for applying the law, it is not surprising Satan plays a significant role in Paul's faith system. Just as the law can drive us to sin, rather than save us (Rom. 7:7-12), so the attorney can tempt us rather than guide us (7:5; 1 Chron. 21:1). Satan then belongs to the old age, to that time when we seek our own way (flesh) and cannot respond affirmatively to the revelation of God (sin). To deliver the man to Satan, then, is to return him to the old age (see summary essay, 234). He has prematurely arrived in the kingdom, the new age.

The faith community should deliver the man to Satan for the destruction of his flesh. Flesh (see summary essay, 257) for Paul refers primarily to human aspirations (Rom. 7:13-25). Paul knows nothing of a dualism in which the spirit is good and the flesh is evil. To be sure, sin enters through flesh (Rom. 8:3), but that is only because we seek our own self-fulfillment (Rom. 8:6-8). God will grant us our fulfillment if

---

[1]William F. Orr and James Arthur Walther, *I Corinthians*, Anchor Bible 32 (Garden City NY: Doubleday, 1977) 186.

we live by the Spirit (Rom. 8:12-14). The man in question lives primarily for his own freedom. He does not live in consideration of the faith community as led by the Spirit of God. Paul says he needs to be "sent back" to the old age so he can learn that his self-concern will only lead to deeper dissatisfaction. His flesh, his living according to his own, personal sense of fulfillment, needs to reach its limits. The man needs to know he cannot live that way (Rom. 7:24). When that happens his flesh (*sarx*) will have been destroyed.

Finally all of this leads to the saving of the spirit (*pneuma*) at the endtime. Again, translation problems reflect the difficulty of interpretation. The Greek does not designate whose spirit will be saved. So, unless there is some reason otherwise, the translation would be, "in order that the spirit might be saved in the day of the Lord." Older translations (KJV, ERV, ASV) follow the Greek literally, but more recent translations (RSV, NRSV, NASB, NIV) read, "in order that his spirit might be saved in the day of the Lord." It is not likely Paul would have spoken of the man's spirit being saved. The person was a unity in Hebraic thought. The whole person would be saved at the endtime (see summary essay, 237). But even if that were not true, it would be, in more Hellenistic thought, the *psuche* ("soul" in earlier English) that would be saved on the last day. Consequently one is forced to suppose Paul speaks of the spirit of the congregation, more specifically the Christ house church. It is necessary for the Christ house church to recognize its own spiritual arrogance, to see the danger involved, to forego its spiritualistic, gnostic leaning, and to remove this man from life in the new age, the faith community. Only if that is done can the spirit of the congregation be healed (saved or made whole) at the endtime.[2]

In order to make this difficult and important passage clear I offer the following translation.

> It is heard everywhere that there is among you an illicit relationship, a type of relationship that does not even exist among the Gentiles— a man is married to his stepmother. And you have been arrogant! Ought you not mourn, so that the one who has done this thing is cast out from your midst? For I, though absent in body but present in the spirit, have already decided, as if present, that when you assemble as

---

[2]James Benedict, "The Corinthian Problem of 1 Corinthians 5:1-8," *Brethren Life and Thought* 32 (1987): 70-73.

a congregation with the power of our Lord Jesus, and with my spirit, that the one who has done this thing in the name of the Lord should be delivered over to Satan for the destruction of his flesh, so that the spirit will be whole on the Day of the Lord.

5:6-8 From his Jewish background Paul offers an analogy to illustrate v. 5b. Immorality in the faith community is like old leaven in a lump of unleavened bread. Admittedly the analogy could confuse the reader. Old leaven was the yeast taken from the previous lump of dough. Without it the new dough would not rise, of course. In that sense Christians (e.g., children of the kingdom of God) are the yeast, or leaven, of the world (Matt. 13:33). Nevertheless, leavened bread or meal was forbidden as a sacrifice or offering to God (Lev. 2: 4-5, 11; Ex. 23:18). Whatever the origin of this prohibition against leaven, its rationale stemmed from the haste with which the Hebrew people left Egypt (Exod. 12:34, 39). And the analogy was frequently used to illustrate how evil could spread among the faithful. Jesus spoke of the teaching of the Pharisees and Sadducees as destructive leaven among the Jewish people (Matt. 16:5-12). So, in sharp contrast to the good leaven of Matthew 13:33, unleavened bread was a symbol of holiness and leaven itself an agent of pervasive corruption.

The Christ house church has boasted of itself (see summary essay, 220), by analogy, as a new lump. But there remains a little leaven which they must not ignore. Or, at least, they ought not boast as if there were none. Verse 7b is a remarkable intrusion. Reflecting on the Jewish Feast of Unleavened Bread, Paul shifts, by association, to the climax of the feast, the Passover. Whereas the Feast of Unleavened Bread originally celebrated the new crop of grain, the Passover meal with its lamb celebrated the death of the firstborn in Egypt (Exod. 12:21, 27). Just as Paul thinks of the new age as the time of Unleavened Bread when the people are holy, so he can say the new age began at the offering of the Passover lamb, none other than Christ himself.

A very rich chord is struck by the seemingly offhand inference that Jesus was the paschal or Passover lamb. The Johannine literature especially refers to Jesus as the Lamb. Well known are the numerous references in Revelation to Jesus as the lamb that was slain (twenty-eight times in chapters 5-22). One assumes that the lamb slain was the Passover lamb, a lamb that ushered in the endtime, though some early Christians identified it with the suffering lamb of Isaiah 53 (as in Acts

8:32). The Gospel of John itself has been organized to identify Jesus with the Passover lamb. John the Baptist introduced Jesus as the "lamb which takes away the sin of the world" (John 1:29). The passion narrative of John was so composed to show that Jesus died on the cross at the same time the lambs for Passover were being killed by the priests in the temple (19:31). And the soldiers avoided breaking the legs of Jesus in order that his death would be analogous to that of the Passover lamb (19:36; Exod. 12:46). In the Synoptic Gospels the Passover comes on Friday (rather than the Saturday of the Gospel of John), so the disciples eat the Passover, and the Passover lamb, with Jesus. So in the Synoptics Jesus anticipates the coming endtime as he eats the Passover meal (Mark 14:25), while in the Gospel of John Jesus as the Lamb embodies the endtime (John 14:9). Or better yet, as in Revelation, the Passover Lamb, as a sign of liberation, describes the life of the endtime.

Paul's thinking about Christ, the paschal lamb, has not reached the level of the Johannine material. In v. 7b Paul only means that Christ the lamb has signaled the shift from the old age, the leavened lump, to the new age, the unleavened lump. If here we see the Christ who brings the kingdom identified with the Passover lamb, we see Christology at one of its earliest levels (see summary essay, 229). In any case, Paul calls on the Corinthian Christians to celebrate the change from a life of evil and immorality to a community of sincerity and truth.

5:9-13 By this time Paul has become aware that his words can be seriously misunderstood (see introduction above, 9-10). He recognizes that his admonition to the Christ house church could have an undesirable effect. Their radical conversion to the new age might lead to spiritual arrogance. In fact he suspects his previous words about disassociating from immoral people might have already contributed to their sense of intense separation from the world. Those previous words had been written in a "previous letter" (v. 9; see introduction, 10). Though many associate the previous letter with the misplaced section 2 Corinthians 6:14-7:1, it seems more likely that the letter has been lost. Nevertheless, the arguments put forward for the authenticity of 2 Corinthians 6:14-7:1 could help clarify the content of the previous letter. While the legalism of 2 Corinthians 6:14-7:1 hardly matches the language and thought of Paul, it could be that he did report to the Corinthians the results of the Jerusalem Council. The agreement spelled out at that meeting (Acts 15:19-29) may well have appeared to the Corinthians to be a call to extreme purity.

In v. 10 Paul makes it clear he did not mean that Christians should withdraw from the world, from the arena of the immoral, greedy, robbers, and idolaters. That would destroy the redemptive function of the faith community. The origin of this list (see summary essay, 257) cannot be determined. It refers primarily to financial gain: greed, use of sex for profit, and robbery. Even idolatry may very well point to the same sense of greed. Though idolatry referred to worship of gods other than the true and living God (1 Thess. 1:9), in the New Testament it refers also to a self-centered way of life (Col. 3:5; Phil. 3:19; 1 Pet. 4:3; 1 Cor. 10:7-8). The list does not correspond to the requirement of the Jerusalem Council (prohibitions against idolatry, adultery, and murder). In 6:11 Paul does hint that the list describes some of the Corinthians in their former way of life. If that is true, the meaning of the lists here, in v. 11 and in 6:9-10, may simply be a random reference to certain persons in Corinth.

The Greek word *egrapsa* in v. 11 presents us with a problem. In Greek the verb "to write" is in the aorist tense. As a tense it does not correspond exactly to anything in English. It means an action done at a point in time, whether past or present. Normally one should translate it "I wrote." But Greek letter writers were in the habit of writing from the perspective of the reader. Anticipating the reader would have a letter already completed, they frequently said "I wrote" where we would say "I write." In v. 11 we cannot now tell the difference. Did Paul mean he wrote this in the "previous letter," but they misinterpreted what he said (NASB, RSV)? Or did he mean that he did write one thing in the previous letter, and now he would like to correct that (NRSV, NIV)? It seems like most of the slogans we encounter in 1 Corinthians did originate from Paul (see explanatory notes on 4:6-7), so Paul is constantly caught between admitting what he said, but denying the interpretation. So "I wrote" would be the correct translation.

Paul meant to say that such persons should not be allowed to participate in the fellowship of the church. They should not assume acceptance in the new age without a radical transition from the old age. So the Christ house church should cease offering fellowship to such persons, particularly the man living with his stepmother. In summary, the church does not make discipline judgments regarding those in the old age, but only toward those in the faith community. Quoting Deuteronomy 17:7b, Paul insists that the man must be disciplined.

THE TEXT IN ITS BIBLICAL CONTEXT

This section is one of the key texts in any discussion of church discipline. At stake are such concerns as the nature of church discipline, excommunication, and the purpose of any corporate action toward an individual member. In the Hebrew Bible and in Judaism at the time of the New Testament it was the issue of God's holiness as expressed in the people of God. The people, certain spaces, and certain vessels all were *qodesh* or holy, as we translate it. Violation of God's holiness made a person unclean or common and profane. Such people were not to be included in the assembly of Israel. For violation of things devoted (*cherem*) God caused the earth to swallow Achan and his whole entourage (Josh. 7:10-26). Even in Judaism at the time of the New Testament some people were not allowed access to the faith community because they were unclean (Acts 10:28), though often the person was said to be possessed by an unclean spirit or disposition (Mark 1:23; 5:2). Other violations of the faith community could also lead to discipline. Most dramatic were the violations of hospitality shown in Sodom (Gen. 19:1-28) and Gibeah (Judges 19-20). The Holiness Code of Leviticus 17-26 lists both ethical and tribal expectations, which, if violated, would lead to discipline, excommunication, or even death.

The issues were different for the first Christians. Most narratives of church discipline move toward reconciliation. The famous passage Matthew 18:15-22 stresses a process of reconciliation. Eventually, if reconciliation fails, the person may need to be treated as a nonmember (v. 17). And, as in 1 Corinthians 5:1-5, the church has the power to make that decision—for the Lord is in the midst of the assembled congregation (Matt. 18:18-20). Nevertheless, for the follower of Jesus, forgiveness has no limit (vv. 21-22).

First Corinthians 5:1-5 follows very much the same pattern, except the reconciliation here comes through the destruction of the flesh, a strong self-will, rather than discussion and encounter. In both systems the person in question is asked to submit again to that radical change which has created the faith community. Even in the rather harsh passage 1 Timothy 1:20, Hymenaeus and Alexander are handed over to Satan for the purpose of correcting behavior which wrecks the community (i.e., loss of conscience, v. 19). Eventually they will return to the faith community.

To be sure, there are in the New Testament some dramatic examples of discipline which match that of Achan in the Hebrew Bible. The case of Ananias and Sapphira can hardly be called reconciliation (Acts 5:1-11). As noted in 1 Corinthians 11:27-32, failure to discern the body, that is, the work of the Spirit, implies death. In both instances the emphasis lies on the failure of discernment, not the gravity of any particular act or behavior. Failure to discern the Spirit shows such a depth of alienation that illness or even death results. From a psychosomatic perspective one cannot easily make distinctions between alienation, illness, and death.

Discipline in the New Testament follows two lines: most often for the purpose of reconciliation, but sometimes because discernment of the Spirit is lacking. In the former case one assumes the eventual return of the person disciplined. In the latter case death has already occurred. Such spiritual death may be visibly substantiated by actual illness or even death. 1 Corinthians 5:1-13 belongs to the first type: repentance is expected. The man living with his stepmother should be sent back to the old age for another chance. Unless that is done the Spirit cannot act in the faith community for the good of all.

THE TEXT IN THE LIFE OF THE CHURCH

The church of Jesus Christ often waivers between "cheap grace" and stern legalism. Like the church at Corinth we find it difficult to "speak the truth in love," that is, to be honest with each other, to speak with the intent to reconcile rather than to judge. To the credit of the historical church this passage has been used as the basis for a church discipline which recognizes certain behavior as inappropriate, yet is applied in such a way that the individual can or will be restored. This system, called penance, however, became so predictable and trite that, to some extent, it triggered the Reformation.

Some Reformation groups did not reject the practice of discipline as a means of encouraging repentance. In fact most congregational type groups could not exist without some sense of community discipline.[3] The intent was to create a climate for development and formation which

---

[3]William Klassen, *The Forgiving Community* (Philadelphia: Westminster Press, 1966).

would keep all persons open to the spirit of the community.[4]

In our day some type of church discipline is necessary for at least two reasons. "Cheap grace" can allow the individual person access to the faith community without facing reality. For example, an alcoholic learns to depend on those who will overlook the problem. Such dependency only exacerbates the situation. Personal growth depends on realistic relationships. Secondly, the progress and health of a community will be thwarted when divisive or alienating dynamics (flesh) are not faced. They need not be solved (legalism), but they do need to be acknowledged. In that way the Spirit can continue to work for wholeness.

THE OLD CANNOT INHERIT THE NEW 6:1-11

PREVIEW

In sharp contrast to the Christ house church, another group in Corinth had not yet entered the new age (see summary essay, 248). Or, at least, they did not understand the meaning of life in the new faith community. They still held on to the security of the old age. One sign of that failure is mentioned in 6:1-11—the use of the local judiciary system. The lawsuit apparently involved fraud (vv. 7-8). It was presumably an unintentional fraud since Paul does not chastise the defendant. Whatever the issue, it does not appear to have had any bearing on the nascent Christian faith.

Paul's concern (vv. 1-3) is quite clear, even if his rationale has confused many readers. The old age has no authority or capability for making decisions in the new age. The old is passing away (2 Cor. 5:17) and the new represents the fulfillment of God's promises. On what basis would that which is failing (old) make decisions for that which is entering the kingdom (new)? The logic is impeccable. None! In fact the reverse is true. The new age will judge the old. Put another way, the values and criteria of the new age will be those which enable the old to perceive and enter the new. To submit to the values of the old age not only misses the point of the Christian life, but it subverts the mission of the faith community. To paraphrase: "Do you not know that by their

[4]Marlin Jeschke, *Discipling the Brother: Recovering a Ministry of the Gospel* (Scottdale PA: Herald Press, 1988).

life-style the saints of the Christian community (*koinonia*) critique the world of the old age?"

Since the saints will judge the world it seems unbelievable that the house churches do not have leaders who can decide on these trivial cases (vv. 4-5). Failing that, or, perhaps instead of that, why are there such cases in the first place? Applying the teaching of the Sermon on the Mount, Paul suggests they could well afford to accept the wrong rather than formally accuse a brother or sister (vv. 7-8). With some sense of drama, Paul reminds them that there are criminal types in the old age. Consequently, that age could not possibly inherit the kingdom of God, a kingdom the Corinthian Christians have entered by baptism in the name of the Lord Jesus Christ and by the power of the Spirit (vv. 9-11)

• OUTLINE •

6:1-4 Persons of the new age will judge the old age
6:5-6 Persons of the new age can settle their own cases
6:7-8 In the new age there should be no formal lawsuits
6:9-11 Those living according to the old age have no access to the new

---

EXPLANATORY NOTES

6:1-4 While chapter 5 apparently addresses the Christ house church, there is no indication in chapter 6 which group has the lawsuit. Whereas the Christ house church lives above the law--even the law of the Gentiles (5:1), this group has submitted to the law—even the law of the old age. So this case study must have been directed toward one of the other three house churches. The cause of the lawsuit must not have been important. Paul did not chastise them for whatever caused it, nor did he admonish the one who committed the legal infraction. There is none of the vehemence noted in the case of the man living with his stepmother. As a matter of conjecture, probably one member unwittingly sold another a defective piece of property or made an inappropriate contract. So the legal suit involves unintentional fraud, and Paul knows nothing of a deliberate crime against another sister or brother.

Paul is only concerned about the relationship of the new faith community to the old age. How could the new community allow the old age to make decisions for it? How could the unrighteous (*adikoi*) make judgments for the justified (*dikaioi*). The reverse is true.

Paul begins v. 2 with "Do you not know?" a formula common to Greek letters and to Paul (3:16; Rom. 6:3). It brings to the attention of the reader what is obvious. The constant repetition of the formula in this chapter (vv. 2, 3, 9, 15, 16, 19) stresses the apparent truth of his arguments, though the implications may not have been so obvious. It is the saints (faith community) who will make judgments for the world, the old age. How could it be otherwise? Those who give allegiance to the Lord could hardly submit their disputes to local authorities. Those who know the interpersonal reconciling action of Jesus Christ could hardly accept the impersonal justice of a magistrate. If all this is true then surely the faith community can solve its own minor issues (v. 2b).

It is v. 3 that has confused the issue for many. At first it would appear that the new community will not only judge the old age but also the divine world. But we have already seen that the Greek term *angeloi* refers not only to divine messengers or angels (see summary essay, 222), but also the "sons of God" who "organize" or represent large human institutions, especially nation states (see explanatory notes on 4:8-13). All *corporate* human endeavors are, in a sense, of God. The image of God (Gen. 1:26-27) in humankind expresses itself as the drive toward universal community. Put quite another way, the religious a priori can be seen in us as the constant pull to community.[5] Paul will say later that all authorities (*exousia*) have been instituted or appointed by God (Rom. 13:1). So states and other human institutions are really divine gifts, messengers, if you will. In relationship to God they are secondary or penultimate, nevertheless, they do serve God because they create human community.

Historically these penultimate institutions have gone astray. That is the meaning of the strange narrative in Genesis 6:1-4. The "daughters of men" can seduce the "sons of God" (or vice versa in later intertestamental literature). In any case, human institutions are a gift of God, but they can and will be subverted. The ultimate expression of human community will be the kingdom of God, where the Son of God is Lord. Meanwhile the Christian faith community does imperfectly anticipate

---

[5]Josiah Royce, *The Problem of Christianity* (New York: Macmillan, 1913; rpt. Chicago: University of Chicago Press, 1968).

and make known that kingdom yet to come.

If this is true, then the faith community cannot ask the subverted institutions of the old age for judgments. If, finally, all the nations will be judged by the kingdom, then the faith community contains within itself the means of settling disputes, particularly everyday kinds of matters (*biotika*: trivial cases, NRSV; matters of this life, NASB). Only the faith community understands that the common life can be organized according to love. Only the faith community can solve disputes by means of reconciliation (see v. 7). Eventually the organizing principle of love will transform even the "angels," the divinely appointed human institutions.

6:5-6 These verses mark an important point in early Christianity. Following the example of contemporary Judaism,[6] Paul suggests they organize their own judicial system. Rather than depend on the untrustworthy or unbelievers (v. 6), the faith community should appoint some wise persons within the church to make the judgments. For the most part Paul asked the first Christians to rise above (be disengaged from) their past culture (see explanatory notes on 7:29-31). One of the key effects of the pending endtime is to render irrelevant the institutions of the present age (7:29, 31b). Seldom, in light of the coming endtime, does Paul suggest the restructuring of a parallel society. But here he does. He suggests a parallel judicial system. Insignificant, perhaps, but a clear recognition that Christians must live in this world, must buy and sell, marry and bury. What started here eventually became visible as a parallel or even competitive social structure. By 180 CE Christian meeting places, Christian art, banking functions, burying societies and church administrations were visible to the Roman empire.[7] Whereas Paul meant to say the institutions of the old age, with its unrighteousness, cannot make decisions for life in the new age, it appeared later to some that he was establishing the church over against the world (sectarianism).

6:7-8 Though Paul gave advice regarding the settling of disputes in vv. 5-6, at heart he cannot understand why sisters and brothers in Christ

---

[6]Jean Juster, *Les Juifs dan l'empire romain: leur condition juridique, économique et sociale* (Paris: Librarie Paul Geuthner, 1914) 2, 110-11.

[7]Snyder, *Ante Pacem*, 2.

would even have such disputes. The Jesus tradition called for reconciliation before that stage (Matt. 5:23-24). Indeed, the faith community has the responsibility to establish a system of reconciliation (Matt. 18:15-22). Moreover, ought not persons reconciled to God through Jesus Christ be willing to accept a wrong or fraud (v. 7b)? Though Paul does not say it, he surely thinks that God accepted our wrongdoing and nevertheless acted to reconcile us (through the cross). So how could sisters and brothers do wrong or defraud each other (v.8)?

6:9-11 These verses present a puzzling summary to the case study. Paul had complained about letting the unrighteous (v. 1) and those disdained (v.4) make judgments for the new age. One assumed the unrighteous were those who operated out of self-interest (flesh) or out of loyalty to penultimate values (idolatry). In the list we could have expected corrupt officials, judges who take bribes, slave owners, tax collectors, greedy merchants—these would be the leaders in Corinth who might make judgments for the house churches. It is a shock to see rather a list of criminal types, people who would be outlawed by the Corinthian legal system—not people who form it. Clearly Paul was not concerned here with the alleged case of fraud, nor was he primarily concerned with establishing an ecclesiastical judicial system. Paul was only concerned that life in the new age not be determined by life in the old age (v. 11).

To characterize that old age he listed some of the more unsavory types—a list not unlike that of 5:9-10. Even more surprising is the side comment of v. 11. Some of you were among those listed in vv. 9-10! From the data available (see summary essay, 231), there is no reason to suppose the church at Corinth, or any other, was composed primarily of social misfits or criminals. Assuming there were indeed some criminal types whose life-style was radically altered by the gospel, the function of the side comment in 11a is to enhance Paul's point in v. 11b: once they were in the age of unrighteousness, but no longer.

The list, likely from a contemporary ethical list, needs some clarification. We have already seen that the Greek word *pornos,* translated immoral, probably refers here to persons who profited from sex (see explanatory notes on 5:1-5). In addition to the more profit motivated crimes of 6:10, Paul includes in this list adulterers, homosexuals, drunks and abusive people. The presence of two terms which have been translated "homosexual" requires further explanation. Two Greek terms, *malakos* and *arsenokoites,* have presented translation and interpretive problems. The first term means soft and therefore, by extension, effeminate (so NASB; male prostitutes, NRSV, NIV). It probably refers to boys used in the practice of pederasty. The second term refers more directly to males who have intercourse with males, therefore homosexuals (homosexual offenders, NIV). Yet the term "homosexual," same-sex sexual preference, does not adequately convey Paul's meaning.

First, just as the term *pornos* here refers to sex for profit, so also these two terms likely refer to male prostitution. Second, Paul probably thinks of the Greek practice of pederasty, not a sexual orientation toward a person of the same sex, nor even intercourse between two adult males. In the Greek world some (upper class?) adult men considered sexual intercourse with women unnatural. They preferred the companionship of preadolescent boys. Such arrangements were construed by some to be mutually beneficial for the boy who might receive an education and financial security, though others would have considered the practice a form of child abuse. In any case, pederasty obviously could be used for financial gain.[8]

On the other hand, the Jewish world apparently had little acquaintance with the practice of homosexuality. At least it is not often mentioned in the Hebrew Bible or in the Mishnah. Male-female relationships were considered normative (Gen. 1:27) and family life was highly protected (Deut. 5:16). The only really explicit admonition against homosexual intercourse among Jewish men occurs in Leviticus 18:22. That section defines the limits of legitimate sexual relationships. Homosexual relationships lay outside those boundaries. Like his Jewish foreparents and in contrast to Greek intelligentsia, Paul considered homosexuality, of whatever form, a violation of natural relationships (Rom. 1:26-27). In summary, Paul shared the view of the Jews and others that homosexuality was unnatural and therefore a perversion. Despite his clear opposition to homosexuality it seems likely male prostitution and pederasty for profit, not homosexuality, are the specific immoral acts mentioned in this passage.

In v. 11 Paul summarizes why the Corinthian Christians are no longer among the unrighteous, even though once they were. First they have washed (were washed, RSV/NRSV, NIV, NASB). Washing is some-

---

[8]Robin Scroggs, *The New Testament and Homosexuality: Contextual Background for Contemporary Debate* (Philadelphia: Fortress Press, 1983).

thing you do to yourself (middle voice in Greek). The Greek word *apolouo* (wash away) is found only here and in Acts 22:16, where Paul recalls he was asked to be baptized and wash away his sins. The author of the Gospel of John used the root term *louo* (Greek) in exactly the same way (13:10). In the religious sense washing away the past is a choice or decision. To be sure, one cannot baptize one's own person, but leaving the old age (washing away the old) is a personal act.

On the other hand, sanctifying and justifying are not activities we can do for ourselves. They are done for us. In Greek they are always passive when they refer to what happened to the Christian. But washing away the past age is an adult decision. Paul says they were once in the old age of unrighteousness, but they have chosen to wash that away. Now they have been (passive) sanctified and justified. As we have already seen (see explanatory note on 1:3) sanctification was not a synonym for purity (see summary essay, 231). Being holy was to participate in that which is devoted to God (see commentary on 6:1). Having been claimed by God they are justified also. Although Jesus Christ was called the righteousness of God in 1:30, this is the first and only reference in 1 Corinthians to the justifying action of God. Considering the incredible importance of the term in the later letters Galatians and Romans, this single occurrence here appears striking. In later Pauline letters justification occurs by faith. Persons cannot justify themselves. That is, one cannot do anything which makes one just or pleases God to make you just. Being deemed righteous is a matter of faith, or trust. For religious perception the importance of sensing justification can hardly be overestimated.

For the Jewish people of the Hebrew Bible, *tsedeqah,* or righteousness, was the deep sense of acceptance by God in the faith community (Hab. 2:4). Without the sense of acceptance, life would be frustrating and even thwarted. Although the Law (Torah) was given by God to guide us in righteousness, it was never meant as a tool to gain acceptance (Rom. 3:20). A person cannot gain acceptance by doing right or correct things. If this were true the faith community would be based on mutual admiration. It is essential that the church be based on acceptance by trust rather than acceptance by merit. The church could not extend trust to others except that the faith community itself has been created by God's acceptance (Rom. 1:17). So in this reference to divine justification, Paul mentions a theme he will develop later: as persons are claimed by God (sanctified) they are justified by God (accepted).

Nevertheless, the context of this early statement on justification requires further consideration. Some have said justification in v. 11 does refer to the moral life. It is true that the members of the new faith community are contrasted with the morally unrighteous of the old age (vv. 9-10). But both the decision to leave the old age (see summary essay, 237) and the claim of God precede justification. All the Corinthian Christians were of the old age and some were immoral, but they have been changed by the process of redemption. Now, having been justified, they do live a corporate moral life in the new age. One cannot easily distinguish between faith and moral living unless morality becomes simply a matter of individual piety and purity. As long as trust continues, justification (acceptance) can be seen. As long as trust continues reconciliation will be at work within the faith community. Using the courts of the old age to enforce morality would be of no value.

THE TEXT IN ITS BIBLICAL CONTEXT

According to Jewish tradition the Hebrew people first organized under the advice of Moses' father-in-law Jethro (Exod. 18). Moses was no longer able to make decisions for neighbors at odds with each other, so Jethro suggested a division of the people of Israel into formal groups. Each group should have a capable administrator who would make judicial decisions. Actually, as the story of the Hebrew people develops, the judicial system seems less formal than what Jethro suggested. Though there was a court of final appeals in the palace of the king (1 Kings 3:28), normal judgments were made by wise elders at the city gate. In his wretchedness Job dreamed of the days when he walked to the gate of the city and rendered respected judgments (Job 29:7-25). When Boaz wished to arrange for his rights as next of kin to Ruth, he made the arrangements with the elders at the city gate (Ruth 4:1-2). In the faith community, disputes between members were adjudicated by elders, wise persons with weightiness (*kabod* in Hebrew; see summary essay, 244).

In the New Testament such elders (*presbuteroi*) are known as the local leaders of congregations. They were persons of experience and wisdom who could represent the congregation (James 5:14), make decisions for the whole community (Acts 15:22), and appoint leadership (1 Tim. 4:14). Such elders were just beginning to appear in the budding Pauline congregations (Acts 14:23), but apparently they either did not yet function at Corinth or else the people had not yet transferred judicatory powers to them.

The church very early developed political and economic structures parallel to the Roman state. It could well be that Paul's own collection for the poor of Jerusalem (16:1) was the beginning of a bank which eventually competed with the Jewish Temple Bank. Jews were allowed to cross national boundaries with the silver. Christians shared that possibility. In a third-century document addressed to the brothers in Arsinoe, a Christian writes of sales in Alexandria. The sales receipts were deposited with the papa of Alexandria.[9] In Rome the bishop Zephrynus established a Christian burial society by 200 CE. The church eventually established it own laws and judicial system. The relationship of the church's judicial system to the state has varied from time to time and place to place. Churches from the Radical Reformation have fairly consistently refused to settle disputes in secular courts of law—either among themselves or with others.

There are several reasons for this reluctance to utilize the courts. Some Christians believe firmly in the separation of church and state. Though stated differently, this conviction stems directly from Pauline assumption that the old age cannot make decisions for the new age. Some believe the state cannot make judgments for the church because it has a legitimate function which does not correspond with the redemptive function of the church (Rom. 13:4). The state strives for justice in this world, while the church strives for love.[10] Others think the state should also express God's will in love, but believe the state has fallen. In the latter case the function of the love in the church not only serves to reconcile within the faith community, but also witnesses the will of God to the old age.

In any case Paul has called the church to a process of reconciliation which would avoid conflicts which must be settled in a court of law. In order for the church to settle differences by reconciliation, an educational process must be established. At an early age children need experience in process reconciliation. This can occur in church school, camp

---

[9]Snyder, *Ante Pacem*, 153.

[10]Walter Klaassen, *Anabaptism: Neither Catholic nor Protestant* (Waterloo, Ontario: Conrad Press, 1981) 45-48.

and youth groups, peace academies, and colleges. For a church to live in the new age it must practice and train its members in such a style of trust. As long as communication can be maintained, any problem might eventually be solved.

The faith community not only trains its members in the art of reconciliation, but it makes available the process of reconciliation to the world at large. Such projects as conflict management seminars, victim-offender reconciliation programs, and college and university peace departments witness to the life of the new age as well as offer a new way for those caught in the old.

THE BODY OF CHRIST IS ULTIMATE 6:12-20

PREVIEW

In chapters 1–4 Paul has responded to the problem of divisions at Corinth. In 5:1-13 he gave a case study on the problems of an endtime reached too quickly: an immorality done in the name of the Lord. In 6:1-11 he addressed, by means of another case study, those who were still living in the old age: a failure of trust within the faith community. Now, before starting the answer to their questions (7:1), he draws this "letter" to a close with a unifying summary. Both elements of the Corinthian church are addressed in one image—that of the body. In the first section (vv. 12-14) Paul agrees with the Christ house church. "All things are lawful." But all things do not build up the body. Finally only the body of Christ matters (v. 14). On the other side, to those not yet certain of the new age, the body cannot be prostituted by living in both worlds (vv. 15-18). The body of Christ is now the temple of the Holy Spirit. All believers are to glorify God in that body (vv. 19-20).

• OUTLINE •

6:12-14 The corporate body of Christ is ultimate
6:15-18 Members of Christ's body are one with the Lord
6:19-20 Glorify God in the body of which you are a
member

EXPLANATORY NOTES

6:12-14 Concluding the section chapters 1–6, Paul expresses his opinion with a single metaphor: the body (see summary essay, 227). He looks first at the Christ house church. They have been quoting and living out a slogan: "All things are lawful for me." One supposes this is one of the slogans used by Paul in his first preaching at Corinth (see summary essay, 241). He may have used it to emphasize the useless-ness of the law for salvation. If not, the Christ house church may have created the slogan to identify their own disdain for human laws and cus-toms (see explanatory note on 5:1-5). Whatever the origin of the slo-gan, it remains that the Christ house church used the phrase and Paul agreed with it. Paul's reply does not deny the validity of the claim. His response is to modify its value. He has two objections: (1) not every-thing is useful; (2) one can be enslaved by one's own sense of freedom.

Paul does not explain his first objection. Consequently, we must suppose the second objection clarifies the first, as in 10:23. "All things" are not helpful, because even the marks of freedom can enslave or over-power a person. We are at the threshold of one of Paul's most remark-able observations. That which marks for the individual person her or his own freedom can often become the point at which she or he becomes reenslaved. The point was well made for the Christ house church.

In the letter of chapters 7–16 Paul mentions several such marks. In chapter 8 some people who possibly had not been free to eat meat of-fered to idols, now insisted on that freedom. They ate such meat re-gardless of the situation or the company. Their freedom to eat the meat offered to idols was more important than the effect such eating had on others. All things were not helpful. In chapter 11 some women who previously had covered their hair now felt free to appear publicly with-out a covering. Their freedom to wear what they wished was more im-portant than the effect it had on others in the house church. All things were not helpful.

Some Corinthians were enslaved to the freedom of eating meat of-fered to idols; some were enslaved to the freedom of dressing as they wished. Their marks of freedom had become ideological; that is, the mark of freedom had to be expressed in order for their freedom to be realized. For Paul this individualized ideological freedom is no freedom at all. It is not clear to us now whether Paul first saw this in the church at Corinth. When he said "All things are lawful," he had surely meant "All things are possible in the context of the faith community." But the Christ house church took the slogan to mean "Anything goes."

Paul responds by attacking yet another slogan: "Food is for the belly, and the belly is for food." Again we do not know the origin of this phrase, but it expressed the attitude of the Christ house church regard-ing meat offered to idols. All food was created to be eaten, and the hu-man stomach was created to accept any food known. Surely Paul had indeed taught them that food laws would not commend them before God (10:26; Rom. 14:13-23). For Paul the same freedom which accepted the validity of any food (note 1 Tim. 4:4) also took away the significance of any food. No food commends one to God; no food can produce freedom. Eventually God will destroy both the belly and the food. Neither has ultimate value. It is not the belly which has ultimate value, but the body (v. 13). The meaning of body at this point is critical not only for the interpretation of this important passage, but for the entire letter (see summary essay, 227).

It is well known that the Greek word *soma*, body, had an extended, metaphorical meaning for Paul and other Jewish writers. While it does occasionally refer to the human body (9:27), more often than not Paul uses *soma* to refer to the intimate human network. The concept of body as human network cannot be easily described in a language which stresses individuality. In contrast to the people of the Bible, we think of ourselves as a body with a soul rather than a *psuche* or person in a network called *soma* or body. We often think of that soul as if it had an existence separate from the body in which it resides. That becomes most self-evident when we speak of the immortal soul and the perishable body. We cannot find this understanding of body in the Pauline epistles (or even in the New Testament).

Paul speaks of body as the primary network of persons who create our identity. Most obviously that refers to the faith community, but it need not. For example, Paul can speak of a destructive network as a body of death (Rom. 7:24). That identity which comes from involvement in the primary relationships is called by Paul the *psuche* (translated soul, life, or person). The metaphorical use of *soma* can best be seen in such passages as 1 Corinthians 12:4-31 and Romans 12:3-8. Once body is understood through such obvious passages as these, then other passages, such as the eucharistic formulas (10:17), can be interpreted metaphorically, too. At this point most readers would agree. But, when there is no specific mention of the body of Christ, it becomes much more difficult to know whether Paul meant *soma* literally or metaphorically. This is one of those uncertain passages (see summary essay, 220). Some readers will want to understand this passage as literally referring to the human body and prostitution. Others will read it, as in this commentary, as a metaphorical use of the body, the body of Christ.

In v. 13b it would seem reasonable that the human body was not made for sexual immorality. Readers have generally assumed Paul shifted quickly and without explanation from the issue of food to that of sexual immorality. This shift then sets the stage for the warning against prostitution in vv. 15-16. But a literal understanding of body in the passage has several problems: (1) except for the case of the man living with his stepmother, there is no specific mention of sexual immorality as a problem within the Corinthian church. (2) Like the term *soma*, the term *porne* has a strong metaphorical meaning. In the Greek version of the Hebrew Bible it frequently referred to Israel in her unfaithfulness to the Lord (Judg. 2:17; Jer. 3:6; Ezek. 6:9, 23:1-48; Hosea 4:12). In the New Testament it can be used in the literal sense (Matt. 21:31-32; Luke 15:30), but better known is the metaphorical picture of corporate unfaithfulness in the old age, Babylon (Rome) the harlot (Rev. 17:5, 19:2). (3) Though Paul does use *porneia*, sexual immorality, in a literal sense (5:1; 7:2), he also uses it as a metaphor for unfaithfulness to the Lord (10:8). (4) There are several phrases in 6:12-20 which cannot easily be taken as a reference to the human body: "the body is for the Lord and the Lord is for the body" (v. 13b); "God raised the Lord and will raise us" (v. 14a); "your bodies are members of Christ" (v. 15a); "the one united to the Lord becomes one spirit with the Lord" (v. 17); "your (plural) body is a temple of the Holy Spirit among you (plural)" (v. 19); "glorify God in your (plural) body" (v.20).

The passage 6:12-20 cannot be taken simply as a warning against sexual immorality. It is better understood as a teaching about the corporate life of the new age. Given the nature of the divisions in chapters 1-4 and the misunderstandings of the body in 5:1-13 and 6:1-11, it seems reasonable to suppose Paul closes this "letter" (chapters 1-6) with a metaphorical summary on the nature of the body of Christ.

In v. 12 Paul agrees that all things are permissible. But not all things are helpful, and Paul does not wish to be enslaved by anything. To be enslaved by the marks of one's own freedom (ideology) not only gives one a false sense of freedom, but it destroys the corporate body. For Paul genuine freedom comes from justification before God and trust within the body. A person cannot earn acceptance by deeds of merit, nor can one live in freedom based on supposed free acts. The former is legalism, the latter is enslavement to the marks of one's own freedom. If a person must eat certain formerly forbidden foods in order to experience freedom, then enslavement has occurred. Such a person can no longer serve the Lord, no longer receive the leading of the Holy Spirit, and no longer experience the joy of acceptance in the faith community. Instead, the life of the Christian will be guided by the marks of his or her own freedom. Such an allegiance to an ideology has the same affect as "idolatry."

Therefore, says Paul, the corporate body is not made for immorality (an alienating or competing allegiance). Rather, the corporate body is made for allegiance and loyalty to the Lord. Paul uses the term *kurios,* Lord, to refer to the ruler of the new age (and so by inference all things in this world; 8:6). As such the Lord carries over the functions of Yahweh in the Hebrew Bible. But Paul's term also implies the Christian counterpart to the many lords of the Hellenistic religious world (8:5). In the Hellenistic world, the corporate assembly of the believers belongs to the lord of that cult. Specifically, when the faithful meet to eat the cult meal, that "table" belongs to the lord (10:21). In reference to eating whatever they wish (v. 13), the Christ house church has forgotten that the corporate body belongs to their Lord (see summary essay, 231).

Paul's succinct proof of that comes in v. 14. In contrast to the destruction of the belly and the food in it (v. 13a), God has resurrected the Lord and consequently us. Without at all denying that Paul can think specifically of the resurrection of Jesus and an empty tomb (see explanatory note on 15:3-11), here one thinks more of the resurrection of the Lord as the beginning of the new age (see explanatory note on 15:20-28). The resurrected body of Christ is a corporate spiritual body which eventually includes us all (15:44-45). The resurrection of the Lord is the creation of the kingdom's spiritual network (as in Rom. 6:5-11) and our redeeming participation in that new community. Whereas the belly and the food will be destroyed, the spiritual network, the body, has ultimate value. In this way Paul relativizes all religious and social practices (see explanatory note on 7:29-31). Only that which contributes to the corporate life of the universal faith community, the resurrected body of Christ, can be considered ultimate. So actions which indeed might be permissible may not contribute to the life of the body (precisely the point of the same argument in 10:23). Having used the body analogy to instruct the Christ house church, Paul now uses the same analogy to address the others.

6:15-18 Using the same analogy and the same language, Paul now flips to the other side of the coin. While, in body language, *porneia* (immorality) refers to a loyalty to something other than that of the Lord of the faith community—the ideology of freedom in this case—it can also refer to allegiance to the "old body," the body of sin, or the body of death. Paul makes the transition in v. 15 by speaking of their function as members in the body. And that is the transition from the ideology of freedom in the Christ house church to the lack of faith evident among some in the other groups. Now the issue becomes the extent to which the early Corinthian Christians have actually shifted from the unrighteous age to the community of the endtime.

First, though, he asks all of them if they understand that their own sense of body depends on their membership in the body of Christ? That, of course, is the key question of the entire letter. If their sense of body (Greek, *ta somata*) comes from their association in the old age, then their self-identity (*psuche*) belongs to the age of unrighteousness. Only if they place their sense of body in the body of Christ can their self-identity (*psuche*) be transformed to the "mind of Christ" (note Rom. 12:1-3). The message is clear: self-identity occurs where the body is being formed.

Having established one of the major theses of the letter, Paul now emphasizes its importance with a rhetorical question. If you have found your identity in the body of Christ, you could not possibly return to the body (formative network) of the old age, could you? In v. 16 Paul continues the rhetorical question, beginning with the introductory phrase (see summary essay, 241) so common in this chapter, "Do you not know?" This time the question moves more toward substance than toward caricature. He moves back to the basic Jewish statement on the body. When a woman and a man join together in sexual intimacy they become two persons with a single intent (one flesh). That single intent defines the nature of a body: a pluralistic community with one mind (1:10). Of course the literal meaning of the statement is also intended (the vehicle of the analogy; see summary essay, 220). The Jesus tradition (Matt. 19:3-9; Mark 10:1-12) uses the same text to indicate the parallel literal truth: a man and a woman joined together cannot be separated (i.e., there can be no reversal of that self-identity established through the formation of one sexual body).

The truth expressed in this creation statement (Gen. 2:24) applies not only to legitimate, intentional relationships, but also to illegitimate, incidental relationships. Of course, one can and will become one flesh with a marriage partner. One will also become one flesh (body, *soma* in Greek!) with a prostitute (v. 16a). That lesson was not easily heard in the churches at Corinth. Perhaps even Paul lacked clarity. For example, he and they doubted the functional existence of idols (8:4). Consequently eating food offered to idols could have no meaning (10:19). Yet he had to admit that eating at the table fellowship of any other than the Lord Jesus Christ could be damaging (10:21). Body formation can and will occur even in unauthentic circumstances. A man who is joined to a prostitute will become one flesh with her. They will be joined in a common purpose, and a common self-identity will be established.

Some readers have confused the literal analogy (the vehicle) with the actual situation addressed (the tenor; see summary essay, 220). Paul was not addressing a case of immorality at Corinth. Granted the analogy bears truth and there were likely some cases of immorality in the Corinthian church, nevertheless the topic is the return of some Corinthian Christians to the old age of unrighteousness. Depending on the old age for body-network functions (legal judgments in this case, 6:1-8) creates or preserves a self-identity outside the faith community. To be sure, association with the old age is required (5:10), but one's self-identity (*psuche*) comes from the community of the endtime. It comes from joining to that community where Christ is Lord (v. 17). The spirit of that community can be none other than the Holy Spirit (vv. 17b, 19).

Regardless of one's interpretation of the passage, v. 18 presents considerable difficulty. If the reader has taken the section literally and supposes the issue at Corinth is sexual immorality, then the reader is forced to ask why only sexual problems are sins against the body. Why not gluttony? Why not drunkenness? There is no available answer.

If, however, the reader assumes a metaphorical use, then some of the problems are immediately clarified. Sin as a condition (not sins as wrong deeds) occurs only in the process of formation. Sin, by definition, is alienation or brokenness in the way we relate to God and therefore to each other. If Paul meant to say that Sin occurs primarily in our unfaithfulness to the Lord (loyalty to false gods or ideologies) or in our failure to live in the new age (allowing body formation to occur in the age of unrighteousness), then obviously faith immorality (the *porneia* of v. 18) is indeed the only way one could sin. Sins are attitudes or acts of destruction against one's own formation body or faith network. If this is true, and it is congruent with the intent of the passage, then v. 18 presents yet another problem. What are those sins which are outside the body? By Paul's definition there is no such sin!

Sin for Paul primarily stands for a condition, nearly a force (Rom. 6:14; 7:13). As such it seldom occurs in the plural. Though Sin (capitalized in this commentary when Paul means a condition) as a word describes an alienation (peccancy), there are, of course, actions which result from this condition of alienation. These alienating actions (peccadillos) are also called sins (15:3), though that meaning of the word occurs rarely in what Paul wrote (Gal. 1:4?; Rom. 3:25). Since sin (Greek *hamartia*) so seldom means wrong deeds in Paul, we can rightly ask if it means a wrong action here. Actually, heretofore in his extant letters Paul has said little about Sin as such. He spoke of the misdeeds of the Jews in 1 Thessalonians 2:16 as *hamartia*—the only use of that term prior to 1 Corinthians 6:18. The misdeeds mentioned earlier in this chapter were either named specifically or done by persons who were *adikos* (unrighteous; 6:1; 6:9). Paul here puts forth his own definition of Sin as a condition. Sin is corporate *porneia* (immorality)—the frustration of or pollution of the body network. Anything else that people might call sin is outside the body. That is why Paul can say, "All things are permissible." So-called food regulations, dress regulations, cultic regulations and religious laws do not define sin per se. By breaking these laws one does not necessarily sin. But any action which pollutes the interrelationships of the body comes from Sin. Therefore the one who frustrates the body network releases the power of Sin against his or her own relationship to the body. At the bottom line all Sin is an act of self-destruction. Even more powerfully, only the creation of distrust within one's body network should be called Sin.

6:19-20 The metaphorical interpretation of 6:12-20 becomes self-evident in v. 19. Leading once more with his rhetorical formula, "Do you not know?" Paul speaks again of this body network as the temple of the Holy Spirit. We have already seen Paul speak of the nascent church as a building (3:10-15). In 3:16-17 that building is identified as the temple (see explanatory note on 3:16-17). At no point in the Bible does a writer identify the temple with an individual person. Even the Johannine "destroy this temple, and in three days I will raise it up" (2:19), must refer to the resurrected body (2:21) of Christ. Only in the early second-century writings of Ignatius of Antioch do we find the individual identification (I Eph. 15:3). As in 3:16-17 here the temple houses the Holy Spirit (see summary essay, 256). In Pauline thought it is the Holy Spirit which guides the corporate body in its common life (1 Cor.

12:4-31). Each Christian belongs to the body and therefore the Spirit. That belonging or ownership was costly. Paul uses the analogy of a slave purchase to pull together the whole section. In v. 12 Paul insisted that his freedom must not be destroyed by any necessity to express marks of that freedom. Indeed, in a later writing, Paul will insist that such slavery to predictable courses of action actually defines slavery to Sin (Rom. 7:13-20; 8:15). Genuine freedom in Jesus Christ brings flexibility and openness in the body of Christ. Freedom from slavery to predictable and unwanted actions does not come easy. Paul speaks of each Christian as one who was bought from this slavery—bought by a price. He does not here explain how that purchase was made nor what price was paid (see Gal. 5:1).

Verse 20 summarizes not only vv. 12-20, but also the entire first section, chapters 1-6. The message is simple. In the life of the body Christians do not act for themselves or for their own self-interest. Christians give honor and obedience to God—in that way the body will not be divided against itself.

THE TEXT IN ITS BIBLICAL CONTEXT

Central to biblical thought is the belief that only body formation has lasting value. In contrast to other points of view, biblical writers suppose personality is developed by one's social environment. Consequently, the individual's primary relationships are highly valued and sharply protected. Since human consciousness, and even divine awareness, result from the social network, these relationships are of ultimate importance. They define what it is to be human. Such primary relationships in life usually involve the sexual dynamic or often the sexual dynamic is used as an analogy. So the Priestly account of creation speaks of humanity formed in the image of God—male and female (Gen. 1:27). The other account tells of Adam's search for such a primary companion (Gen. 2:18-20), a search that ended finally in the oneness of woman and man (2:24). The biblical narrative continues with stories of families and their highly intricate networking. One thinks of Abraham and Sarah, Isaac and Rebecca, Jacob and Rachel; Joseph and his brothers; Saul and Jonathan; David and Bathsheba with the narrative of succession; the kings of Israel and Judah. Nearly absent are the legendary feats of divine-human warriors, mythological struggles, and miraculous adventures that so characterize ancient Greek and Near Eastern scriptures.

Needless to say, these family narratives included the whole Hebrew people. The people were described with corporate terms like family, nation, flock, and tribe. Only in the New Testament did the term body come to play any importance. The reality behind the body metaphor was there from the beginning. Without it, one cannot understand Sin (as alienation in the body), redemption (as return to the body), or resurrection (as purification of the body). In that sense 6:12-20 becomes a central passage in the entire letter of 1 Corinthians.

The problems at Corinth may have been rather new for the people of God. Heretofore God's people had known Sin— brokenness within the body—as caused by individuation over against the nature and/or authority of the community or community representatives (rebellion). They knew Sin as a rigid interpretation of covenant which placed order above relationships (legalism). They even knew Sin as lack of trust in the values of the community (idolatry). But Paul may never have encountered Sin as the placing of principle above divine community (ideology). How Paul dealt with the problem has deeply influenced later faith communities.

THE TEXT IN THE LIFE OF THE CHURCH

Though the church today may not face precisely the problems of the Corinthian church, the situation generally does not differ. The body of Christ constantly has been broken by the Sin of rebellion and the Sin of legalism, but ideology and idolatry also are always with us. Churches which stress a congregational type community life frequently have been plagued by legalism. Questions of dress and issues of lifestyle can all too often override the nature of the community—the very community such rules try to preserve. But congregational type Christians can also shift rather easily into ideology. Some of the ideologies lie at the heart of our convictions. Most obviously the peace position espoused by some can shift into ideological pacifism. Such persons do not work for peace through development of relationships, but by encounter and confrontation. For them the true position of the church must be maintained at all cost. Other ideologies, such as separation from the state, identification with the poor, or justice for women can often disrupt development of the faith community.

Very few groups escape the problem of slavery to freedom. If a previous generation of women wore veils, then freedom can be shown by not wearing veils. If a previous generation of men wore beards, then freedom can be felt by not wearing beards. If a previous generation of men shaved cleanly and used shaving lotion, then freedom can be experienced by growing a beard. If a previous generation of women wore dresses to social functions, then the next can express freedom by wearing slacks. If some men wear neckties, then some men can find freedom by never wearing them. If some like classical music, others find freedom in rock. If some like country music, others show freedom in their love of opera. There is no ultimate meaning in any of these things. For Paul they may simply became another form of slavery. True freedom allows the Christian to do what functions well in the situation. The Christian who is truly free is always free to do whatever builds the faith community (9:19-23).

The faith community has constantly fought against idolatry of this age. It appears to us that much of Christendom has tried to straddle the two ages—giving credence to the new age, but still living in the old. That perception applies particularly to the so-called mainline churches, where state functions are upheld by Christian virtues. Consequently, the radical nature of the new age does not become as evident to the world as it could. Paul spoke of the form of this world passing away, but, on the positive side, he used body language to describe the power of formation in the new age. The decison to enter the new age must be made again and again. It cannot be inherited.

FIRST CORINTHIANS 7:1-40
REGARDING MARRIAGE AND REMARRIAGE

INTRODUCTION

Having completed his response to news of quarrels among the house-churches at Corinth, Paul now turns to the first of the questions put to him in the letter from the Corinthians. He chose to start with the slogan "It is better not to touch a woman." We have already noted how often slogans appear in 1 Corinthians (see explanatory note on 4:6-7). Again, we suppose this slogan may have originated with Paul, but has been misappropriated by some of the Christians at Corinth, particularly members of the Christ house church. Furthermore, readers of this passage have continued to misappropriate it for centuries. Historically, it has been understood as an attack on marriage and call for celibacy. In more recent years that ancient interpretation has been seriously questioned. Now we see in chapter 7 a series of responses to the whole gamut of marriage relationships.

The chapter falls easily into two divisions—a discussion of issues involving marriage (vv. 1-24) and a discussion of the unmarried state (vv. 25-40). Both sections are introduced by the Greek phrase *peri de,* a formula used by Paul to refer to questions from the churches (1 Thess. 4:9; 5:1; 1 Cor. 7:1, 25; 8:1; 12:1; 16:1; 16:12). Within each division there is an endtime discussion which supports Paul's responses, a discussion which is broader than the issue of marriage. In vv. 17-24 he discusses social change and Christian freedom and in vv. 29-31 he advocates disengagement from the involvements of this life. Placed as they are in a specific reflection on marriage, we can learn much about Paul's understanding of the endtime as applied to everyday life.

In the section on marriage Paul deals first with the issue of sexual intercourse in marriage (vv. 1-7). Apparently the more spiritually minded at Corinth had taken the slogan of v. 1 and Paul's teaching on sexuality as an encouragement to limit sexual intercourse. Paul has to correct that impression. Following his discussion of sexual intercourse he takes up separately the marriage problems at Corinth. First comes the question of remarriage (vv. 8-9). The earliest church doubted the possibility of remarriage and therefore advocated a celibate life after the loss of a spouse. Paul undoubtedly had advocated the same teaching (v.8), but was unhappy with the results at Corinth. Consequently, in this passage he allows remarriage to occur. In vv. 10-11 he deals with marriage and divorce in a manner reminiscent of the Synoptic teaching. The "rest" of v. 12 catches up those who are married, but not to a Christian spouse. In vv. 12-16 he reflects on the power of unilateral covenant relationships.

Verses 17-24 are puzzling. They follow the *peri de* of 7:1, yet clearly the question of social freedom leads directly to the teaching on marriage in the vv. 25-38. Noting this transitional nature of the passage, we will consider vv. 17-24 a separate section. The *peri de* of 7:25 leads to a lengthy discussion of a first marriage. Paul moves into a new area of reflection and, for better or worse, concludes that marriage is good, but delay of marriage would be better. He bases his conclusion on endtime teaching. In vv. 39-40 Paul returns to the argument of vv. 7-8—remarriage is acceptable, but remaining celibate after the death of a spouse would be better.

• OUTLINE •

7:1-16 Response to those who are or have been married
7:17-24 Social status and Christian freedom
7:25-38 Response to those not yet married
7:39-40 Permission to remarry

REGARDING THOSE MARRIED 7:1-16

PREVIEW

We are dealing with one of the most controversial sections of the New Testament. Historically, it has been taken as an authoritative call to celibacy, or at the best a reluctant permission to marry. Such a negative attitude toward marriage runs counter to Paul's otherwise positive evaluation of marriage and quite contrary to the biblical understanding of body formation (see summary essay, 227). The section fits much better in Pauline thought if we see that vv. 1-7 deal primarily with the issue of sexual intercourse in marriage. He does not depreciate marriage, but, to the contrary, strongly urges Christian wives and husbands not to limit unduly sexual intercourse with each other. Such a limitation is not only contrary to the nature of body formation (vv. 3-4), but a temptation to immorality (v. 2a). In a specific statement to the demarried (persons once married but no longer) Paul again prefers they could remain unmarried, but admits they probably should remarry (vv. 8-9).

His statement to the married (vv. 10-11) follows primarily that of the words of Jesus: neither a husband nor a wife should separate or divorce their spouse. If that does become necessary then they should not remarry. In the section on mixed marriages (vv. 12-16) Paul argues that the family bond (intimate network) may positively affect the faith of the family—the unbelieving husband or wife, as well as children as they grow up. Therefore the family unit should stay together.

• OUTLINE •

7:1-7 The importance of intercourse in marriage
7:8-9 Remarriage is permissible
7:10-11 Marriages "in the Lord" should not be dissolved
7:12-16 Marriages "not in the Lord" should be maintained if possible

---

EXPLANATORY NOTES

7:1-7 We begin now that part of the letter first written by Paul. Chapters 1-6 were appended to this letter after Paul heard of the divisions plaguing the house churches in Corinth. The "letter" begins with a specific reference to the correspondence from the Corinthian church—not only the characteristic *peri de* (see above, 11), but a fuller reference to what they wrote. We have no right to say there was a letter from the church at Corinth. The "church at Corinth" could not have written a letter to Paul. Are we to understand that a pastor or administrator, such as Apollos, wrote the letter on behalf of all the house churches? Is it possible that only one of the house churches wrote the letter? Most of the questions involve the practices of the Christ house church. Did they write to Paul for confirmation of their style of Christianity? Or did some other house church write to ask if the Christ house church was out of line? We are not certain.

The first issue involved the validity of the slogan "It is better for a man not to touch a woman." In form the slogan looks like a "better than" saying.[1] "Better than" sayings were used in Jewish wisdom literature to express a particular observation about life. The author of Ecclesiastes was especially fond of such sayings: "Better is a poor and wise youth than an old and foolish king" (Eccl. 4:13). Often the sayings are directed toward the listener: "It is better for a man to hear the rebuke of the wise than to hear the song of fools" (Eccl. 7:5). During the period before the formation of the New Testament "better than" sayings became more exaggerated and often included some endtime threat. There are a number of these in the New Testament. The best known are collected in Mark 9:42-47. For example, "It is better for you to enter life lame than with two feet to be thrown into hell" (9:45). The first part (protasis) of the slogan makes an exaggerated statement about being lame, and the second part (apodosis) makes a threatening endtime statement.

There are two such "better than" sayings in 1 Corinthians 7. The one in 7:9b does not appear as exaggerated as those of Mark 9. But if we recognize that Paul and the early Christians frowned on remarriage then the saying "Better not to marry at all than to burn" does sound similar to other New Testament "better than" sayings.

The other "better than" saying in chapter 7 is the slogan in v. 1. At least it had been such a saying. At one time it likely read, "It is better for man not to touch a woman than. . . . " Than what? We do not know. Presumably it was some endtime threat. Was it "than to enter into hell with many sexual conquests" (the *tas porneias* of v. 2a)? Probably it does not matter. What does matter is that some Corinthians, presumably members of the Christ house church, took the first part of the saying as a literal teaching rather than an exaggerated "better than" saying. They used the saying to promote sexual asceticism.

---

[1]Graydon F. Snyder, "The *Tobspruch* in the New Testament," *New Testament Studies* 2 (1976): 117-20.

The meaning of the saying as it stands is clear. The word "touch" was often used in the ancient world as a euphemism for sexual intercourse (Gen 20:6; Prov. 6:29). A good translation could read, "Why, it is better for a man never to have intercourse with a woman at all than. . . . " Since the term man (*anthropos*) is generic and normally means "you" in a "better than" saying, we might then read it, "It is better for a person never to have sexual intercourse at all than. . . . " Certainly the NIV translation— "It is good [better] for a man not to marry"—completely confuses our understanding of the passage.

As we have seen, when the Christ house church misappropriated a slogan or teaching Paul immediately corrected it (see explanatory note on 6:12-14). He uses the same procedure here. Even though some of the Christ house church husbands and wives may be limiting or even eliminating sexual intercourse (v. 5), Paul insists that serious problems (immorality) could arise unless each husband goes to bed regularly with his wife and each wife goes to bed regularly with her husband. The terms used in v. 2 are "have her own husband" and "have his own wife." These phrases have often been understood to mean "marry," but that can be misleading.

The act of marrying is expressed in Greek by the word *gameo*. In this chapter when Paul speaks of a single person marrying he consistently uses *gameo* (vv. 9 [remarry], 28, 36, 39). Married persons are referred to by the participle of the verb *gameo* (vv. 10, 33, 34). In contrast he uses the terms "have a man" or "have a woman" to indicate the state of a man and a woman living together, normally as husband and wife (vv. 12, 13, 29). Yet there is frequently a slight taint in the use of the phrase. The man and woman of vv. 12 and 13 are not married in the Lord. The other use of the term by Paul, the man living with his stepmother, was called an immoral situation (see explanatory note on 5:1). The author of the Gospel of John spoke of the Samaritan woman as having husbands (4:17, 18), rather than being married. John the Baptist told Herod it was unlawful for him to have her (his brother's wife, Matt. 14:4). In Greek of the time the same possibility of a tainted situation existed. The terms seem to stress more the living together than the being married (note, for example, Deut. 28:30 and Ex. 2:1). Consequently we understand v. 2 to mean that immorality could develop if husbands and wives do not live with each other as sexual beings.

In v. 3 Paul makes his point quite clearly. The husband should give his wife her conjugal rights and the wife should give her husband his rights. At issue was the function of intercourse in the marriage relationship. Perhaps the specificity of Paul's statement seems strange to us. We do not talk openly about the frequency of sexual intercourse between husbands and wives. Perhaps they did not either, but in the Jewish Mishnah (collection of Jewish opinions from the time just after the formation of the New Testament) the issue was discussed at length. Sailors had one set of obligations, camel drivers another, and the unemployed yet another (*Ketubot* 5.6). If the obligations were not met the wife had a right to divorce. From his Jewish context, Paul could speak of the debt or obligation (*opheile*) a husband had to a wife and a wife had to her husband.

Verse 4 could be taken as a legal restatement of v. 3. That is, the wife has the power over the husband to define conjugal rights and the husband has the power over the wife to define conjugal rights. Certainly the Mishnah reads that way. But it is difficult to believe Paul would use Jewish law to solve such a sensitive problem. It is much more likely he would explain why conjugal rights were necessary. Assuming that intent, we should take the use of body (*soma*) here in its extended meaning (see explanatory note on 6:12-14 and summary essay,   220). It refers to the intimate social network which defines the person (*psuche*). While the social network is broader than the husband-wife relationship, the intimate sexual relationship determines in an intense way the nature of one's body. Individual persons cannot determine their own sense of body. It is a gift, a gift of God, given through human relationships (see explanatory note on 1:26-31). Because we are women and men, the human network (body) constantly involves sexuality. At the center of God's gift stands sexual intimacy. At no other point does dependency on another for identity appear so absolute.

Because the sexual relationship is so central to personality formation and the quality of one's body network, it is little wonder that the early Christians protected so carefully both the family of origin and the family of choice. Divorce was considered nearly impossible. Remarriage was frowned upon. Here Paul struggles with those who might allow marriage, but deny sexual intercourse. Our most intimate relationship determines the meaning of the body network. Every husband must understand that his wife determines the nature of his body network, and every wife must understand that her husband determines the nature of her body network. For that reason abstention from sexual intimacy within marriage could do irreparable damage to the formation of a person (*psyche*).

In v. 5 we finally learn the cause of the problem. Some couples have agreed to refrain from sexual intercourse as a part of their spiritual discipline. Sexual abstinence for specific purposes was not uncommon among Jewish men or even in the Greco-Roman society. At the giving of the Decalogue the Hebrew men were warned not to go near a woman (Ex. 19:15). The description of recovering from sexual uncleanliness in Leviticus 15:16-18 presumably applies to such occasions as worship or holy war (see 1 Sam. 21:4-6; 2 Sam. 11:11-13). In contrast to cultures that combined human intimacy with divine intimacy (equating the social network with divine universality, Deut. 23:17-18), the Jews, and subsequently Christians, believed the divine network ought not be confused or limited by the human, specific network. Consequently, sexual intercourse was forbidden as a part of divine worship. Indeed, intercourse should be sufficiently separated from holy times to avoid any such confusion.

Paul, as a Jew, surely must have taught them the distinction between a divine network and the human (*Test. Naphtali* 8.8), but did not anticipate the more spiritually minded would eliminate intercourse altogether. It is not clear why the Christ house church came to this conclusion. Was it intense spirituality? Was it the incipient gnostic disdain for the material world? Was it the substitution of principle for relationship (see   below, 104)? Or was it a premature realization of the endtime? Whatever the cause, Paul grants them the possibility of a short time of abstinence (in the Mishnah the "short time" is one, or at most, two weeks) and then they should "go at it again" (v. 5b).

Paul calls for a mutual decision if husband and wife opt for a mutual discipline. The entire passage has emphasized very highly the equality of women and men in their relationship to each other. Each should have their own spouse; each has power over the body identity of the other. Any alteration in their sexual relationship should be by mutual agreement. Perhaps no statement from antiquity matches the sexual mutuality expressed in these five verses.

The reason for "each person going to bed with his or her own spouse" (see v. 2) is reaffirmed in v. 5b. It is the fear that Satan might tempt them at a weak moment (when they lack *akrasia* or self-control). We need to remember that for Paul, as in the Hebrew Bible, Satan functions as the prosecuting attorney for God's law (see summary essay, 255   ). For him the temptation of Satan does not come as a moral weakness or a burning lust, but as a reaction to law. The shift from mutual agreement between the couple to a potentially legalistic discipline could have the opposite of the desired effect. One or both members might be driven by reaction to find their intimate human relationship with someone else. Paul is fully aware that both the human and the divine relationship are necessary. By establishing a sexually delimiting spiritual discipline within marriage, the members of the Christ house church are playing with a potentially destructive fire.

Paul agrees to a time of abstinence only reluctantly. In fact, he doesn't really agree to it—it is only a concession to their particular situation (v. 6). And to underscore the seriousness of their misunderstanding, he repeats his intent—there is certainly no command from him to abstain from intercourse.

Those who consider this passage a call for celibacy would match the concession of v. 6 with v. 2. According to their interpretation Paul advocated celibacy for Christians, but did allow marriage, as a concession, when people could not control themselves. As we have seen, this destroys seriously the flow of vv. 1-7, and runs counter to Paul's otherwise high estimation of marriage. The interpretation of this difficult passage culminates in v. 7. Paul wishes that all readers were as he is, though he recognizes that different people receive different gifts from God. What was the situation with Paul? Because it has been widely accepted that Paul was single, then, despite the obvious difficulties with vv. 3-5, it has been assumed Paul here called all Christians to celibacy, even though not everyone had his self-control.

Was Paul really never married? In this chapter the question depends on the interpretation of v. 8 rather than v. 7. There Paul appears to define his marital status. He addresses the *agamoi* (Greek for unmarried or demarried) and widows, and he wishes they would remain as he is. Normally in the Greek language a person never married is known as a *parthenos* (often translated virgin; see summary essay, 258). That language occurs in v. 25 (see also Acts 21:9). On the other hand, *agamos* hardly ever means a person never married (cf. vv. 32, 34). And, in fact, *agamos* in v. 11 cannot possibly mean "never married." So in v. 8 the *agamoi* are widowers, or demarried men, paired with the other category, widows. As Paul addresses them, the demarried and widows, he wishes they could remain as he—once married, but not in need of remarriage.

Paul was once married and has lost his spouse. Nowhere do we find any indication that Paul was a bachelor. To the contrary all the evidence points to a previous marriage. In 9:5 Paul regrets that he cannot take with him a wife like the other apostles. His apparent understanding of sexuality reflects the marriage experience (see explanatory note on v. 4). And many believe Paul could hardly have carried the type of responsibility he did without having been married. In Jewish circles not to have been married was the exceptional circumstance that should have been mentioned. The language of v. 7b reminds one of Matt. 19:3-12. There Jesus warns the listeners that anyone who divorces and remarries will commit adultery. The disciples are astounded by such a strict teaching on remarriage and exclaim that a person would do better not to remarry at all (reminiscent of 1 Cor. 7:1 and 7:9b!). Jesus replies that not all can handle the teaching on remarriage, though the possibility is given to some (v. 11).

7:8-9 Paul now shifts to specific groups of married people. The first are those who have been married, but are no longer. Presumably they are widowers and widows (see explanatory note on v. 7), although the term *agamos* does not designate how the person became demarried (e.g., v. 11). These people are urged not to remarry, just as Paul has not. The first Christian teachers strongly discouraged remarriage. The Jesus word on divorce made subsequent remarriage a matter of adultery (Matt. 19:9; Mark 10:12; Luke 16:18). Within the period of the New Testament, however, a gradual shift on remarriage can be detected. We have already seen that Jesus, in Matthew 19:3-12, on eunuchs for the sake of the kingdom, admits that sexual abstinence after the loss of a spouse is a special gift (see explanatory note on v. 7). In v. 7 Paul makes the same concession. The situation in vv. 8-9 is not quite the same as vv. 1-7. Paul wishes the demarried could live celibate as he does. But if they do not have self-control (NASB) they would do well to remarry.

Verse 9 has been much debated. One problem has to do with "exercising self-control." Many translators prefer "if they cannot exercise self-control" (RSV, cf. NIV). That sets the stage for a particular interpretation. If the demarried *cannot* control their basic desires, then they had better marry, for it is better to marry than burn with passion. But the text can hardly say that. And Paul simply does not advocate marriage as a last resort against human lust.

In the first place the "cannot" does not belong in v. 9a. Paul is making a statement of fact, not an observation on lust and marriage. The Greek reads, "if they are not exercising self-control, let them marry" (cf. NRSV). Paul doesn't mention any particular scandals, nor do we hear of any. Paul is only protecting his celibacy advice. Persons not inclined to remain single should get married again. In that case the "better than" saying of 9b makes more sense. The problem lies with the Greek word *pyroo* (burn). When the "cannot" is used in 9a then *pyroo* is translated in terms of lust: "aflame/burn with passion" (NRSV, NIV). If the "cannot" is not used, then the translation may read, "better to marry than to burn" (NASB). Basically there are two considerations.

First, *pyroo* does not mean burn with passion anywhere in the biblical literature. The closest would be 2 Maccabees 4:38: inflamed with anger (cf. 2 Cor. 11:29). Normally it simply means burn, though in the New Testament there is often an endtime quality (Eph. 6:16; 1 Pet. 4:12; 2 Pet. 3:12; Rev. 1:15; 3:18).[2] In the second place, if v. 9b is a "better than" saying, as we have suggested (see explanatory note on 7:1), then the "burn" ought to be of an endtime nature. For these reasons we prefer this translation: "But if they are not maintaining self-control, let them (re)marry. For it is better to (re)marry, than to burn in the endtime." The exaggerated nature of the "better than" saying occurs only in light of early Christian teaching on remarriage. It parallels Matthew 19:10b.

7:10-11 The next two verses address those married "in the Lord." Though Paul does not say this directly, he does not discuss marriages between believers and nonbelievers until the next section (vv. 12-16). For the category "married in the Lord" he leaves the realm of personal opinion and reflection. Instead, he gives a command (NRSV, NIV; instructions, NASB; charge, RSV) from the Lord. References to words or commands of the Lord seldom occur in the letters of Paul. Besides this reference we note 14:37 regarding order in worship; the account of the eucharist in 11:23; an allusion to wages in 9:14; and an endtime description in 1 Thess. 4:15. Paul makes practically no reference to Jesus simply as a historical person. Though he protects the priority of Jesus

---

[2]M. L. Barré, "To Marry or to Burn: *Pyrousthai* in 1 Cor 7:9," *Catholic Biblical Quarterly* 6 (1974): 193-202.

(see explanatory note on 12:3), still he recognizes that historical knowledge does not suffice for faith (2 Cor. 5:16). In addition to these few direct statements, there are echoes of the words of Jesus in the letters of Paul. One thinks of Romans 12:9-18. But these echoes are never attributed to Jesus, nor are any such words or deeds used as authoritative.

Some readers are disturbed by this lack of reference to Jesus (see summary essay, 249). Two things should be noted. 1 Corinthians is one of the earliest written parts of the New Testament. Sometimes we forget that. Only 1 Thessalonians should be dated earlier (James and 1 Peter could be about as early). The Jesus tradition has not yet reached written form (ca. 64 CE). We cannot be sure how stable it was in oral form. Nor can we determine the authoritative power of that tradition. In the earliest letters we have mentioned (1 Thessalonians, 1 Corinthians, 1 Peter and James—add to that Galatians, Romans and 2 Corinthians), there is very little indication of an authoritative Jesus tradition. One can be certain the gospel tradition had not yet reached a definitive level.

More important is a second consideration. The theology of Paul, and the Hellenistic-Jewish community, had not reached the point of needing a Jesus tradition. The Pauline tradition had started with an intense endtime expectation. That can be seen in the early summary of that community's faith: 1 Thessalonians 1:9-10. There Paul called on the Gentiles to serve the living God and wait for the coming Son. That Son was identified with Jesus. The intensity of that endtime expectation can be seen in 1 Thessalonians 4:13-5:11. Eventually that endtime expectation began to include the death of Jesus as the end of the old age and his resurrection as the beginning of the new age (see introduction, 7-8).   Such a theology of death and resurrection does not appear so explicitly in 1 Corinthians 1, but becomes quite clear in 1 Corinthians 15. Christ was the first of many (1 Cor. 15:20-28). Only when it was understood that Christians were already living in the new age, by virtue of the resurrection of Jesus, did it become necessary to describe the nature of life between the times.[3] The Jesus words and narratives provided that kind of guidance. That need for an authoritative Jesus arose from the questions raised by Christian groups like the house churches at Cor-

---

[3] J. Paul Sampley, *Walking between the Times: Paul's Moral Reasoning* (Minneapolis: Augsburg/Fortress, 1991).

inth (see summary essay, 249). Paul's use of the words of Jesus when addressing those married "in the Lord" foreshadows the eventual use of the words of Jesus as the primal authority.

The words of Jesus to which Paul alluded must be those found in Matthew 5:32, 19:9, Mark 10:11-12, and Luke 16:18. All of these, except Mark 10:12, forbid a husband to divorce his wife. And, though variously stated, if he does divorce his wife, she will commit adultery if she remarries. The word in 1 Cor. 10b addresses the wife, not the husband. The only comparable Jesus word occurs in Mark 10:12, where Mark records a warning to the wife, a warning which is similar to the one usually given the husband. In 1 Corinthians 7 Paul addresses the wife first and then, almost as an afterthought, includes the husband. The reason for this must be contextual. As we have already noted (see explanatory note on 1:11, and the Summary Esssay, 260) many women were attracted to early Christianity. There must have been many women enthusiastic for the new faith whose husbands were only lukewarm. Did the problem of separation or divorce arise among these women? So, although women normally did not have the right to sue for divorce, has that become a new social possibility in a faith community which stresses the equality of men and women?

It is most instructive that Paul could adapt the Jesus word as a word of the Lord for the faith community at Corinth. Clearly, he understood the words to be authoritative, yet neither he nor his community considered these words something written in stone. They understood the Jesus sayings as words of the risen Lord speaking to the Corinthian Christians in their time. Centuries later it may be difficult to fathom the fluid state of what since then has become an inalterable, printed tradition. But properly understand we can see here the formation of the gospel traditions, even the development of the synoptic Jesus. Out of a historical tradition stemming from Jesus the various areas of the early church developed adaptations which served their communities as authoritative guidance. From those adaptations three quite similar gospels have survived. The Gospel of John was a more radical adaptation, or perhaps it was based on somewhat different tradition.

The early Christian opposition to divorce states the moral dimension of that body formation we have already noted in 6:12-20 (see summary essay, 227). One's self-development depends on one's intimate network (body). A major joy and difficulty in life is that one's body relationships are neither reversible nor erasable. It is not possible for a person to roll back one's formation by saying," I wish it had not been so." Because one cannot reverse development, from the biblical perspective, formation must always be appropriately handled. The commandment to honor one's father and mother makes that clear. Whatever the parents may have been like, eventually, to be healthy, a person will need to "deal with" and recognize those who formed his or her initial personhood (*psuche*). Wholeness does not lie in going beyond our family, and thereby managing to establish a new identity. Wholeness lies in understanding and accepting the function of our family in both our personal development and our trust in God (Deut. 5:16).

We find in the words of Jesus that same perception of marriage. When one person can determine the other's body identity (see explanatory note on 7:4), that relationship could not possibly be reversed. Normally speaking wholeness in marital life requires working through a marriage, not opting out. Opting out leaves the issues unsettled. Add to that the second critical fact: body (network) relationships are not erasable. The inability to erase relationships appears in these and other New Testament sayings as the warning not to remarry. If it is necessary to separate or divorce, then one should not remarry. In v. 11a Paul wishes the separated persons not to remarry because they should work for reconciliation. Again, health comes with working through the relationship rather than aborting it. In the synoptic words of Jesus remarriage constitutes adultery. This is true because a primary relationship cannot be erased. The divorced person takes with her or him the body network of the previous spouse. That previous spouse will be a part of his or her body identity forever. It cannot be erased. So anyone who remarries commits adultery—that is, mingles a previous primary relationship (husband-wife body identity) with a new primary relationship. The words of Jesus, therefore, speak of remarriage after divorce as adultery. Paul does not, though he has wrestled with it in 7:1-2 and 7:8-10. Eventually the early church did give its blessing to marriage after the death or loss of a spouse, but only reluctantly affirmed marriage after divorce (see the adjustment in Mt. 19:9).

In the preceding verses the power of the primary community in forming personhood was assumed. Now in vv. 12-16 Paul speaks plainly. Having addressed the demarried and those married in the Lord, he speaks to the remainder of the married people: those not married in the Lord—couples in which only one converted to Christianity. Even though the covenant relationship would be not be mutual, Paul still advises the Christian husband or wife to remain with his or her spouse. The lack of a Christian covenant (see summary essay,   235) leaves the couple without an articulate method of reconciling differences. More important, the couple lacks a compatible faith community in which their marriage and family can be rooted. Without that institutional support system the couple constantly faces fracture—being pulled apart by two different senses of body identity.

But the failure to articulate a reality does not negate that reality. It only renders it inaccessible for conscious use. The fact that a couple cannot verbally express a common covenant—or any covenant at all—does not mean that the marriage lacks "body." Quite the contrary. All close relationships are formative, whether that is recognized or not. Even on the basis of an inherent, unconscious covenant, Paul can advise Christian wives and husbands to stay with their spouses, unless the spouse is unwilling (v. 15). Though there is no guaranteed success, the formation of the Christian partner could eventually encompass the formation of the unbelieving partner. Then, in effect, if not fact, theirs would be a marriage in the Lord.

Paul's conviction at this point runs deep. He believes in the power of the covenant. He also believes in the unilateral power of covenant love. The cross is such an expression. In order to be redemptive, God's love on the cross did not require our consent. It was effective anyway (Rom. 5:6-8). Much of the Pauline Christian ethic assumes the power of a unilateral love. As we have seen in chapter 6, Paul believes the loving action of the community of the new age can alter the life of the old age (see explanatory note on 6:3-4). Consistent with his conviction Paul argues that the Christian wife or husband might "convert" the unbelieving spouse (7:12-14a, 16). As an argument for his position he uses an analogy they apparently will accept. If the covenant life does not affect others, even unconsciously, then their children will be untouched by their faith. The Corinthian Christians obviously believe that the new faith will indeed successfully determine the formation of their children.

Despite the power of the argument from Christian nurture, Paul grants that it might not work in the case of adults. In that sense he is willing for separation to occur (v.15). The Greek term used by Paul means only separate, not divorce as in vv. 11b, 12, 13. We cannot quite tell whether such Christians would then join the category of demarried or the separated category of v. 11a. In any case the Christian sister or brother ought not be enslaved by oppressive rules. Let the unwilling partner go. Let the remaining spouse live in that *shalom* to which Christians are called. Still Paul cannot quite give up his deep sense of covenant, so he asks the Christian who is considering separation, "How do you know for sure?"

THE TEXT IN ITS BIBLICAL CONTEXT

A uniform picture of marriage in the Bible cannot be drawn. However, the description of marriage as the formation (body) of personhood (*psyche*) occurs throughout the Bible. Man and woman were created for such a relationship (Gen. 1:27; 2:18, 23). In these texts practically nothing is said of sex and marriage as primarily a means of procreation (except in the first account of creation, Gen. 1:28). The purpose of marriage and family as a means of body formation made mixed marriages most questionable. It is true that the son of Abraham and Hagar, Ishmael, was not the son of promise, and therefore unacceptable. But he was also the offspring of an Egyptian. When the Israelites entered the promised land they were constantly tempted to take as wives women of the prior inhabitants. Because of the conflict of "body network" this often resulted in the worship of the gods of these wives (Judges 3:6). It was forbidden. Solomon was constantly censured for his foreign wives (1 Kings 11:1-8), and one of the first actions of Nehemiah, on returning to Jerusalem from the Exile, was to send away the foreign wives (Neh. 13:23-30; Ezra 9:1-2). Granted there were problems of conflicting networks, the Hebrew Bible also contains marvelous examples of crosscultural love (Ruth). Few books from the ancient world express more beautifully the ultimate value of companionship between a man and a woman than Song of Songs (8:6-7), a love that bridged racial boundaries (1:5-6).

Although the Hebrew Bible does not stress procreation, it is understood that a person's being extends not only through one's peers (the body network of the New Testament), but also into the next generation. In fact, if a person does not extend into the next generation, then that person has been cut off from Israel. For that reason it becomes necessary for every person to be married and have children. Therefore, to ensure participation in the ongoing community of faith, singleness and celibacy are unthinkable. If a man failed to have children because of death his family was obliged to furnish him and his wife progeny (Gen. 38; Deut. 25:5-10). The book of Ruth is based on that presupposition (Ruth 4:1-8). For her own extension into the next generation a woman would presumably remarry (Ruth 1:12-13). A barren couple presented anguishing problems for the faith community. Frequently it was seen as a divine punishment which would cut them off from the ongoing people (Gen. 30:1-2; 1 Sam. 1:5b, 11). Sometimes the barrenness was removed by an act of God, or because of a vow (1 Sam. 1:11; Judges 13:2-7). In the patriarchal stories a barren wife might use a maidservant as a substitute (Gen. 30:3).

Despite this fairly clear picture, the practice of the Hebrew people was not at all consistent with what we have seen. In the first place polygamy was apparently widely practiced until the time of the Exile. If through marriage a man and a woman came to a unified identity, then how could a man have more than one wife? Eventually, in the New Testament, monogamy became the norm, both for men and women. Why did the obvious become practice only after the Exile? Furthermore, divorce initiated by the husband became fairly easy to obtain. Given the power of family life and tradition, this seems quite incompatible. Jesus and the first Christians noted the deep inconsistency (Matt. 5:31-32). In their first statements they left no room for divorce. Following the implications of their Jewish heritage they recognized that separation within the family body would be impossible (Mark 10:2-12). It would appear then that Christianity, in respect to sexuality and marriage, appropriated the intention of Judaism. Even to this day it discourages divorce as a way of settling marital conflict. At no time in earliest Christianity was that understanding relaxed. In fact, church leaders and most writers leaned more toward celibacy than toward laxity regarding divorce. Remarriage for any reason presented a problem, for it meant the merging of one body system with another. But within the New Testament period remarriage was being accepted as a social necessity. Paul states it point-blank in 7:39-40 and his rather strange analogy of the law in Romans 7:1-3 makes the same point.

THE TEXT IN THE LIFE OF THE CHURCH

Everyone lives in a body network. That network can be made articulate in two ways: covenant and contract. A covenant acknowledges the mutuality of a relationship. There are parameters to such relationships and they are known. Usually they are expressed by stories which are repeated over and over. Making a contract normally marks the demise of a covenant relationship. The contract strives to protect the relationship and those involved. The parameters of this relationship are expressed by laws. Often such laws are expressed by a condition: if this happens, then that will happen. Body networks normally begin as covenants, but invariably take on contractual elements. Eventually the network can become so rigid or legalistic that it acts to destroy the relationship rather than protect it. This was the heart of Paul's criticism against Judaism. Jesus had called for a return to the covenant intended by God. Paul saw in the death of Jesus an end to legalism and the possibility of covenant life in a new age, a life directed by the Holy Spirit.

Although Christians can see in Judaism that a contractual legalism had replaced the original covenant, they have been unable to prevent the process from occurring in their own lives. That is nowhere more true than in marriage and family relationships. As in previous generations, we have come to a strong reliance on contract to maintain the most intimate of relationships. It cannot be done. The basis for marriage lies in a covenant in which two persons mutually agree to the process of intimate involvement in each other's identity. The joy of such a mutual love cannot possibly be guaranteed by contract; nor by law can terrible anguish be prevented. Maturation does not come by obedience to the contract, but by working through the relationships. The Christian church knows this is true, but frequently fails to convey it. Consequently, when faced with the demand of covenant we are frequently advised to seek our freedom, to express our own individuality, to take care of ourselves, on the one hand; or, on the other, to live according to the traditions and requirements of the church and our society. But it is the formative power of this most intimate relationship that needs to be stressed, not protection of individuals or institutions.

Nearly all Christian groups have stressed the sanctity of marriage. Congregational types have especially stressed the sacredness of the family, since they depend primarily on the family as the locus of Christian nurture. In regard to divorce the issue of remarriage still remains the key problem of pastoral care. That is, the uniting of persons already formed by an intimate relationship will present problems not faced by two persons previously unmarried. An even more complex issue involves those who have been divorced and have an exspouse still living. In such a case the remarried person must not only deal with two or more intimate formations, but also with two ongoing body processes at the same time. As the secondary body network for such persons, the church should be deeply concerned with the health of both the family and the faith community. Universal laws will not likely cover each instance.

ON SOCIAL STATUS 7:17-24

PREVIEW

As if the first sixteen verses were not controversial enough, Paul now begins to tackle the question raised about the marriage of single persons. Verses 17-24 may be considered a transitional reflection as he moves toward that difficult issue. Or put another way, we find in vv. 17-24 the reason why he will answer the marriage question as he does.

As we shall see, this section has been the basis for a widely accepted theory regarding Pauline ethics: a radical private relationship with a socially conservative public policy (see summary essay,   233). It is argued that Christian love destroyed any inequalities between persons, but that Christianity did not directly confront injustices at the social level.[4] Paul does say that seeking a change in one's social or racial identification will not affect one's relationship to God. In vv. 17-19 he advises Gentiles not to seek a "racial" change by becoming Jews. At the same time he advises Jews not to deny their Jewish identity. In vv. 20-24 he applies the same reasoning to the problem of slavery. Freedom ought to be accepted, but *seeking* freedom does not characterize a Christian. All must submit in any case (v. 22b). However, since God has paid the price for our freedom, we should not submit to human ownership (v. 23). Whatever the nature of that nonownership it does not necessarily require social change (v. 24).

Why does this passage appear in the middle of a discussion on sexuality and marriage? Paul realizes the controversial nature of what he is about to say in vv. 25-38, so in vv. 17-24 he lays the basic theological groundwork. He argues the same in each case: in regard to race, slavery, and marital status it is theologically inappropriate to seek a change, though socially quite appropriate to accept change. We can be certain of this procedure because Paul consistently addresses social issues in terms of this trilogy: race, slavery, and gender. Most obvious is the repetition of the three in Galatians 3:28, in the same order. In this passage Paul states his position on race and on slavery before he tackles the difficult problem of gender and marital status.

---

[4]Ernst Troeltsch, *The Social Teaching of the Christian Churches* (London: Allen & Unwin, 1950) 1, 82.

```
• OUTLINE •
7:17-19 On altering racial identity
7:20-24 On altering social status
```

EXPLANATORY NOTES

7:17-19 The very first verse announces the difficulty of the passage. Not only should the Christian not seek to alter her or his racial, social or marital status, but actually that status has been allotted (*merizo*) by God—indeed, she or he was called (*kaleo*) there. Considerable damage to persons has been done by claiming their social position results from God's will. But, because human development stems from one's primary network, it is quite appropriate, in terms of faith, to speak of one's social place as the calling of God. Indeed, the only way to find peace in the primary community is to recognize the ultimate value of one's own development or formation. To say you are called to a given place in life is finally to say that you have found your peace with/in that place.

Even more significant is to know you have a lot (*meros*) in life and that lot or share has ultimate significance (a divine allotment). Dissatisfaction with that allotment can cause the very individuation Paul fears. Just as the ego can rebel against the law, so also the ego can rebel against its own social formation. Rebellion against the law leads to aberrant behavior, while rebellion against one's own formation leads to negation of self. The first is marked by arrogant pride, the latter by gradual loss of self-esteem. Though no one has the right to tyrannize another person with a divinely enforced racial ghetto, social caste, or sexual inferiority, still theological health cannot be divorced from a personal recognition that one is Jew or Gentile, slave or master, male or female—and there is meaning in that. Paul stresses the universal importance of his argument with the formula "in all the churches," v. 17 (cf. 14:33; 11:16). At the same time the formula backhandedly admits the teaching does not derive its authority from the Lord. Instead it is authoritative because it has been taught everywhere, that is, it is not an occasional argument.

The issue of Jew and Gentile, though complicated, was perhaps the easiest of the three cases. Was there any advantage in being a Jew or a Gentile? Some said it was necessary to become a Jew before becoming a Christian (Gal. 5:2-12), but Paul steadfastly resisted those critics.

Within the New Testament we find no Jews desiring to become Gentiles, though in the Maccabean period there were those who had tried to remove the marks of circumcision (1 Macc. 1:14-15). But the situation may be more complicated than first appears. Despite Paul's protest against Judaizers, the first Christians were not aware of their separation from Judaism. Only at the time of the Jewish war (67–70 CE) did it become clear that Christians were not a Jewish sect. Surely Gentiles who had been attracted to Judaism (God-fearers) assumed, when they turned Christian, that they were in some sense adhering to Judaism. The acceptance by Gentiles of Jewish religious customs and regulations may have been deeper than simply a matter of pressure from Jewish legalists. Actually, as we have seen, the faith of Paul may not be discernible except from the Jewish perspective. This tension will appear in issues such as eating meat offered to idols, wearing the prayer veil, the common meal, church order, and the resurrection.

Paul cuts through yearning for piety (Greeks) and display of religious form (Judaism) by stressing obedience to the true and living God (1 Thess. 1:9-10). For Paul the result of the faith must be radical obedience to the one, universal God, rather than any human penultimate power (v. 23). Paul does not designate what commandments are to be obeyed. He speaks only of obedience (v. 19). Yet one suspects the original intent of Law (Torah) cannot be far from his mind. Like Jesus of the Sermon on the Mount (Mt. 5:17-48), Paul does not divorce the community of the new age from God's original intention for the people of God. Race, social position, or gender cannot "inherit" the kingdom of God—only living as God intended will do (see Romans 2:12-14; 4:31; 13:8-14).

7:20-24 Both slavery and gender become much more complex even than racial or ethnic adherence. Paul believes peace comes through understanding of one's formation. For some, rebellion against that formation brings distrust and death. Eventually, perhaps, God effects for them a resurrection through Jesus Christ (Rom. 7-8). But others may be captured in a formation network which proves destructive. Preservation of the network requires the individual to submit to penultimate powers, for example, humans or human institutions. Slavery certainly and gender, perhaps, can cause such entrapment. Paul deals first with slavery. What does a Christian do when her or his primary network has led to slavery?

At the time of Paul slavery was not indentured servitude. A slave was owned by the master. But the reasons for slavery varied considerably. Often the slave was a captive. These slaves were not necessarily less skilled or less educated than their masters. Quite the contrary, much of the imperial administration must have been lodged with slaves in the household of Caesar. But slaves could also be persons who had voluntarily accepted slavery as a means of avoiding or recovering from bankruptcy. Slavery then was a position of political or economic servitude. Being a slave did not necessarily imply inferiority of origin, skill, or education.[5]

As with the Jew-Gentile question Paul encourages enslaved persons to remain in their formation or primary network. Becoming a Christian does not change that ("when you were called," v. 21a). To be sure, unlike the Jew-Gentile issue, Paul does admit freedom from slavery would be preferable. The Christian should not turn down the opportunity to leave a situation which requires unilateral submission to human authority. Paul can, however, encourage people to stay as they are because becoming a follower of Christ relativizes political enslavement. A person who indeed has been enslaved will be free in Christ. A person who was supposed to be free will now submit as a slave to the lordship of Jesus Christ (v.22). A new type of network is formed which does not recognize the distinction between dominant and submissive. Though the thesis here is clear we are not told how it happens. The answer first occurs in vv. 26-31.

One thing becomes quite evident. Paul's message cannot be construed as socially conservative. A new Christian may remain in the position she or he was found, but under no circumstances should the Christian submit to human enslavement (v.23). Ernest Christians have wrestled for centuries with how one could remain in human institutions, yet not be enslaved by them. That is, how can one be in the world, yet not of the world? For Paul it is critical to affirm one's formation without letting it tyrannize you.

----

[5]S. Scott Bartchy, *MALLON XPHSAI: First-Century Slavery and the Interpretation of 1 Corinthians 7:21* (Missoula: University of Montana, 1973).

THE TEXT IN ITS BIBLICAL CONTEXT

The Bible strongly protects the process of life development. The fourth commandment states firmly the necessity of affirming family origins. Without stating laws, biblical narratives invariably describe life as following progressive patterns. The oldest son inherits the family wealth and authority (Gen. 27). The oldest daughter has the first right of marriage (Gen. 29:25). To interrupt the process of life can have dire consequences (Gen. 37:4; 1 Sam. 17:28-30). In the Hebrew Bible the process of life can only be interrupted by God's use of the unexpected—Jacob, Joseph, Gideon, David, for example. In the New Testament we find in the gospels and Pauline material that same sense of process in life. But the process can be interrupted by the nearness of the endtime. The nearness of the endtime suspends normal values without destroying the fabric of society. Families will be set against each other (Mark 13:12) and even motherhood will become a curse (Mark 13:17). Even the non-eschatological Gospel of John recognizes the necessity for a disengagement from the values of this world (John 17:15-17). In 1 Corinthians 7:17-24 Paul allows the fabric of society to remain, but asks the Christian to live under the lordship of Christ. In vv. 26-31 his social ethic will become more evident.

THE TEXT IN THE LIFE OF THE CHURCH

Both the difficulty and value of this material for our day can hardly be overestimated. Western culture admires the autonomous person. Such a person must be free of determinative or oppressive networks. The truly happy person must have freedom. Our culture often advises persons to seek that freedom regardless of cost to family and society. It is best to "do it my way." Paul's thought stands in sharp contrast to the autonomous thinking of the western world. For Paul there is no freedom except in peace with one's social network. At the same time freedom cannot be gained by changing one's background or dropping out of tyrannical institutions. Freedom comes through allegiance to the Lord of all, Jesus Christ.

An extraordinary price was paid for that freedom. That price released each of us from slavery to localism and penultimate human institutions. Freedom comes from adherence and obedience to the one, true, living God. Then one lives out of what is ultimate. Such a life cannot be bound to any form of slavery except that obedience to God.

The Christian calling is not to social change. The calling is to a faith in the ultimate Lordship of Christ. Such a faith makes secondary all human institutions. Such a relativization of human lordship can, has, and will create radical social change. Those who say Paul's ethic is privately radical, but socially conservative, have made an error. Paul's ethic stance calls for a radical community which, in daily contact, makes a parabolic, endtime critique of the institutions of the old age.

An example in recent times of relativizing human institutions is the civil rights movement in the United States. As long as black persons allowed white people to define black as inferior and subservient, then blacks were indeed submitting to a tyrannical relationship. No laws or civil rights legislation could change that. When black people began to redefine their color and culture as "beautiful," then the tyranny of slavery was broken, although the institutions of white dominance only slowly fade away.

REGARDING THE UNMARRIED 7:25-38

PREVIEW

In v. 25 Paul begins his answer to the second question posed by the Corinthian Christians. The first dealt with sexual relationships, with particular regard to those who had been married. The second question does not deal at all with sexuality or sexual relationships, but with the human institution of marriage (and gender differentiation). From this distance in time it is difficult to determine what instigated the question. We can see what Paul says in response. If his response accurately reflects the question, then the Corinthians were asking about the viability of marriage in light of the kingdom present and the kingdom coming. If vv. 36-38 also belong to the question, then the focus finally settles on the third element (Gal 3:28) in Paul's endtime ethic: equality of Jew and Greek, equality of slave and master, equality of woman and man.

Following the posing of the Corinthian question, Paul again states his theological position (vv. 25-31). The famous "as if not" (*hos me*) passage states Paul's belief in endtime social disengagement. In vv. 32-35 Paul approves marriage but makes it clear that marriage as an institution does hold a man or a woman in this age. It is difficult to serve the universal lordship of Christ and be responsible to a marriage partner. And finally Paul addresses the parental question. Knowing that women are enmeshed in a male-dominated society, Paul advises a parent (father in this case) not to further the subjection of a daughter by arranging a marriage for her (vv. 36-38).

• OUTLINE •

7:25-31 Living "as if" this world were "not"
7:32-35 Marriage can divide loyalties
7:36-38 A parent ought not promote enmeshment

EXPLANATORY NOTES

7:25-31 The section begins with Paul's response formula, *peri de* (see above, 11). The topic concerns *parthenoi*, a term often translated "virgin," but here refers to persons never married (see summary essay, 258). Paul immediately admits he has no authority from the Lord regarding the marriage of a single person. Paul is extending his faith system into an occasional problem. He does not call on the authority of tradition (word of the Lord) nor universality of practice (in all the churches), but on his own reliability as one graced by God with the ability to extend the will of God into a new situation. Apparently Paul did consider the question occasional, that is, a particular question raised only by some factions of the Corinthian church. It is important for the modern reader to distinguish between general teachings and occasional teachings. Paul's answer to the Corinthian question has value to us primarily for the way in which he engaged the problem. The answer itself has less value for us than the method used. Yet one must be careful even with this statement.

Granted the church should not have turned Paul's occasional answer into an ecclesiastical preference for celibacy, still the problem addressed by Paul cannot be limited to the Corinthian church. The relationship of marriage and family to the coming kingdom still puzzles the individual believer and the church. And especially the subordination (enmeshment) of a woman to male domination plagues a church which learned from Paul that men and women are equal (Gal. 3:28). So the reader must be careful not to draw unwarranted conclusions from this passage, yet take seriously the manner in which Paul addresses a problem very much alive in our time.

As already started in vv. 17-24, Paul is working up to his answer. He has already argued for Jews and Greeks, slaves and masters, to stay as they are, because a change of racial or social position does not bring with it divine approbation (race) or freedom (political status). Now he underscores his reasoning with endtime expectation (v. 26). The use of eschatological language has confused readers of the New Testament in general and specifically in this verse (see summary essay,   237). Many have supposed biblical writers, since the dawn of apocalypticism (see summary essay,   261), literally expected an end of history. But apocalypticism was never that simple. The apocalyptic writers believed the values and institutions of this age were passing away and that God was establishing a new type of kingdom not based on the values of this present age. There is nothing in apocalypticism to make us suppose history itself literally would come to an end. To the contrary, there was always a new life ahead. But some readers have taken endtime thought as chronologically literal. Consequently they often read the radical ethical demands of the New Testament as interim ethics—a life-style that can be advocated only because the end of history will occur very soon.

Paul did not describe a life-style which was valid only because the end of history was at hand. Rather, Paul spoke of a life-style that characterized the coming new age. In that new kingdom there would be no racial preference, no social caste, and no gender superiority. It is the immediate presence of the Kingdom of God which permits and calls forth this life-style of the new age. As throughout Paul's writings the Christian lives between the ages, between the times. That "between the times" is called here "present distress" (*enestosan anagken*). Life for the Christian in the present distress must be one which participates in this age, yet also participates in the coming age. Alterations and changes in one's life in the old age does not and will not gain advantages for the new age. So, says Paul in v. 27, becoming celibate provides no advantage in the new age. At the same time, seeking marriage ties a person to this age in a way that interferes with life in the new age. So one should remain as called.

But just as the slave would well accept freedom, so a single person would well accept marriage (v. 28). Paul says the person who marries does not sin. Obviously Paul could not have referred to marriage as a sinful act. In what sense could he or the Corinthians have countenanced marriage as a sin? The two sections, vv. 17-24 and vv. 25-38, make it clear there is more than one sense of sin in the letters of Paul (see summary essay, 234). Most readers define sin in Paul as alienation. That understanding of sin, so well stated in Romans, describes the individual rebelling against her or his covenant community. Due to the human drive for self-fulfillment, persons protect themselves with contracts rather than live more freely in covenant. They regulate life with prescriptions (laws) rather than descriptions (stories). Eventually that drive will cause the individual to feel isolated from his or her primary network (body) and even lead to the use of law for one's own supposed benefit. When the covenant relationship, that which is life itself, is abused for individual self-interest, we call that Sin (often capitalized to distinguish, with Paul, from improper behavior). It is a condition of alienation which results in antisocial behavior. This well known understanding of Sin, so frequent in Galatians and Romans, does not appear sharply in the first two letters of Paul, 1 Thessalonians and 1 Corinthians.

In these two more eschatological writings, to the churches at Thessalonica and Corinth, Paul describes our human problem (Sin) as entrapment in an old age which is passing away. As we have seen, according to Paul, one cannot change values or structures in the old age in such a way as to escape its entrapment. So the coming of the new age does not call simply for a shift in racial, political, or marital status. The presence of the new age calls for disengagement from the old. But, in answer to the Corinthians, Paul cannot say that marriage, an institution also of the old age, would be Sin. He can only recognize it does indeed deeply anchor a person in this old age and can lead to a stultifying social enmeshment. The potential Sin, then, is neither an antisocial act nor alienation, but self-destructive enmeshment (trouble in the flesh, v. 28, KJV) in this age. Paul's faith answer to such enmeshment is to proclaim the imminent present power of the new age. The presence of that new age is breaking up the institutions of the old age, therefore the time (*kairos*) is foreshortened. In light of that presence of a new age, the Christian should live *hos me*—as if not. In a rhythmic cadence Paul repeats the *hos me* five times: in reference to marriage, to death (mourning), to weddings (rejoicing), to business dealings, and to relations with this world in general. That is, the Christian is to live in the world, but not as if it were ultimate. Paul calls for an endtime disengagement from life in this world.

The Christian disengages from life in this world, not only because, in Jesus Christ, the new age has begun, but also because the form (*schema*) of this world is passing away. Paul was a true apocalyptic writer: not only is the endtime at hand, but the present age has reached its limit. That is the actual social critique of an apocalyptic thinker. The old forms are bankrupt. Pauline-style faith starts with the realization that the present age provides no possible solution for life. Later, in the powerful Romans 12:1-2, Paul urges Roman Christians not to cooperate with this age, but rather to shift to new forms. Some have taken this distrust of the present age as an invitation to anarchy or sectarianism, but Paul meant for the new Christians to live in this age without conferring ultimate value on its institutions.

7:32-35 There is little new in this section. Paul repeats the problem of enmeshment: the unmarried can give full loyalty to the Lord, while the married person must constantly be concerned about family and matters of this age. Paul simply notes this fact, but makes no mandate to remain celibate (v. 35). However, Paul does add a new element to his discussion which now puzzles us. In v. 32 he wishes Christians to be free of anxieties (*merimna*).

In early Christianity, anxiety apparently was considered inappropriate for the life of a believer. The Jesus words of Matthew 6:25-34 indicate the uselessness of anxiety. The author of 1 Peter urges the new born Christians to cast their anxieties on the Lord (1 Pet. 5:7). So we are prepared to hear that Christian existence should be without anxiety (v. 32). But almost immediately Paul speaks of a proper anxiety for the Lord, as compared to anxiety for this world and for one's spouse. How can Paul simultaneously wish for Christians to be free of anxiety and then want them to be anxious for the Lord?

It may be there are two senses of anxiety, as there are two senses of sin. Existentially one speaks of a condition of *Angst. Angst,* or anxiety, characterizes all persons as they face their destiny (death) in light of present existence. Did Paul wish and expect that all Christians would and should be free of Angst in the endtime? Yet "between the times" one cannot be free of concerns and cares. Would it not be better to have anxiety (concern) for the coming kingdom than for the old, disappearing, present age? On the other hand, perhaps Paul does not intend any distinction in the use of the term. In the endtime there will be no anxiety at all, though now there is. Anxiety, or anticipation, for the coming kingdom could be freeing for those enmeshed in this old age. But anxiety for the old age encourages even deeper enmeshment with family and spouse. In any case the *merimna* of v. 33 characterizes the person who has become enmeshed in this world and cannot escape.

7:36-38 The key to the entire section lies in these three verses. Two well-known and quite different translations have been made. In one the husband is advised that not marrying his betrothed would be better than marrying her (NRSV). In the other, made popular by the ASV, it is the father who is advised that not giving his daughter in marriage would be better than arranging a marriage for her. In terms of the Greek language a decision between the two would be hard to make. In v. 36 the man acts unseemly (*aschemoneo*) toward the unmarried woman. At first glance that hardly fits the relationship between father and daughter. On the other hand, in v. 38 Paul clearly speaks of someone (i.e., the father) giving the unmarried woman to be married rather than of a man (i.e., the betrothed) marrying her.

All things considered, the father-daughter interpretation seems best. Paul has been speaking of enmeshment in the old age. While he has not spoken specifically of women as an enmeshed group, we know from the later Galatians 3:28 that he considers women to have an unequal place in the Greco-Roman society. While the man might leave home in that day, that was hardly a possibility for the young woman. For a man salvation could be understood as a leaving and a grace filled return (e.g., the prodigal son). For a woman there was only continued social entrapment. The father simply arranged for the woman of age to marry an appropriate man. Her entrapment merely shifted from one man to another.

If we consider the intent of this passage to encourage celibacy, then the betrothal translation makes more sense. But if we consider the intent of the passage to discuss enmeshment in this age, then the father-daughter translation fits better. A Christian father is advised not to continue or create his daughter's entrapment in this age; though, if it seems socially unseemly not to give her in marriage, then he should feel free to do it.

If this interpretation is correct, the action in v. 36 refers to the social obligation of the father to arrange for his daughter's marriage. His failure to act is inappropriate in that culture because his daughter is past the age for marrying (*huperakmos*). Paul says it is okay for him to let his daughter marry, but if he can withstand the social pressure, he would do even better not to give her over to a man in marriage (v. 37). Presumably he means it would be better for the woman to decide for herself, rather than have life decided for her (that is, be pledged in marriage by her father). The best translation would be

> If anyone thinks he is dealing inappropriately with his unmarried daughter, since she already is past the age for marrying, and therefore ought to do something, let him do as he wishes. He doesn't sin; let the couple marry. But the one who can stand firm in his heart, without any distress, having the power to do as he wishes, and has already made up his mind not to pledge his unmarried daughter, he does well. So the one who gives his daughter in marriage does well, but the one who does not give in marriage does even better. (Cf. alternate translation of NRSV, and notes on 7:36-38 in *The New Oxford Annotated Bible*.)

THE TEXT IN ITS BIBLICAL CONTEXT

This section ploughs new ground in biblical theology. As Paul indicated, there is no traditional way to answer the question regarding the marriage of single persons. In Judaism a single person would normally have expected marriage, so there is little discussion of the matter. Likewise the problem of social enmeshment for either man or woman appears not to have attracted attention. The social position of women in the Hebrew Bible can be easily seen. In such stories as that of Jacob one can see that women are expected to stay in the social network as established by father and husband. That is, Laban shifted Leah and Rachel to Jacob. It was even the obligation of Laban to give Leah in marriage first. In the story of Ruth, it was heroic for Ruth, as a non-Jew, to accept the network of her deceased husband. Men leave home and yet find acceptance. Women do not leave home. Their sin is failure to produce for or be faithful to the social network. The story of salvation in the Hebrew Bible is a man's story. It deals with promise, faithlessness or rebellion, repentance and mercy.

While the social network was well protected in ancient Judaism, little is said about one entrapped in the tribal matrix. It took the experience of the Exile to change that. When the *entire* culture, both men and women, was subjugated, the theology changed remarkably. An apocalypticism (see summary essay,   237) developed which devalued present existence and placed ultimacy in the coming kingdom of God. Subjected people were freed from tyranny by relativizing the present.

That is the theology to which Paul was converted and which we find so pronounced in 1 Thessalonians and 1 Corinthians. A few years later a more redemptive ("masculine") theology appears in Galatians and Romans. In 1 Corinthians 7:25-38 Paul addresses both sexes—and both sexes can and will fall into enmeshment. But Paul finally addresses primarily the problem of women. Persons entrapped in the social matrix can only live *hos me*—as if not. Paul may be the first biblical writer to see this and perhaps the only biblical writer to address the issue. Later Christian writers returned to the masculine model. But the art of the early church, as it arises from the local experience of Christians suppressed by the powerful Roman Empire, reflects the problem of social entrapment and a Christology which can free persons without isolating them from the rest of society (like Daniel in the lions' den, or the three young men in the fiery furnace).[6]

THE TEXT IN THE LIFE OF THE CHURCH

This passage has long puzzled scholars. It has normally been interpreted as a strong encouragement for celibacy. Some have taken that literally. Others have dismissed it because of what they consider an unwarranted and mistaken endtime expectation. But seen in light of social subjugation, the passage takes on quite another meaning. It speaks of a Christian freedom within the social network—a freedom that is rooted in the coming new age.

The problem of social subjugation is just as real today as it was in the time of Paul. In the world at large, and even in the Christian world, women, minorities and third-world people feel subjugation as a problem much more than alienation or personal guilt. Yet the Christian message continually proclaims redemption for the powerful (masculine)—a process involving alienation, repentance, and grace. The church needs to reread 1 Corinthians 7:25-38 carefully and, like Paul, speak of a Christology which frees from subjugation without destroying the fabric of society in which we live. That is the Christ who died to the old age and lives in the new age *hos me,* as if not. And with Paul the church today needs to urge those who do have authority (the fathers of vv. 36-38) not to continue the enmeshment of those subjugated but to find ways for Jew and Gentile, slave and master, male and female to be free

---

[6]Snyder, *Ante Pacem,* 55.

together in the coming new age.

ON REMARRIAGE 7:39-40

For reasons now unclear to the reader, Paul shifts to a topic which ought to have been treated earlier: remarriage after the death of a nonbelieving spouse. He reaffirms that a woman must not leave a husband while he is alive. Perhaps he refers to a believing wife and a nonbelieving husband. If so, v. 39a comes across more sharply than 7:13. When the unbelieving husband dies, the wife may remarry, but only to a believer (in the Lord). But, as he has said several times (vv. 1, 7, 8), she would do better to remain unmarried.

FIRST CORINTHIANS 8:1–11:34
ON EATING TOGETHER

INTRODUCTION

The third question from the Corinthians regards eating meat offered to idols. We suppose most meat available for eating must have been dedicated by some religious group. Perhaps all meat would have been processed by a religious association. The new Christians at Corinth did not know how to deal with idol-meat issues. Since idols had no reality, were they free to eat as they saw fit? Some did eat, while others did not. Who was correct? Paul understands both sides, and, as previously, opts for unity in the community rather than any sense of rectitude.

Most readers would not assume the unity of chapters 8–11 as Paul's answer. Some reflection on Paul's method makes us think Paul did not start a new topic until 12:1. Paul's style becomes most clear in this section, though it can be seen also in chapters 12–14. Paul states the problem (8:7). He reflects on the problem, then moves to an analogy (chapter 9). The substance of the analogy (wages in 9:1-18) may have little to do with the actual problem, but it has parallel implications. Having reflected on the analogy Paul turns to his solution (10:1-11:1). Then he hangs on the argument some parallel problems, not raised by his questioners (head covering in 11:2-16 and the Lord's Supper in 11:17-34). Chapters 8–11 are divided as follows.

    8:1-13 Regarding Food Offered to Idols
    9:1-27 All Things to All Persons
  10:1–11:1 The Power of Religious Community
   11:2-34 The Conduct of Worship

REGARDING FOOD OFFERED TO IDOLS 8:1-13

PREVIEW

The issue of eating meat offered to idols was contributing to tension in the church at Corinth. Paul was asked to make a judgment on the matter. Should they eat the meat and risk splitting the church wide open? Or, for the sake of the community, should they forego meat for reasons no longer meaningful to Christians? In a parallel passage (10:23-30) Paul speaks to the issue of table fellowship and its effect on the participants. But here he speaks more to the issue of actions which might divide the faith community.

The problem of eating meat offered to idols must have been raised by the Christ house church (see summary essay,   252). Paul responds to the question in terms of their claim to have *gnosis* or special knowledge (vv. 1-3). His reflection on knowledge and love has become a classic statement. Then Paul attacks the issue of idols (vv. 4-6). His rather incidental confession about God and Jesus Christ is one of the earliest statements we have. But in vv. 7-13 Paul moves to the real issue: how to live in the same community with different perceptions of key problems. Some are "free" to eat food offered to idols while others believe eating food offered to idols actually involves one in idol worship. How shall these two beliefs exist side by side?

```
• OUTLINE •

8:1-3 Love of God is true knowledge
8:4-6 No God but the one
8:7-13 Freedom in the community context
```

EXPLANATORY NOTES

8:1-3 Again Paul introduces the chapter with *peri de,* his formula for responding to a question or inquiry. The topic is food offered to idols (Greek, *eidolothuton*). Literally the Greek term refers to a sacrifice (*thutos*) to an idol (*eidolon*). Since a sacrifice of this nature normally would involve the taking of life or spilling blood, one supposes the topic is meat offered to idols. That presupposition is buttressed in 1 Corinthians by the use of the Greek term *makellon,* meat market (in 10:25). But our knowledge of Roman cities places this in doubt (see **above, 3**). There are indeed eating establishments where certain divinities are honored. But the connection of eating establishments with butcher shops cannot be established. Neither can butcher shops with certainty be connected with religious sacrifice. That is not to say such links were not there, but Greece lacks archaeological evidence for eating associations like that of Mithraism in the Roman world.

It was the Christ house church that raised the question. It was a matter of their *gnosis* or knowledge. Paul quotes their slogan, or his: "we all have knowledge." The slogan makes good sense. If one has become a Christian, if one has left living in the old age and entered into the new, then one must perceive some of the depth of religious truth. Why otherwise would one make the social and personal sacrifice required to become a member of the new faith community? Paul does not deny this. He ought not to—he likely coined the phrase.

Instead of retracting the slogan, Paul placed *gnosis* over against love. It is not clear to what extent he felt it necessary to "downgrade" *gnosis*. *Gnosis* was a key element in Paul's theology,[1] but, as in 13:2, Paul is forced to subordinate knowledge to love without negating *gnosis* itself. *Gnosis* puffs up the person; it is ephemeral. But love, agape, builds up the person; it is lasting. *Gnosis* is the perception of divine truth. Love is that covenantal caring which marks a healthy social network. While a religious movement could hardly exist without perception of divine truth, that interpretation comes through the community of faith, not a personal revelation. Insofar as individual Christians suppose their understanding of truth is a personal matter they can be puffed up (*phusioo*). Therefore, Paul can say that *agape* develops the person in community, while *gnosis,* as a private perception of truth, will eventually give a false self-understanding.

Paul's classic statement of that difference appears in vv. 2–3. If a person thinks he or she is knowing, then that very self-perception indicates knowing is no longer, or not yet, complete. A person who is self-conscious about her or his religious knowledge has already privatized the faith. That person supposes she or he has a private knowledge. If that is true the individual does not yet "know" appropriately. The

---

[1]Walther Schmithals, *Gnosticism in Corinth: An Investigation of the Letters to the Corinthians,* trans. John E. Steely (Nashville: Abingdon Press, 1971).

source of *gnosis* is not in one's understanding, but in being understood. A primary function of any community is to build a common self-understanding, normally in narrative form. Since the individual is developed by primary networks (see above,   100), then the epistemology, or way of knowing, depends on the common story of the primary community. One's self-perception depends on how one is understood in that story. That understanding comes from the community. Its validity depends, in part, on the person's acceptance of the understanding (faith) and acknowledgement of its correctness *pro me* (conversion, rebirth).

Divine truth enters our consciousness through the faith story of the primary community. For the Jewish believer the Hebrew Bible was a powerful common story as God's chosen people. The Christian story stressed a formation in Jesus Christ which creates a present story as well as a story yet to come (hope).[2] People who cannot care for others in the faith community and cannot understand them (articulate their place in the divine story), have themselves lost access to *gnosis*. Without mutual care in the faith community there is no way to be known and understood. Any knowledge one then possesses has lost its anchor in revelation (the divine story). Such private knowledge "puffs up," but does not build up mutual self-understanding.

Paul states the principle in v. 3. If one cares for others as designated by the Other, then one is known by the Other through those "others." In the Hebrew Bible knowledge as mutual self-understanding occurs primarily in sexual contexts. The Hebrew term *yada'*, translated in the Greek of the Septuagint as *ginosko*, was used frequently for sexual intercourse (Gen. 4:1). The writers of the Hebrew Bible seldom spoke of humans knowing God, but, as in 1 Corinthians 8:3, spoke of God knowing them (Ps. 139:1-6, 23). Perhaps no religious sensation could be more satisfying than to be known by God—that is, that as an individual to know one's role and place in God's intention. Paul may not have originally understood that the reversal of this process—our knowing God—would result in a growth of individual piety at the expense of community formation.

8:4-6 The Christ house church at Corinth possesses *gnosis* about the nature of God. Quoting Deuteronomy 6:4 some Corinthian Christians note

---

[2]Warren Groff, *Christ the Hope of the Future: Signals of a Promised Humanity* (Grand Rapids: Wm. B. Eerdmans, 1971).

that idols cannot possibly exist (v.4). If idols do not exist, the Christians ought not act as if they did. Eating food offered to idols has no meaning; it would be offensive to think or act otherwise. Paul cannot possibly disagree. At an ontological level, Judaism constantly attacked the reality of idols. Most notable were the attacks during the exile. Isaiah of the Exile cynically ridiculed idols who needed to be carried by the people rather than carry the people (Isa. 46:1-4). The author of Daniel showed the same scorn. When asked to worship Nebuchadnezzar's golden image, Shadrach, Meshach, and Abednego said theirs was a God who could deliver them from the fiery furnace. But even if that were not true, they said, they certainly would not worship a piece of metal (Dan. 3:16-18). Paul continued that attack in his own preaching. He called for the Gentiles to worship a true and living God (1 Thess. 1:9; see also Acts 17:29). The Corinthian Christians surely heard this message from Paul. He will not deny that conviction. Quite the contrary, he reaffirms there are indeed many so-called gods and lords, but only one God from whom comes life.

At the time of Paul the Greco-Roman world had entered a period called by some "a failure of nerve."[3] During the classical period (ca. 400–300 BCE) the Greeks portrayed the human spirit and form as supreme. As the powerful Greek city-states declined so did the Greek spirit. So Hellenistic (and subsequently Roman) thinkers spoke of a world in which the environment was overcoming the human. Religion shifted from the Olympic divinities to religions of personal salvation, primarily mystery religions. These religions were represented in every town by small temples, meeting places, or homes. The mythical divinities of these mysteries were called "lords." Everywhere were found religious associations for Lord Serapis, Mithra, Isis, and many others. Paul denies the reality of these "gods" and "lords," and turns to a confession of the one God.

It should be noted that Paul misses two issues. He does not deal with the social function of polytheism. Whatever the ontological attack against idols, polytheism enabled a tolerant pluralism to exist.[4] The Roman Empire was marked by a sense of pluralism loosely held together under Roman administrative and military power. Little did Paul

---

[3]Gilbert Murray, *Five Stages of Greek Religion* (New York: Columbia University Press, 1930).

[4]David L. Miller, *The New Polytheism* (Dallas: Spring Publications, 1981) 81-94.

know that the Christian attack on idols would appear to Romans as an intolerant monotheism.[5] Secondly, Paul misestimated the power of a community or network even if based on a nonreality such as idols. At Corinth he saw that error and corrected it (in chapter 10).

But here in v. 6 Paul states his faith in the one God. The key to the statement lies in the two Greek prepositions, *ek* and *dia*. Otherwise the two phrases are quite parallel: one God . . . from whom; one Lord . . . through whom. God the parent is the source of all things and the Lord Jesus Christ is the agent of that creation. One God as the source of all things prevents any type of dualism or gnosticism (where the world is considered evil). In the Judeo-Christian tradition it is not possible to place the source of evil in a parallel power which works against the divine power. So in Pauline thought there is no sense that a person is hopelessly caught between two impulses, between two opposing forces, or between heaven and earth. There is no use in yearning for a heavenly existence instead of life in the created world. For Paul the human predicament reflects the Sin of alienation or the Sin of entrapment rather than the error (sin) of making a wrong choice, or being in the wrong place.

Likewise, there is one Lord through whom all comes into being. The *kurios* (Lord) rules the human community. As Yahweh was the Lord of Israel, so Jesus Christ is Lord of the church and the universal new kingdom. The community of humankind came into being through Jesus Christ. The tolerant pluralism of the "many lords" allowed the human community a genuine multiplicity. The lordship of Jesus Christ brought all things, human pluralism, into one ecumenical community. The unity does not depend on toleration, but on the single lordship of Jesus. That unity was well stated in Ephesians 4:5—one Lord, one faith, one baptism.

The ultimate lordship of Christ is eschatological. It is not yet fully realized. For Paul we Christians stand between the failure of the old age and the coming of the new. Why then do we have a creation statement about God and the Lord Jesus Christ? In the Hebrew mentality a finale never appears *de novo*. Life exists on a continuum of promise and fulfillment. Paul could only understand the coming new age as a fulfillment of God's promise to all the nations (Genesis 12:1-3). On a deeper basis Paul could only understand the reality of the new age as a fulfillment of the creation. Creation statements are promises of an endtime

---

[5]Snyder, *Ante Pacem*, 164.

reality. Creation statements are not meant as a description of beginnings to which we must return for salvation and peace. Rather, they are statements of divine intention. The Christian stands in the tension of life as it is and life as God intended it. Though pluralistic in customs, languages, and perceptions, life was intended to be lived under a single lordship. Theologically speaking, the formation of the Christian culture about 200 CE was a victory of the one Lord, with its many different expressions, over the many lords of the Greco-Roman world.

The confession refers only to God and Jesus Christ. Since it has characteristics of a common formula, one wonders why there is no reference to the Holy Spirit. Although the activity of Father, Son, and Holy Spirit had been articulated, there was not yet, in 53 CE, a formal trinitarian statement. Still, despite claims that the contribution of Judaism to world religions was monotheism,[6] both Judaism and Christianity understood God as a unity, but not an arithmetical oneness. In the Old Testament they spoke of God and the divine court with its several God functions, the sons of God (Job 1:6). Paul knows three God functions and perhaps a fourth, Wisdom (see summary essay, 261). Eventually early Christianity would develop a threefold formula. The faith community knew the necessity of a trinitarian formula. Mono-formulas would result in a God-based human tyranny. Binitarian formulas would lead to a human dualism. Only trinitarianism made it clear that the human community could be plural, yet united. Surely Paul recognized the necessity for a trinity even as he penned 8:6, yet had not formulated it in confessional terms (see 2 Cor. 13:14).

8:7-13 The issues raised by the Corinthian church are classic. This one ranks as a constant problem of the faith community: "not all possess knowledge." Though the idols clearly have no existence, and for those with *gnosis* it cannot be otherwise, some do not share that knowledge. Up to this time they have been accustomed to idols, so they eat as if it really were food offered to idols (v. 7b). Then, without any prior warning, Paul speaks of their weak conscience being polluted. It is the first known use of the term "conscience" (*syneidesis*) in Christian history (see summary essay, 233). The term has no history in the Septuagint, the Greek Hebrew Bible. Surely the sensation of what we know as con-

---

[6]William F. Albright, *From the Stone Age to Christianity: Monotheism and the Historical* (Garden City NY: Doubleday Anchor Books, 1957) 272.

science was known to the Jewish people. What was it called? Perhaps the emotional attachment to others connected with bowels (*splagchna*) represents the same phenomenon. In the Greek world the verb *suneidon* had more to do with self-knowledge than with an individual's corporate awareness. We have already seen that the individual finds his or her own identity in the corporate memory (or narrative) of the faith community. The interior understanding which bonds an individual to the corporate was called by Paul "knowing with" (*sun* [with] *eidesis* [knowledge] in Greek; *con* [with] *scientia* [knowledge] in Latin). The person's self-perception was indeed bound with this "knowing with others." To break with the community of interpretation creates a sensation of pain. The content of conscience depends on the community in which it was developed; the phenomenon of conscience is universal.[7]

Those at Corinth who did not understand that idols did not exist were said to have a "weak conscience." The phrase has been extremely difficult to interpret. Weak conscience normally refers to a person who has a poorly developed sense of morality and appropriateness. That can hardly be the case here. Those with a weak conscience have more scruples than those who do not. It is also difficult to define "weak conscience" by means of this particular social situation. Those with a weak conscience suppose the food has been offered to idols. Does Paul mean their formation up to now forbade, and therefore made abhorrent, the eating of meat offered to idols? If so, those with such a background would be Jews. Even in the new community of faith they simply could not overcome that abhorrence (see Acts 15:29).

But Paul implies those with a weak conscience had, up to now, been eating food offered to idols (7b). That surely eliminates a Jew. Those with a weak conscience must be Gentiles who have been eating food sacrificed to idols. Conversion meant for them a break with that past. To leave Isis for Jesus meant foregoing all association with the Isis community and joining with the new Christian community. Eating food offered to Isis or Serapis denied their conversion to Christianity. Yet we cannot possibly make this a "racial" issue. Not all Gentiles had a weak conscience. If that were true then all those with a "strong conscience" would be Jews. Few would dare suggest the Christ party was a strong

---

[7]Donald F. Miller, *The Wing-Footed Wanderer: Conscience and Transcendence* (Nashville: Abingdon, 1977).

Jewish group (with a gnostic tinge!). So, in the final analysis, those with weak conscience cannot be a particular ethnic group, either Jew or Greek. They are converts not yet assimilated into the Christian community. The conversion of their means of "knowing with others" has not been completed, i.e., they have weak consciences.

Paul agrees with the Christ house church that eating or not eating food offered to idols is a moot point (v. 8; see explanatory note on 6:13). Yet that eating can have serious adverse effect on the development of new converts. Paul says such an act can defile (*moluno*) their consciences; can be a stumbling block for them (*proskomma*; see explanatory note on 1:23); can destroy (*apollumi*) them (v. 11); can be a sin against them (*hamartano*, v. 12); can pummel (*tupto*) their weak consciences; and can cause them to fall (*skandalizo*, v. 13; see explanatory note on 1:23). With the perpetration of such violence, little wonder Paul urged the Christ house church to be careful!

Paul will pursue further the occasion of eating food offered to idols in chapter 10. Though the issue has hardly been settled, we will assume the *eidoleion* of v. 10 should be understood as an eating establishment attached to the precincts of a temple or any place where religious practices occurred. In such a public place another member of the congregation, in particular, one with a weak conscience, could see the fellow Christian eating the questionable food. The problem is not offensiveness. The problem is that the sister or brother with a weak conscience would then, following the example of the one with gnosis, also eat food offered to idols.

Since there is nothing wrong with eating such meat (though note Acts 15:29), what damage has been done? Those with a weak conscience are still sufficiently in the community of the old age that to eat food offered to idols still would be worship of those divinities. Put another way, even restaurants attached to temples have become a part of the *hos me*, the "as if not" (see explanatory note on 7:29-31). The Christian lives with them, and eats in them, as though they had no final value. But some have not been sufficiently integrated into the new endtime community. They cannot suspend what they are doing. For them the idols (or their communities) are still real.

In such instances the "weak" are damaged because they are not freed from the enmeshment of the old age. In fact, their new faith will have betrayed them back into their old patterns. Instead of being freed (suspended) they will become only more deeply enmeshed in their prior culture. Furthermore, large numbers of such persons eating food offered to idols without *gnosis* would eventually drag the new faith community back into the old age.

The problem is indeed a classic one. How does the community of the new age deal with itself as a community in process? Paul's answer is clear, though not definitive and certainly not an easy one. Those who have *gnosis* ought not cause the downfall of sisters and brothers just starting in the faith (or incapable of further development). In no way should the strong (formerly arrogant?) underestimate the difficulties of the weak (formerly enmeshed?) as they seek to escape from the old age. Knowledge alone does not build a faith community in which both weak and strong are accepted. Love does (v. 1).

Theologically speaking, the death of Christ was just such a love. If God in Christ died on the cross in love (v. 11), then those more mature can sacrifice their own gnosis, their own freedom, and their culinary habits for that same sister or brother. To do otherwise would be Sin (alienation) against Christ (v. 12). For that reason Paul would rather not eat meat at all (v. 13).

THE TEXT IN ITS BIBLICAL CONTEXT

Chapter 8 of 1 Corinthians ploughs new ground. To be sure the problem of idolatry can be seen in much of postexilic biblical literature. And Paul's confessional distinction between God as creator and Lord as sustainer was deeply rooted in the biblical faith. But the issue of voluntary association with a new community of faith (based neither on tribe nor race) does not arise until the New Testament. How did one, as an adult, voluntarily change from servitude to the old age to the freedom of the new age? In the New Testament only Paul deals directly with the issue. We have already seen how he called us to forego any ultimate investment of our life in the forms of this age (in chapter 7).

Here he calls for older members to show love and patience with newer Christians, until they can be freed from the enslaving patterns of the old world. In the midst of that discussion Paul offers the concept of conscience as that element of personhood which marks and monitors the increasing unity of the individual believer with the faith community. Here and in 10:23-11:1 he argues that those with the stronger conscience should care for those whose consciences are weak. They should not so act as to confuse the "weaker" group, nor should they isolate them (cause individualism). In Romans 14 he writes the same way about those "weak in the faith." In that passage debates have arisen regarding not only food, but also times of worship. All should work for peace and mutual upbuilding (Rom. 14:19).[8]

Through all this Paul still defends *gnosis*. Those who understand the depth of God should not let their love of sister and brother confuse them. There are no acceptable and forbidden foods (Rom. 14:14). Times for worship and religious observances are matters of human conviction (Rom. 14:5). And idols, or false gods, do not exist (1 Cor. 8:4). The Christian must make concrete decisions in love without losing *gnosis*.

THE TEXT IN THE LIFE OF THE CHURCH

Every congregation of today has problems parallel to that of food offered to idols. Every congregation contains some who perceive the depth of the Christian faith and some who do not as yet, or perhaps may never. How do the two, with many variations, relate to each other? How do congregational members participate in the faith community when some tithe and some do not, when some attend worship and some church school, when some serve alcohol and some punch, when some support evangelism and some disaster relief, when some believe in verbal inspiration of the Bible and others do not, when some like the pastor and some do not, when some prefer formal worship and others like flexibility, when some speak in tongues and others do not—when some think they are following Jesus Christ in their way and others are not?

The greatest test of congregational life may be the answer of 1 Corinthians 8—care for each other despite the variation in growth or the differences in faith perception. At the same time it must be clearly understood that the new age is not to be compromised. The congregation cannot fall back into mere acceptance of each other, or move in a corporate direction which cannot be distinguished from the life of the old age.

ALL THINGS TO ALL PERSONS 9:1-27

PREVIEW

Chapter 9 provides a personal analogy to the problem of eating meat offered to idols. At first glance it may appear to be an insertion, since chapter 10 continues the discussion of food offered to idols. But Paul likes to move from question to personal analogy and back to conclusions. In chapter 7, in a much shorter form, he reflected on his personal

---

[8]Robert Jewett, *Christian Tolerance: Paul's Message to the Modern Church* (Philadelphia: Westminster Press, 1982).

experience about remarriage (7:7-8) before he turned to his more complete advice to the Corinthians. In the analogy of chapter 9 Paul points out that he, too, is free (free as an apostle, as analogous to their freedom to eat meat offered to idols, 9:1-18). Yet, for the sake of the gospel Paul limits his freedom, even enslaves himself (he becomes all things to all persons), just as they should exercise restraint in their eating of meat offered to idols (9:19-27). He had argued in chapter 8 that the people with weak consciences should be treated with love and patience. But doesn't this curtail the freedom of those who "know" the divine truth? Apparently such a discussion with Paul has occurred before. There must be historical reality behind the analogy. Some of Paul's critics have charged that he himself has lost his freedom and has become enmeshed in local congregations!

Paul responds that he is free. As an apostle he is free of the local congregation because he founded them. Does his freedom from the local congregation mean he has no rights or authority? No! In vv. 3-6 he answers those who might think he lacks the rights granted other apostles: to eat and drink what he pleases, to bring a wife on the missionary journeys, and to receive compensation as an evangelist. For reasons not now clear the latter claim troubled Paul the most. In vv. 7-14 he shows why the person who works for the church should be paid by the church. Despite all of this he admits that he has not used the privilege of eating and drinking as he pleases, nor has he brought along his wife, nor has he received pay for his work. He was called to preach the gospel. That call comes out of freedom, not enslavement or enmeshment (vv. 15-18).

Nevertheless, Paul will, for the sake of the gospel, give up his freedom. He will eat and live according to the standards and customs of the people with whom he works (9:19-23). It takes self-discipline to exercise the call to apostleship (vv. 24-27).

• OUTLINE •

9:1-2   An apostle is free
9:3-6   Is Paul's freedom limited?
9:7-14 The minister has a right to compensation
9:15-18 Paul will not be limited by dependency
9:19-23 But Paul will limit himself to preach the gospel
9:24-27 To reach the endtime one must submit to discipline

EXPLANATORY NOTES

9:1-2 Following the discussion of eating meat offered to idols, Paul seems to digress rather radically from the questions posed by the Corinthian Christians. While he does seem to have injected his own agenda, still the issue remains the same. He is giving an analogy from his own experience—likely his own experience with them. It is not his apostleship that has been questioned, as reflected in 2 Corinthians 10-13. It is his own freedom. As an example of how one could have knowledge and yet submit to the necessities of the congregation, he offers himself. "Am I not free?" The second question is not parallel to the first. It is a rhetorical question with an obvious answer: I am an apostle and apostles are free. To support that statement he claims, in the third question, to have seen Jesus the Lord, and, in the fourth, to have formed new congregations.

The claim to have seen Jesus the Lord comes as something of a surprise. In his conflicts over apostolic legitimacy (2 Cor. 10-13; Gal. 1-2) he does not offer contact with the historical Jesus as a proof of his apostleship. To the contrary, he argues we should no longer know Jesus according to the flesh (*kata sarka,* i.e., historically [?]; 2 Cor. 5:16). And in Galatians Paul insists his gospel and its authority came from no man, but by direct revelation of Jesus Christ. In v. 1 Paul is not referring to the historical criterion of Acts 1:21-22. It is not Jesus he has seen, but the *risen* Lord (15:6; Gal. 1:12, 16). Paul differs from the Twelve, then, because of his postresurrection calling rather than a calling by Jesus during his ministry (Mark 1:16-20).

Normally Paul connects the authority of his apostleship to his God-given function. He was called to preach the gospel. He rests his case on that fact and its effectiveness (1:17; Gal. 1:16). Here he also rests his case on apostolic effectiveness. The fourth question, then, serves two purposes. On the one hand, it affirms the apostleship of Paul—one for whom the preaching of the gospel has resulted in the creation of faith communities. On the other hand, the rhetorical question reaffirms Paul's freedom. Since he founded the congregations, especially that at Corinth, he can hardly be enmeshed in his own handiwork.

9:3-6 Though Paul is drawing an analogy, the analogy has a basis in painful fact. He has been accused of an inappropriate relationship to congregations. At first glance it would appear he has been accused of accepting payment from the house churches. In the next paragraph (vv.

7-12) he defends the right of public servants to receive wages. But that is not really the issue! Paul does not wish to receive payment. It curtails his freedom (v. 12b). His accusers are actually questioning his lack of dependence on the local congregations! By not accepting wages he has avoided that enmeshment which would make him financially responsible to the new congregations. Yet he and Barnabas (two who lack the historic marks of apostleship?) must work so they are not a burden (v. 6). Does that not make them lesser apostles?

Peter was married (Mark 1:30) though we know nothing of his wife nor anything regarding the marital status of the other apostles. We know that Paul had been married, but now was demarried (see the commentary on 7:7). Yet v. 5 reads as if Paul had been refused the right to travel with his spouse. Given this information one can only conjecture that Paul's wife had died before the writing of 1 Corinthians, yet was still living when his missionary journeys began.

9:7-14 On the basis of reasonable behavior, and scriptural analogy (Deut. 25:4), Paul argues that the spiritual leader has a right to receive support from the congregation. As a warrant for his position Paul makes allusion to a word of the Lord—the statement by Jesus to the seventy that they should receive food and lodging wherever they are welcomed (Luke 10:7).

9:15-18 Paul will have no part of this strange doublesided attack (e.g., he has no right to wages, yet his independence makes him arrogant). Though he has a right to be supported by the congregations, he will not accept a salary for preaching the gospel. Receiving wages makes, for him at least, preaching the gospel simply a service to the faith community, a task or profession. It takes away his deep sense of commission or call which compels him to preach.

9:19-23 Despite his freedom, parallel to the Corinthian Christians' freedom in Christ, Paul has and will subject himself to the people with whom he works. At first glance it would appear Paul has dismissed the law by making it relative. The Christian should simply adapt to the culture of which he or she is a part. But understood as a personal analogy, Paul simply says the one who is free in Christ may—or should?—also be free to avoid conflicts due to cultural differences. The free Christian may curtail her or his own preferences for the sake of the emerging faith community. In this sense Paul can submit to the Jewish law (Acts 21:26) in relationship with Jews (v. 20). Yet he assures the Corinthians that he is not himself under the law.

Verse 20 comes as a shock to the reader. For the great apostle to the Gentiles to submit to the law seems hypocritical. It was Paul who in his letter to the Galatians describes how he castigated Peter for reverting to the Jewish law when both Jews and Gentiles were present (Gal. 2:11-21). According to Paul his own sense of justification by faith derived from that experience in Antioch with Peter (Gal. 2:15-16). That sense of justification by faith in Christ rather than justification by the law does not yet appear in the Corinthian correspondence. It seems more likely that Paul, by becoming a follower of Jesus Christ, was converted from a Judaism limited by Jewish ceremonial law (temple centered) to a new form of Judaism (synagogue centered) open to the Gentiles without such laws (Gal. 1:15-16). In that case it was primarily the ceremonial law which was set aside (Acts 15:28-29). So we are not to assume that Paul has backed off from "justification by faith"—something not yet fully formulated (see introduction,   8).   Nor has he set aside the Torah, or the Ten Commandments. When the occasion called for it, Paul was even willing to resubmit to the ceremonial law—as, indeed, he probably did (Acts 21:26).

On the other hand, it is equally shocking to hear a blue-blooded Jew (as he would write to the Philippians, 3:2-6), state that he no longer lives under the law. The Jewish law was more than rules (see summary essay,   235). It was the revelation of God to the chosen people. It was the story of their election, their formation, and their covenant. Paul could not have set this aside. By the law of Christ he means the law (covenant) itself would be fulfilled through this new faith he proclaimed (see Rom. 7:12).

Just as Paul would submit to Jewish ceremonial law when necessary or appropriate, so he would live without the law when that was useful (v.21). The story in Galatians 2:11-21 illustrates his point. When the opportunity arose to participate in a fellowship consisting of Jewish Christians and Gentile Christians, he would set aside ceremonial and food laws. While the Jewish understanding of God, and the moral law resulting from it, attracted many Gentiles, the religious laws were not so obvious or appreciated. The Roman satirist Juvenal told his readers that the Jews in Rome's Jewish area kept the Sabbath laws out of laziness rather than conviction (*Satires* 14.96-106). The case in Corinth exemplifies precisely what Paul says: you don't always need to avoid meat offered to idols, for we know there is only one living God. Yet not eating meat offered to idols was precisely one of the three regulations mandated by the Jerusalem Council (Acts 15:20)! Paul is not willing to let Jewish ceremonial laws interfere with the growth of the new church.

As a parenthetical note (v. 21) Paul reminds his readers of what we have already noted—in no way does Paul wish to imply he lives apart from the law of God, though he speaks of it as the law of Christ. But it would be most inappropriate to suppose people are redeemed by Christ in order that they might live according to the law of God. We are redeemed in order that we might have right relationships with God and with each other (righteousness). Such relationships cannot be "earned" by living according to law. At this point we see a hint of Paul's famous "justification by faith." But it would be equally fallacious to suppose right relationships do not have requirements. And it would be equally fallacious to suppose those requirements are not found in the Hebrew Bible, especially the Ten Commandments. Put this way one could hardly suppose there is any substantive difference between the law of God and the law of Christ. But the law of Christ describes the nature of the redeemed community.

So now we can understand the famous v. 22: I have become all things to all people. In the analogy Paul says he is free, but will limit that freedom in order to preach the gospel. Because of that overwhelming constraint to "save," Paul will adapt to the society in which he finds himself.

9:24-27 This passage, though a favorite of many speakers, has puzzled the serious reader. The mention of a race should not surprise us. The stadium of Corinth was located at nearby Isthmia. The famous panhellenic Isthmian games ranked second only to the immortal Olympic games. Beginning in the 6th century BCE, games were held every two years. The Romans did not alter this pattern, and likely added to it. We can hardly overestimate the importance of these sports events. Surely every Corinthian understood the races. Surely such Greek events gave the new churches opportunities to meet and to preach the gospel. The fact that women also had their races reflects the freedom women must have enjoyed in the ancient city of Corinth.

The illustration does not surprise us, but the implications do. How could Paul, the great apostle of grace, use an illustration which stresses discipline, competition, work, and winning? In order to understand this strange passage, we should make several interpretive observations. (1) 1 Corinthians was written before the apostle Paul had fully formulated his crucial "justification by faith." We cannot expect the earlier writing of Paul to be absolutely consistent with what he wrote later to the Galatians or the Romans. To be sure, the roots of "justification" are already present even in this passage (v.21), but Paul would not have supposed this illustration contradicts what he would later write to the Galatians. (2) The racing illustration closes an analogy. All too often we take a passage out of context. The racing illustration ought not be taken as a general teaching of Paul. It functions only as the final point in Paul's personal analogy about eating food offered to idols. This frequently misunderstood passage illustrates two important points about interpretation: The writings of Paul do have a chronological progression which cannot be ignored. Each passage must be understood in its context.

To reiterate: the intent of chapter nine is to give an analogy from personal experience that speaks to the question about eating meat offered to idols. Paul has argued that he is free, but for the sake of the gospel he willingly submits to cultural practices. In this final illustration he notes that the one who reaches the goal willingly submits to intense discipline. Those who run in the games compete for a prize. In order to win that prize the runners go into strict training. While athletes do this for a crown which will not last, Christians submit to discipline in order to run for a reward of ultimate value, the development of the Christian community. Verse 26 presents a shift in the illustration. Within the analogy and even in the illustration the point is voluntary submission for the sake of achieving a goal. But v. 26 stresses having a goal. Paul does not wish to run without a track and a "tape," nor does he wish to spend the rest of his life throwing practice punches without hitting anything. There is a purpose. Paul is goal oriented in terms of his thinking. In his earlier letter to the Thessalonians he was much more eschatological or endtime oriented. But that is less obvious in the Corinthian correspondence. We should not be misled, however. Paul still lives for the final goal—the presence of the kingdom in the development of the faith community.

Verse 27 has often been taken to be a sign of Paul's asceticism or disdain of the body. Paul was not an ascetic. He did not favor an ascetic approach to sex (see commentary on 7:5). Nor is there any indication in the letters of Paul that he advocated abstinence from food or drink. The pummeling of the body simply reflects, as a detail of the analogy on discipline, the time-honored practice of developing muscle tone.

THE TEXT IN ITS BIBLICAL CONTEXT

Though chapter 9 serves primarily as an analogy in the discussion about eating meat offered to idols, still there is much to learn from the passage. We can see here how Pauline ethics began. Paul does not believe God gave us laws which are to be obeyed and which, if obeyed, will commend us to God (Rom. 3:20). Laws enter human life at three points: (1) as marks of identity for a people (e.g., circumcision in Genesis 17); (2) as descriptions of the proper relationship to God (e.g., the oneness of God in Deuteronomy 6:4); and (3) as descriptions of human relationships like Exodus 20:12-17.

Though Paul clearly will sacrifice the marks of Judaism (food laws, purity laws, cleanliness, Sabbath, circumcision, etc.) in order to carry the gospel to all people, he would not set aside his understanding of a proper relationship to God. We see in 1 Thessalonians 1:8-10 how Paul saw it was his mission to take the Jewish sense of a living God to those who only knew stagnant imitations. That is why he had to say he was not free from God's law. But ethics, the standards of behavior which guide a society, are a different matter. The basic commandments of the Hebrew Bible are descriptions of the limitations of human relationships. This is especially true of the absolute or apodictic laws. "Thou shalt not kill" and "Thou shalt not steal" are actually statements of facts about life. Individuals and society will be destroyed if they do not stay within these apodictic descriptions. There is nothing in these laws about a God who demands obedience for the sake of obedience, nor does keeping the commandments insure salvation. But the commandments do realistically describe a world in which human relationships can flourish. It is only when people obey the law in order to please God or other people that they become trapped. It is impossible to live in covenant relationship simply to please another.

In the new age there is a new society, the faith community. This community does not simply obey or disobey laws as they did in the old age. Rather these people, the Christians, live in the new covenant relationship. Though they are free of the law's demand, any network of relationships has its requirements. Faced with the possible rupture of a faith community, Paul feels compelled to state what is necessary for the new community to exist. That is the beginning of Christian ethics.

To begin that discussion Paul has used an analogy and an illustration. In the Jewish world particularly, but most societies as a whole, primary ethical teachings are often conveyed by means of analogies, illustrations, cases, and stories. Paul approached this issue by means of an analogy based on his experience. In chapter 7, where he wished to make a similar "ethical" point, he had referred to a word of the Lord (see commentary on 7:10-11). Eventually the words of the Lord were incorporated into a narrative about Jesus the Lord (a gospel). Like the Torah of the Hebrew Bible, the gospels, as stories and analogies, convey the basic ethical perceptions of the new community of faith.

THE TEXT IN THE LIFE OF THE CHURCH

The analogy in this chapter points directly to one of the major issues of our time. We live in a society which treasures its individual freedom. As persons strive for that freedom they often turn to violence. One of the clearest manifestations of such violence comes out in personal vendettas. People who are frustrated with rules or are thwarted by society take matters into their own hands. This often results in mass killings or reckless actions. One person kills fifteen others because he lost his job. Or, now, people, especially young people, turn that violence against themselves. It is as if to say that if I can't have it my way, I will either destroy others or myself. Yet our society does little to correct itself. As a sign of that, we have uncontrolled violence shown on television. Some countries censor violence the same way we censor sex. But the freedom to do it our way has become an American way of life.

Paul claims there is a freedom in Jesus Christ. We are to be genuine persons. We are not to be limited or bound by exterior laws. But in Christ we are to live with others in caring community. In order to do that there are obvious requirements. Paul will submit to those requirements in order that the gospel can be preached and lived. In other words, there is a Christian discipline. In our society it may be too late simply to pass harsher laws or enforce censorship. We need a new story for our time. We need a story which speaks of love and care for those with whom we live. That story is the good news.

THE POWER OF RELIGIOUS FELLOWSHIP 10:1-11:1

PREVIEW

Having worked through a personal analogy regarding freedom and submission and/or discipline, Paul now returns to the question originally asked by the Corinthians (8:1b). This time, however, Paul comes at the issue in quite another way—different enough, indeed, to make us wonder if there were not a second question. Paul had agreed that eating meat offered to idols posed no problem, since idols did not exist. Yet for the sake of the budding Christian fellowship Paul was willing—even compelled—to limit that freedom. The analogy in chapter 9 makes that very clear. But chapter 10 deals more with the power of religious fellowship than with the question of freedom. Paul admits there is no power in the idols, but he insists that *any* religious community can create an overpowering *koinonia* (community).

In order to develop this argument Paul analyzes, by means of an allegory, the formation of Israel. In reality he still would like to argue that ceremonial or religious celebrations do not create ethical behavior (10:1-13). Yet, the fellowship of eating together does have ethical power. And he uses the Christian eucharist as an example (10:14-22).

After all this fascinating reflection, when he finally returns to the question as originally asked, his answer remains the same as before: there is no problem in eating meat offered to idols, but don't let that freedom destroy the faith community (10:23–11:1).

• OUTLINE •

10:1-5　An Allegory of Moses and Christ
10:6-10　The Power of Eating Together
10:11-13　Israel Serves as a Warning
10:14-22　The Meaning of the Warning For Us
10:23–　Be Free, But Not Destructive
　11:1

EXPLANATORY NOTES

10:1-5 In order to reflect more on the problem of meat offered to idols, Paul introduces the function of religious ceremony. To explain his point, he offers an allegory about the beginning of Israel. An allegory uses an authoritative text to express a spiritual truth, or series of spiritual truths, by means of details found in the passage. Normally the truths expressed have little or nothing to do with the original intent of the author. Therefore allegory seems strange to us. We are accustomed to seeking the meaning of the text as the author intended it—or at least as the listeners heard it. But much of the best writing of Paul's time was allegorical. The great Jewish author Philo, contemporary to Paul, used allegory almost exclusively. Many medieval saints and theologians understood the entire Bible as spiritual allegory. Even today ministers, teachers, and laypeople assign meanings to the text that could not have been intended by the author. Had the New Testament been an allegorical interpretation of the Old Testament, as in the writings of Philo, Christianity would have been quite different. It would, for example, have been more rooted in spiritual and intellectual truths than in historical narrative. But that was not the case. There are only two allegories in the New Testament: the one here and the one the Galatians 4:24-31 (though some might include the interpretation of the parable of the sower, Mark 4:13-20).

The phrase "I do not wish you to be ignorant" was used in letters of that time to introduce the substance of a letter. For example, the same phrase in 1 Thessalonians 4:13 signals the main teaching Paul has to share. So we are to take this allegory quite seriously, even though we may not appreciate the way Paul used the Hebrew Bible. Paul speaks of the beginning of Israel in a sacramental way. Instead of the well-known liberation language which speaks of Israel being freed from an oppressive Pharaoh, Paul speaks of the sea and the cloud as a baptism (Ex. 14). Likewise the manna and the water from the rock become the elements of the eucharist (Ex. 16; Num. 20:1-13).

It is true that Judaism had already shifted from liberation to wisdom. That is, the manna was the wisdom of God given to those who ate it (Philo). But Paul allegorizes even further. As the Hebrew people walked through the Red Sea they were baptized as Jews. And the water from the rock was the wine (or blood?) of the eucharist. The source of that wine-water was none other than Christ, just as the bread celebrates the body of Christ and the wine celebrates his blood.

Though all this is simply an allegory on the Exodus and Numbers passages, still there is more to it. To say the source of salvation for the Jews was Christ does not violate Paul's later thinking. One thinks particularly of Ephesians 1:4 and Colossians 1:15 as examples of how Paul's faith includes Christ from the beginning of creation. We have probably too closely defined the historical Jesus, who lived from 4 BCE to 33 CE, as the Christ. The Christ is a way God relates to us (see summary essay, 229).   God is the creator. One does not simply believe in God or a god. We speak of God with such and such qualities, that is, God who created heaven and earth. We cannot really say we do not believe in God. We can only say we do not believe in God the same way someone else does.

The same is true of Christ. Christ is the way God relates to particular people (see commentary on 8:6). Christ brings meaning to life, creates the covenant between God and people. When that covenant is broken Christ saves, delivers, reconciles, makes whole once more. Those are Christ roles. Everyone who lives has some sense of being loved and some sense of being saved or delivered from destructive circumstances. That, for them is "Christ." Christians proclaim the good news that the man Jesus is indeed the Christ. We define all saving in terms of Jesus. Yet the Jews, and other people, also have saving functions in their lives. True they do not have the depth of Christ we have in Jesus. But they do have that role in their lives. So Paul can speak of the rock, the rock of deliverance, as Christ. And we understand he means the action of deliverance was present with God from the beginning.

All the Jews who passed through the sea and the cloud were baptized into (*eis*) Moses. To be baptized in Christ has the same implication and in Romans 6:3 the same preposition *eis* is used. Normally the phrase "in Christ" uses a Greek preposition meaning already within (*en*). To be baptized means to enter *into* a community as defined by a primary person such as Moses or Christ. As a member of that community one lives *in* Moses or Christ.

10:6-10 Paul used the allegory to give the Corinthians a warning. Paul calls the story a type. We learn much from this. These stories are hardly given to us simply to satisfy our historical curiosity. They are definitive types which teach us a lesson—often an ethical lesson. Once more we see the use of narrative to form ethical direction. Paul's lesson is simple: the Hebrew people participated in the sacraments—baptism and eucharist—yet they sinned grievously.

In the original story (Exodus 32) Aaron made a golden calf with an altar in front. The people made sacrifices and gave offerings. Then they ate a ritual meal. Following the ritual meal they rose up to play. Many readers assume the word "play" is a euphemism for sexual fertility rites. The issue was not so much the calf. The calf was not an idol. It was the place where the divinity sat (a sort of saddle or depression would have been built on the calf's back; compare the function of the ark and its "mercy seat," Exodus 37:6). The Lord was angered by the sexual license, the people's involvement in ancient fertility cults.

If the Hebrew people could fail so miserably just after baptism and the "fellowship meal," then obviously religious rites do not "save." In fact, the sacramental meal at the foot of the golden calf may even have led the Israelites to sexual excess.

10:11-13 These stories of the Hebrew Bible were written down as types or examples to serve as warnings for us. We are not to suppose we who are free in Christ cannot be misled. But even here Paul has a comforting word. No temptation can come beyond what, with God's help, we cannot stand. The phrases are pastoral, perhaps even cliches. Yet they reflect the heart of Paul's faith: there is no depth to which we can fall that would separate us from the love of God (Rom. 8:38-39).

10:14-22 Admittedly Paul has used the allegory of the Exodus in at least two ways: religious rites or sacraments do not keep us from temptation, and religious meals can even be the occasion for inappropriate behavior. In this text Paul speaks to the latter issue. The Corinthian Christians should flee idolatry because the table fellowship of the idols can affect, determine, or adulterate their own house fellowships. In order to convince the Corinthians, Paul cites their own experience. Verse 16 reflects the practice of the Corinthian house churches in their Lord's Supper. The words of institution are to be compared with those of 11:23-26 (see summary essay, **239**). The differences are striking and instructive. In v. 16 the cup comes first, as it would in an ordinary Jewish religious meal. And it is the cup of blessing (*eulogia*) as it would have been in a Jewish meal. Drinking of the cup is a *koinonia* in the blood of Christ.

For many of us there is no more important word in the New Testament than *koinonia*. In root form the Greek, *koine*, means to have in common. But it is used in the New Testament for many characteristics of the faith community. When the earliest faith community met it was called a *koinonia* or fellowship (Acts 2:42). For the sake of the poor and the community, they held all things in common (Acts 4:32). When they ate the bread and drank the cup it was a *koinonia* (communion) in the body and blood of Christ. When the Greek Christians shared their resources with Jerusalem they took up a *koinonia* (collection; Rom. 15:26).

In v. 16 drinking the cup together (one cup and one loaf) is a *koinonia*. That fellowship is based on or in the blood of Christ. The association of the cup of blessing with the blood of Christ presents us with rich associations, but complicated problems of interpretation. For persons associated with Judaism to drink the blood of someone or something would have been strictly forbidden, even loathsome (Acts 15:29; see Lev. 17:10-16). In the hellenistic world there were some mystery cults which used blood (the Dionysiac cult and Mithraism). Presumably Christianity could have adopted this practice of drinking the supposed blood of the divinity. And surely some thought the early Christian eucharist was such a practice. But the adaptation of mystery religion practices hardly seems possible. These sentences of institution were written prior to 55 CE. And they must have come from an earlier period. There simply was not enough time for the church to have become so hellenized to speak of drinking the blood of Jesus.

One might think of the blood as the sacrificial blood of the Hebrew Bible ceremonial law. But the objections to this are overwhelming. There is little reference in Paul to Jesus as sacrifice. Most obvious would be Romans 3:24-25, where the blood of Jesus is sprinkled on the mercy seat as a covering for our sins. It is hard to believe the sacrificial system, a part of the law Paul could set aside (see commentary on 9:21), would have formed the central affirmation of the Lord's Supper. And, second, there is no way to explain the drinking of sacrificial blood.

More likely attention should be turned to the cup. The key to the sentence actually is the act of drinking of the cup, not the blood. As with the bread, the believer is asked to "do this" (11:25). The *koinonia* is created by the drinking together of the one cup. As for the meaning of the cup itself, Jesus spoke of the cup of his death which James and John could not drink (Mark 10:38-39). Is it possible that the cup of blessing is a *koinonia* based on the cup of Jesus' death? By drinking of the cup we do share in his death just as we are buried in baptism with him (Rom. 6:3-4).

Most readers suppose we are dealing with a body metaphor. The faith community is the resurrected body of Christ. Sharing the cup and breaking the bread are religious ways of marking participation (*koinonia*) in that body. In such a case the blood of the body corresponds to the life-giving action of the Spirit in the community of believers. The believer dies to self (by drinking of the cup) and shares in a *koinonia* led by the Spirit.

The sentence on bread historically has also caused many problems, but in terms of its context in this letter actually gives us less difficulty than the sentence on blood. Like the drinking of the cup, the breaking of the bread centers on an action which the believer is invited to "do" (see 11:24). Just as the cup may go back to the cup of wrath in Jeremiah and the words of Jesus, so the bread may go back, as a metaphor, to the manna. But we need not seek its origins there, except as a gift of God to a fractured humanity. Verse 17 makes the meaning of the bread clear. It is the one loaf, the loaf which signifies the body. By breaking a piece from that loaf the believer shares in the given unity of the faith community. In this understanding of the bread and cup, the bread, as a loaf, celebrates the unity of the body in which all can participate. The same type of eucharist is described in the *Didache,* an early Christian document of about the year 140. In this earliest of liturgical formulations the bread is described as follows.

> As this broken bread was scattered over the hills and then, when gathered, became one mass, so may Thy Church be gathered from the ends of the earth into Thy Kingdom. (Did. 9:4)

Because the one loaf is not yet a reality we speak of this eucharistic formulation as an endtime hope. One suspects the style of the Didache is the same as found in these verses in 1 Corinthians 10, in Luke-Acts (Acts 2:46), and probably in the story of the feeding of the five thousand (Mk. 6:30-44). Generally speaking, when the cup comes first, calling on the presence of the Spirit, and the bread is second, with its symbolism of one loaf and one body, then we are in the endtime eucharist. The other type of eucharist, the memorial, is described in 1 Corinthians 11:23-26 (see summary essay, 239).

The act of breaking the bread is an act of participation in, indeed, is the *koinonia* itself. The miracle of this meal, and that of the feeding of the five thousand, is the availability of the endtime banquet now for all. Later theologies placed the miracle in the nature of the bread and cup (called "real presence" by some), or in the dramatic repetition of the sacrifice of Christ, or in the transformation of the person who faithfully takes of the bread and cup. But it is participation in and reformation of the community of faith that occurs while eating at the table. This is why table fellowship with any other group can be detrimental, if not dangerous. It is the eating together that creates the faith community. The type of food, the meaning of the food, or even the disposition of the individual partaker—all are finally irrelevant. Historically some Jews (i.e., the priests) ate of the sacrificial food and they became one with Yahweh in that table fellowship (see Lev. 7:1-18; Deut. 18:1-4). The argument seems rather limited but Paul is moving up to his major point: a religious table fellowship has the power to create group and personal formation.

In v. 19 Paul reaffirms, however, what he said in chapter 8. There are no idols, so meat offered to idols has no theological value. But he insists on changing the issue. Eating at the table fellowship can be destructive. Paul understands that community is created and guided by the action of the Spirit (12:7). A community that acts perversely lives under the guidance of an evil spirit. It is likely Paul refers here to the action of the spirit in such a demonic sense. Paul will not grant existence to an idol, even in a demonic sense. He is referring only to the power of a community to function in a way alien to the will of God.

It is not clear what Paul means by his reference to demons in this particular passage. The Greek word *daimonion* refers not only to evil spirits, but also, more positively to the spiritual power of the special dead. For example, the *daimon* of an ancient ancestor was present with the extended family, and could be consulted. Such presence and involvement would occur at a special place of burial. For special people it would be an edifice called a *heroon*. Such edifices led directly to the early Christian *marturia* (sites where martyrs were revered), and the practice of meeting with the saints. Consulting them (prayers of petition) on their death date (calendar of the saints) stemmed directly from this Greco-Roman custom.[9] We know such practices occurred at Corinth as much as at any other city.[10] Besides the special dead it was customary for Greeks and Romans to eat with and have fellowship with their own extended family (see summary essay, 228). Paul would have opposed eating with these benign *daimons* because such a table fellowship held back Christians trying to live in the new age (v. 21).

On the other hand, the term demon here might refer to the power of idols as pseudo divine beings. Jewish writers spoke of all corporate powers as subordinate God functions (e.g., 1 Enoch 6-10). Some were useful, some were not. Idols would be false or misleading (therefore demonic) powers. This interpretation would fit well with Paul's concern that the eating of idol meat at the shops of the divinities could actually alter the Christian's loyalties.

---

[9]Snyder, *Ante Pacem*, 87-115; Jonathan Z. Smith, *Drudgery Divine: On the Comparison of Early Christianities and the Religions of Late Antiquity* (Chicago: University of Chicago Press, 1990) 131.

[10]C. A. Kennedy, "The Cult of the Dead at Corinth," in *Festschrift Marvin F. Pope*, ed. J. H. Marks and R. M. Good (Guilford CT: Four Quarters Pub., 1987) 227-36.

10:23–11:1 Paul returns to the discussion of chapter 8 that food offered to idols need not be shunned, but one ought to act for the good of one's neighbor. Going back to chapter 6 and the issue of freedom (6:12), he quotes once more the slogan of the Christ house church: "all things are lawful." This time he does not pursue enslavement to the marks of freedom, but asks whether the freedom expressed in the slogan actually builds up the faith community. Paul notes, as his lead advice, that we should not strive for our own well being, but rather for that of the other. That defines "building up" the faith community. So he returns then to the argument of chapter 8: eating meat offered to idols is not in itself a matter of conscience (see the commentary on 8:7), but may be a matter of community caring (vv. 28-29). Yet even this caring must not be construed as limitation to freedom (v. 30).

Paul is so oriented toward redemption he hardly mentions creation. In Romans 8:18-25 he will speak of creation being in bondage to sin, and, like humanity, yearning for redemption. Even there the overriding theme lies in God's redeeming activity. But here in these verses we see Paul the Jew expressing his faith in the goodness of God's creation. In v. 26 he quoted Psalm 24:1 to say anything created by God could be eaten (note 1 Tim. 4:3). The logic of v. 30 may be difficult to follow, but essentially it follows the same line. If someone can thank God for what has been created, how could anyone then declare that food forbidden?

Still summarizing the chapters 8–10, Paul suggests that if they find his answer persuasive they should imitate him (the personal analogy of limitation and discipline in chapter 9)—insofar as they recognize in his actions the paradigm of Christ (11:1).

THE TEXT IN ITS BIBLICAL CONTEXT

The theme of this chapter addresses a major element of biblical revelation. What we understand about God has to be important, but obviously does not finally determine our faith. Paul recognizes, indeed insists, that idols do not exist. Theologically speaking there is no meaning to meat offered to idols. But in chapter 10 Paul admits that correct theology does not insure appropriate faith. In the Sermon on the Mount Jesus notes that saying "Lord, Lord" does not insure salvation (Matt. 7:21). The author of James also doubts that belief in the one God produces any special results (James 2:19).

Many have maintained that the distinctive religious contribution of the Jews was theological monotheism. And indeed the shift from polytheism to belief that God is one must be considered an enormous step in the human enterprise. The unity of all life and the oneness of humanity stands in sharp contrast to the fractured and/or dualistic nature of life in the ancient world (Deut. 6:4; see also Acts 17:24). Despite the great theological gain, seldom do we find in the Hebrew Bible disciplinary action for strictly theological reasons. Or, as some have put it, Moses no more organized the Exodus to further monotheism than Jesus went to the cross for "justification by faith." Important as they are, theological assertions as such do not form the people of God, nor do they mark the coming of the new age.

Likewise, actions of piety do not create the true people. Paul claimed that the Hebrew people sinned right in the midst of the Sinai experience. Paul's suspicion of ritual action can be found in the Hebrew Bible, though not necessarily for the same reasons. Jeremiah made his famous temple speech because he felt the Jews had lost their sense of covenant justice (Jeremiah 7). In a similar manner Amos and Hosea spoke of God despising feasts and sacrifices (Amos 5:21-24). Paul's point moves in a different direction. He does not oppose ritual but warns that rituals, i.e., so-called sacraments such as baptism and the eucharist, do not prevent the faith community (i.e., the Christ house church) from falling into temptation.

For Paul the quality of the faith community determines the nature of the faith. Despite their importance, neither right belief nor sacramental orthodoxy can assure the faith community of life in the new age. The people of God have not always wrestled with this problem in a healthy way, but that does not deny its validity. The Exodus occurred to save a repressed people and to set apart an agent of God, the Hebrew people. When the people adulterated themselves with other communities the result was disastrous (Joshua 7; Ezekiel 16). Though Paul does not call for a sectarian Christianity he is aware that the power of formation lies in the primary community. That was true in the old age; it is true in the new age. So despite his insistence on faith in the one, true God and despite his perception of the power of the sacrament, he still realizes the priority of the *koinonia* for faith.

THE TEXT IN THE LIFE OF THE CHURCH

The issues raised in this section are timeless. How will the human community grow toward unity (the kingdom of God)? Will it come together by accepting a great major idea? What will unite us: the Judeo-Christian view of God, the Hindu respect for life, classic capitalism, Marxist or Fabian socialism? Great ideas may call people together and capture their loyalty, but more often they do not finally determine or direct the behavior of people.

It has long been recognized that symbolic acts, ritual, or sacraments more likely pull together people than do great ideas. Religions depend on the celebration of natural events (vernal equinox, winter solstice) and historical or life-forming moments. States depend on holidays (Fourth of July, Thanksgiving) to express the unity of the nation. Or such symbols as flags, banners, hymns, and songs can rally many people. Yet even these can lose their power (as during the Vietnam war).

Finally there is no substitute for primary formation of the community itself. People working, playing, sharing together in a spirit of care not only anticipate the endtime themselves, but afford the opportunity for others to share in that vision. Paul does not call for us to disband right thinking or unifying rituals, but he does call for us to face the nature of the kingdom as it really is: the divine covenant expressed in the human community.

THE CONDUCT OF WORSHIP 11:2-34

PREVIEW

Having dealt at length with the question about eating meat offered to idols, Paul now shifts to other practices of worship in the several house churches. Apparently the Corinthians did not ask Paul about the dress question or the practice of the love feast. But Paul feels the dress question, like the idol meat question, affects how the Corinthian Christians relate to the surrounding social environment. And, since he has discussed meat offered to idols, he might reasonably return again (see commentary on 10:16-17) to the nature of the Christian table fellowship. Still following the thoughts raised by the question of 8:1, Paul gives them unrequested advice on two issues which affect their community life, issues which are parallel to the idol meat question.

This is not a consideration of corporate worship as such. Paul will deal with that question in chapter 14, a chapter which follows the question about the function of the Spirit in the life of the congregation (12:1). So the two issues—dress and Lord's Supper— should be understood as important considerations, raised for Paul by the question of how a caring community acts regardless of theological truth or ritual precedent.

Whatever the reason, Paul left us with a passage (vv. 2-16) that has caused considerable consternation for later generations. The history of its interpretation is replete with derived rigid practices and with explosive social landmines which plague us even to this day. We have no idea who raised the question about clothing or how Paul came to know there was a problem. Using a number of amazing and perhaps confusing arguments, he finally asks for the Christian men of Corinth to lead worship without a covering for their head, and for the Christian women wear a covering on their head when leading worship.

In vv. 17-22 Paul turns to the Lord's Supper or love feast. He is disturbed about reputed divisions, especially at the Lord's Supper, where apparently social stratification has developed. This leads Paul to repeat the tradition of the eucharist in vv. 23-26. The famous passage has become the basis for the Christian practice of communion.

Abuse of the Lord's Supper and eucharist leads to an illness in the body which could have dire results. Paul warns the Corinthians that failure to discern the body (the point of chapter 10) can destroy the nascent faith community (vv. 27-34).

• OUTLINE •

11:2-16 Regarding Appropriate Dress During Worship
11:17-22 Unity at the Lord's Supper
11:23-26 The Tradition of the Bread and Cup
11:27-34 On Discerning the Body of Christ

EXPLANATORY NOTES

11:2-16 Before entering the complexity of a dress code, Paul makes some kind remarks about the Corinthian house churches (v. 2). Normally, in the introduction of a letter, the writer mentions his/her daily prayers for the reader(s). Verse 2 reverses that polite piety (Col. 1:9; 1 Thess. 1:2-3). And the Corinthians not only pray for (remember) Paul, but they have kept the traditions he delivered. Of course they are heavily dependent on Paul for those traditions. What were they, and how did Paul's tradition match that of other parts of the early church? We are not certain. Paul speaks of one such tradition later in this passage—that of the eucharist. In 15:3-7 he repeats the tradition of the resurrection.[11] Other than that we know of several occasions when he mentioned the word of the Lord (see commentary on 7:10).

As we shall see, there are some differences among the various accounts of these traditions, but they agree in their basic thrust. Christianity is a historical religion. Christianity is not so historical that accuracy becomes a dogma, but the historicity of the tradition is essential. Otherwise the faith only exists as an idea or a personal experience.

The discussion begins immediately with the difficult sentence, v. 3. The verse starts a homiletical interpretation of those passages in Genesis 1 and 2 which describe the creation of man and woman (Gen. 1:26-27; 2:21-25). At the time of Paul this Jewish style of interpretation was called a *pesher*. However complex the style, Paul's argument is fairly clear: God created original man from whom came male and female. In Paul's pesher that original man is Christ, not adam (see summary essay, 220). Male and female are equal in Christ, yet there is a sexual difference which the body of Christ cannot ignore. That difference involves, in a given cultural context, appropriate dress.

Paul leads off with the affirmation that the head of every male is Christ ("man" here is *aner*, not the generic term *anthropos*), the head of the female is the male, and the head of Christ is God. The word "head" becomes crucial. Obviously it can mean the head as a part of the body. For example, in v. 7 there is no reason to think otherwise. But in v. 3 it must be used in a metaphorical sense. The Greek term *kephale* (Hebrew *rosh*) can mean chief or person in charge. The Hebrew word for head, *rosh*, when it refers to a leader, is usually translated in the Septuagint by the Greek word *arche*, meaning ruler. At the same time it can also mean source, such as head of a river. The translation "source" seems best for a passage like this that reflects so much on the origin of man and woman in the Genesis creation story.

The words for man and woman are also critical. The words used are clearly those for adult male and female. At the same time the words lend themselves to mean husband and wife. This has caused many readers to suppose the subject is not that of male and female, single or married, but husband and wife only. As we try to understand the passage these options should be considered.

---

[11]E. Earle Ellis, "Traditions in 1 Corinthians," *New Testament Studies* 32 (1986): 481-502.

Paul has the Genesis account of creation in mind. That is clear from v. 8. Though Christ does not appear in the Genesis account we have already seen in 10:1-5 that Paul thinks of God working in Christ to create covenantal relationships and to achieve reconciliation (see commentary on 10:5). Much of the later New Testament thinks of Christ as the means of creation (Eph. 1:4; especially Col. 1:15; John 1:1-14). So we are prepared to understand that the source of Christ is God, and that Christ is the firstborn (human) of creation.

In Genesis, however, that firstborn of creation is generic man (Greek *anthropos*, Hebrew *adam*, Gen. 1:26, 2:7). Here, in v. 3, man is not generic, but an adult male, possibly even husband. Why the shift? In the Genesis account generic man comes from God and, according to the chapter 2 narrative, *adam* first becomes male and female after the rib incident (Gen. 2:22-25). Viewed this way the sentence suddenly becomes clearer. As we have already noted, Paul does not often think in terms of creation (see commentary on 10:26, 30). In the new age male and female, or husband and wife, are not a product of natural *adam*, but a product of the new man, Christ. Paul will eventually make this clear to the Roman Christians (Romans 5).

The prepositions make it clear that Paul is thinking of head as source. We have already noticed that Paul used *ek* (from) as source and *dia* (through or by) as agent (see commentary on 8:6). Here he speaks of God as the source of Christ, Christ as the source of man, and man as the source of woman. In the latter case he makes it clear that woman is *ek* (from) man not vice versa (vv. 8, 12; "bone *ek* my bone, and flesh *ek* my flesh, Gen. 2:23), but woman is the agent through (*dia*, v. 12b) whom man is born.

So the new generic man Christ comes from God. In the new generic man male and female are equal (see v. 11 and Gal. 3:28). But as specific husbands and wives, the wife comes from the husband (Gen. 2:22), as the husband comes from the new man Christ. Putting it bluntly, Christ has replaced Adam in the story. But what does it all mean? That is our problem.

Paul concludes from v. 3 that a man ought not wear a covering on his head while he leads worship (v. 4). Centuries of excellent reflection and scholarship have not produced any reason why this should be true. To the contrary, the practice of wearing or not wearing a covering has varied from time to time. For example, Jewish men probably did not wear coverings at the time of Paul, but did a few decades later. There

are historical and sociological reasons for this, but no particularly inherent faith reasons. We need to look elsewhere for the answer.

The theme of chapters 8–11 has been freedom in Christ and concern
for the viability of the faith community in light of social customs at
Corinth. We can assume the theme continues. There is something about
the dress of men and women as they lead worship which, though irrelevant in terms of faith, may destroy the fabric of the faith community.
And that problem apparently involves husband (or male) and wife (or
female). At that time a Jewish man normally would not have worn anything on his head while leading worship. But we know from archaeological data especially that Roman men wore a shawl or covering as they
directed ritual. Apparently some men in the Corinthian house churches
had adopted the same procedure. Some male leaders of the faith community have placed their role as leaders of worship above their roles as
men, husbands, and fathers. They dishonor, that is, mislead those with
a weak conscience, the body of Christ, the new humanity, by dressing
in the clerical garb of the old age.

Once understood this way, then v. 5 also becomes clear. There is
no faith reason why women should lead worship with their head covered
or uncovered. But some women were discarding their sign of marriage,
a head covering, as they led the congregation in worship. Such a lack
of head covering identified women Christians with religious prostitutes
and entertainers found throughout the city of Corinth. That is, the
women with a strong conscience thought their leadership role and their
freedom in Christ released them, at least temporarily, from symbolic
attachment to their husband and their family. They could dress as they
wished, even like prostitutes or like men (shaved?). Their freedom misled men and women who thought becoming disciples would change their
identity. This seems like the same sexual problem that plagued the
Christ house church (see commentary on 7:5). Paul said then that one's
membership in the new humanity, the body of Christ, does not negate
the relationship between man and woman. For a woman to act otherwise dishonors her family (i.e., husband), and confuses those who are
weak.

Verse 6 follows logically the concern about women leaders. If some
women leaders wish to think of themselves as a unisex in the Lord, then
they might as well do away with their secondary sexual characteristics,
such as hair. In a reductio-ad-absurdum argument he notes they really
would not care to do away with sexual differences, by cutting off their

hair or shaving their heads.

In verse 7 then Paul presents what appears to be an intrinsic faith argument for hair covering. Paul argues that a husband ought to keep his head uncovered (literally) because he is the image and glory of God. Apparently a wife ought to keep hers covered because she is the glory of the husband. Once again he has returned to Genesis, especially the narrative of 1:1-2:4a. In 1:26 generic man, created in the image and glory of God, from the beginning consisted of male and female or husband and wife. They (v. 27) were in the likeness of God. Paul recognizes this equality of man and woman in creation (vv. 11, 12) and in the new age (Gal. 3:28). Yet there are sexual differences. Whether these are cultural for the Hebrew Bible, for Paul, and even for us, may never be known. But Paul does hold the husband to be responsible not only to his wife, but as a man in the public (divine) sphere.

A male leader ought not dress or act in such a way that denies his direct access to God through generic man Christ. That is, he should not take on the role of a priest. A woman also may act in the public (divine) sphere. She also ought not deny her direct access to God through generic man Christ, but as a leader in the body of Christ a wife ought not dress or act in such a way as to deny her relationship to her family and husband. Her leadership role should not override her marriage covenant.

A few words need to be said about glory (*doxa*). The Hebrew word *kabod,* translated in Septuagint Greek as *doxa,* referred to weight or heaviness. Eventually, in an extended sense, it came to mean presence, just as a heavy person often has the power of presence. So the glory of God refers to the overpowering presence of God.

As God's agent *doxa* creates awe or fear. In the Gospel of John it refers to the active, historical presence of God in Jesus Christ. Paul has added this "glory" to the Genesis account. The husband has responsibility for the public presence of God. In addition the wife has responsibility for the public presence of the family (husband).

To make sure we know what he is saying, Paul repeats that the source of the woman is man. In verses 8 and 9 he reiterates his understanding of the creation of Eve in the Genesis 2 account.

The strange, nearly incomprehensible v. 10 finally says what we have already expected. The issue is not power, intelligence, or hierarchy, but sexual differentiation. Men and women are not equivalent in sexual characteristics, therefore their dress, from time to time and place to

place, even in the new age, will naturally differ. If we were to translate
v. 10 as literally as possible it would read, "For this reason a wife ought
to have power on her head because of the angels." Most readers cannot
make sense of this, so most modern translators render the verse, "That
is why a woman ought to have a veil on her head, because of the angels"
(RSV). The word translated veil does not occur in the text nor in any
significant manuscripts. More correct might be the NIV translation: "For
this reason, and because of the angels, the woman ought to have a sign
of authority on her head." Let us take the problems of this famous text
one by one.

First, what are the reasons? Probably there are two which meld into
one. The NIV translation indicates that. "For that reason" refers to the
prior argument: there is a difference between men and women which
affects issues like dress. The second reason, "because of the angels,"
requires more thought. We have already shown that in certain sections
of 1 Corinthians "angel" refers to the corporate existence of humanity,
especially the state (4:9; 6:3; see summary essay, 255 and commentary on 4:9). This is surely one of those instances.[12] We have seen that
some husbands in Corinth who led in worship (the Christ church?) emulated priests of the Roman empire regardless of their married status.
We have seen that some wives led worship and abandoned the marks of
marriage as they did so. For contextual reasons (the angels = society
= state) wives ought not abandon signs of marriage in the new kingdom.

Why the admonition only to wives? Apparently the taking off or
putting on a veil did not greatly affect the sexual or marital identity of
the man, but the taking off of the veil by a wife did make a striking
statement. Following the line of argument regarding the angels there
is yet another reason. In the so-called Watcher myth (a myth is a narrative of the divine in human affairs) a seduction occurs between the
divine powers (sons of God) and humans (daughters of men; see Gen.
6:1-4; 1 Enoch 6-16). The humans (not just women), characterized as
daughters of men, in their desire to seize divine power are described as
female seductresses (*Test. Reuben* 5). The human or even mutual power

---

[12]G. B. Caird, *Principalities and Powers: A Study in Pauline Theology* (Oxford: Clarendon
Press, 1956) 17-18; Clinton D. Morrison, *The Powers That Be: Earthly Rulers and Demonic Powers
in Romans 1.1-7* (London: SCM Press, 1960) 21-25; Walter Wink, *Naming the Powers: The Language of Power in the New Testament* (Philadelphia: Fortress Press, 1984).

of seduction (see summary essay, 255)   appears in the Watcher myth literature as the feminine use of cosmetics, ornaments, hair, and dress. It was not intended to describe a uniquely feminine power of seduction, but admittedly sometimes it must have been so understood (see 1 Peter 3:1-3). The particular phrasing of v. 10 may come from the Jewish Watcher myth—a warning against human seduction of divine power.

In any case, women are to continue in leadership roles, with their power, their authority, on their head. In the eyes of society they will have disgraced themselves if they take off their identifying mark as a woman and a wife. Presumably such a change in dress would identify them with temple prostitutes or other seductive groups in the social life of Corinth. Even women of the new age would be conscious of that kind of a social statement.

Almost as if he recognized how badly he would be misinterpreted, Paul reminds readers of his primary endtime faith—women and men are mutually and equally dependent on each other (v. 11). He does not use the Genesis accounts to imply inferiority or call for submission.[13] To explain this he enlarges the Genesis accounts (v. 12). To be sure, women came from (*ek*) men, but men come into being through (*dia*) women. One is tempted to see here once more the intense nature of human sexual mutuality (see commentary on 7:4). Women depend on the fathering act of a man (source), but men exist only through the birthing and forming process of women (agent). And though there is the sexual differentiation, the source of both remains only one—God (as in v. 3).

With the final affirmation of v. 12, Paul totally changes the basis of the discussion. He calls upon nature itself. Though Paul has perhaps inappropriately changed the argument, we should take vv. 13-14 quite seriously. In the ancient world there was, among intellectuals, considerable conflict over the nature of sexuality. Some Greeks particularly argued that the natural relationship was man to man, or man to boy. For them the heterosexual relationship was unnatural. Others argued for the sexual relationship between men and women as natural. Judaism and Paul would, insofar as they ever entered the debate, naturally argue for the heterosexual relationship. There can be no question about Paul.

---

[13]Robin Scroggs "Paul and the Eschatological Woman," *Journal of the American Academy of Religion* 40 (1972): 28-30; "Paul and the Eschatological Woman: Revisted," *Journal of the American Academy of Religion* 42 (1974): 52-57.

In his letter to the Romans he will argue vociferously for a heterosexuality grounded in the nature of things (Rom. 1:27). So here he appeals to Hellenistic thinking rather than to the Genesis account of creation. For a man to adopt the sexual characteristics of a woman would be degrading. He refers to long curly hair (a reference to pederasty?). If that be true then a woman should also be aware of the power of her hair as a sexual characteristic.

We have seen Paul use at least three types of authority or warrants. In chapter 7 he appealed to the word of the Lord (see commentary on 7:10). At the beginning of this chapter he spoke of traditions (see commentary on v. 2). Again in chapter 7 he speaks of his own authority (see commentary on 7:12), and mentions the universality of his position (see commentary on 7:17). Here again he finally appeals to universality. The teaching is not contextual or occasional; it is the same everywhere, i.e., in all the churches (Jewish Christian as well as Hellenistic?). Women (wives) who take leadership roles wear a veil over their hair, and men do not wear a priestly covering.

11:17-22 Though in v. 2 Paul praised the Corinthian Christians for keeping traditions, here he finds their behavior most inappropriate. Strange that Paul did not chastise the church for breaking a tradition about dress in worship. Obviously the dress issue was a more occasional, contextual issue about which he brought insight from Genesis and universal church practice. Though the Lord's Supper involves contextual problems the authority comes from the earliest level of tradition, the Jesus story. Paul is unhappy with them for violating the very heart of the faith.

The issue is unity in the body of Christ. Paul says he has heard rumors about divisions (*schismata*) among them and he thinks it might even be true. We are surprised by this sentence since Paul spent chapters 1–4 discussing the divisions at Corinth. This is one reason we suppose chapters 1–6 were written after this section had been penned (see Introduction). The term in 1:10, where dissension is first mentioned, is the same as the one in 11:18. Perhaps 1:10 refers more to differences between the house churches, while here we are dealing with actual hardening of social distinctions within house churches.

The probability that we are dealing with social or, perhaps, hierarchical distinctions is heightened by v. 19. Some of the congregation "appear to be somebody" (like the strong of the idol-meat problem?). Paul uses the term pejoratively. He will use it with the same sarcasm in his letter to the Galatians (2:6). He has already expressed his fear that some of the Corinthian Christians will be "puffed up" over against others (see commentary on 3:6-7). It has happened, of all places, at the Lord's table—the locus of unity and equality. As Paul has already observed (chapter 10), even eating a religious meal together does not ensure righteousness.

This is the first and only New Testament occurrence of the term Lord's Supper (kuriakon [Lord's] deipnon [dinner]). Several Hellenistic or Near Eastern religions were formed around a common meal. In excavated towns such as Ostia, Pompeii, and Herculaneum there are many "eating rooms" decorated with religious symbols. For example, in Ostia there are as many as fourteen Mithraic eating rooms found in baths, apartments, or in the business district.[14] Christianity also had a religious meal. It was called the Lord's meal. We know from later Christian writings that the word Lord, though applied to any Hellenistic deity, became the special name for deity in Christianity. So Christians wrote letters to each other in the name of the Lord (not Jesus, though sometimes God). The term "Lord" here marks Christian character of the meal. We know the early Christians ate specific meals together. According to Acts 2:42, 46 the Jerusalem church met daily to eat together in house-churches. In Acts 6:1-6 we find that the apostles cared for the tables and the subsequent distribution to the poor. Whatever the earliest history we know the church of the first four centuries celebrated meals together. These meals were also moments when the faith community shared with the poor and needy.[15] By the late second century some of the meals were eaten with the martyrs of the church and/or the family dead. In the later parts of the New Testament the meal was called the Agape, or love feast (Jude 12; see also the variant reading in 2 Peter 2:13).

In the Agape or Lord's Supper the unity of the church is realized as the members care for each other and the needy of the community. It is not an ordinary meal. It marks the nature of the new faith community. We cannot be certain what went wrong at Corinth, but at some of the meals apparently a few members had an excess to eat and drink, while

---

[14]Samuel Laeuchli, *Mithraism in Ostia: Mystery Religion and Christianity in the Ancient Port of Rome* (Evanston IL: Northwestern University Press, 1967).

[15]Bo Reicke, *Diakonie, Festfreude, und Zelos* (Uppsala: Lundequistska, 1951) 99-100.

others did not receive enough (v. 21). Some translators suppose the offenders ate before the more needy arrived. It need not be a problem between rich and poor. Actually the text should be translated: "For each takes his own meal while eating." That is, apparently the meals were potlucks and people were eating what they brought rather than sharing. That created the disparity. In v. 22 an angry Paul suggests they eat in their own homes if they do not intend to share with everyone. Their action creates divisions, disparaging the nature of the body of Christ and embarrassing those who brought less food. He cannot possibly be pleased with their treatment of this crucial tradition (v. 22). For this reason he repeats what he originally handed down to them.

11:23-26 The abuse at Corinth caused Paul to restate the eucharistic formulas which had been handed to him and which, in turn, he had given to the new churches. Though we have accounts of the Last Supper in the Synoptics (Mt. 26:26-29; Mk. 14:22-25; Lk. 22:14-23), historically the church has used this text as its basis for the celebration of the eucharist. Paul received the tradition from the Lord. As a persecutor of the early church it appears impossible to suppose that Paul received the words directly from Jesus. It makes a farce of the oral tradition of the church to suppose Paul received the tradition as a direct revelation from the risen Lord. So we must understand the phrase "received from the Lord" as a technical reference to the developing oral tradition, a tradition which eventually resulted in the formation of the gospel material. It may be significant that the tradition from the Lord comes from the gospel narrative material rather than the so-called sayings source (German *Quelle,* so abbreviated as Q). The heart of the faith lies in the story about, rather than the words from, Jesus of Nazareth.

The eucharist tradition stems from the last supper (v.23). The celebration was intended to be part of a supper, presumably the Lord's Supper mentioned in the previous paragraph (v.25). Its retelling explained Paul's wrath regarding the abuse of the communal supper.

Jesus took bread and gave thanks. As we have already noted the normal procedure would have been the cup first (see commentary on 10:16). The breaking of the bread first indicates an important faith shift. Historically, the breaking of the body of Jesus occurred before the shedding of the blood. But more important, the death of the body is a preliminary to the work of the Spirit. That is, the body of Christ must continually be broken (contrite) so that the Spirit of God can be effective. The *anamnesis* or remembrance style, in contrast to the endtime style (see commentary on 10:16-17 and the summary essay, 239) always has the bread first, because it recalls the faith paradigm of the death and resurrection. The celebration takes its name from the opening prayer of thanksgiving (*eucharisteo*).

Jesus broke the bread and said, "This act of breaking the bread shares in the breaking of my body for all of you." The emphasis must be on the breaking of the bread. Historically, the bread itself has been the center of the celebration. There are several convincing reasons why this cannot be true. First, we are dealing here with an action, not a substance. As both v. 24 and v. 25 make it clear, we are to do what the Lord says. Second, the word "this" does not refer to the bread. It is widely assumed that bread is the antecedent of the pronoun "this," meaning then "This bread is my body." But in Greek a pronoun normally agrees with its antecedent in number and gender. (As in English: I saw the ship. She was in the harbor.) In Greek the word "bread" is masculine, but the word "this" is neuter. There might be other explanations, but most likely the Greek means either "That is to say" or "This action is." Finally, in Judeo-Christian religious practice, normally the celebration involves a dramatic reinvolvement in the redemptive or paradigmatic event. So the Passover reenacts the Exodus from Egypt. Or Purim reenacts the decision of Esther. One would expect the key celebrative moment of Christianity to be a reenactment—as, indeed, the word remembrance (*anamnesis*) demands.

In breaking bread and drinking of the cup, the faith community participates in the death of Jesus and the new life of faith, by itself dying and being open to the possibility of new life. At an even deeper level the community participates also in the primary redemptive event of the people of God, the Exodus event. The eucharist bread, the bread of the Passover, goes back to the unleavened bread of the Exodus (Ex. 12:14; 13:3-9; Deut. 16:3).

The redemptive nature of the cross and the eucharist can be seen in the words "for you," or "on behalf of you" (v. 24). In the Last Supper the words are "on behalf of the many" (Matt. 26:28). These reflect the wording of the Suffering Servant song in Isaiah 53. The Servant (Israel?) suffers for the reconciliation of the many (53:12). The breaking of the body of Jesus, and the faith community breaking bread—both make the new age available to all.

This breaking of the bread is done as a dramatic reenactment of the passion of Jesus. The act is called in Greek the *anamnesis*. It actively recalls the center of the Christian faith and therefore becomes always the center of the formation and celebration of the faith community.

The cup comes after they have eaten (v.25). We must assume it is shared after eating the bread, but the phrase *meta to deipnesai* implies more than breaking bread. It is translated "after eating supper." Does it suggest a time when the eucharistic cup followed the meal, which, in itself was or included the breaking of the bread?

As the breaking of the body, the end of the old age, makes possible the beginning of a new life, so the drinking of the cup marks participation in the new covenant (new age). This participation in the new age is called a new covenant. Throughout the Hebrew Bible God relates to people covenantally. Nothing is more important in the Judeo-Christian revelation than "covenant" (see summary essay,   235). In the covenant with God we come to know the nature of reality, the way of relating to God, the essence of human relationships, and the function of religious acts.

At the heart of the covenant is a promise. There are many levels of promise in the Hebrew Bible: promises to all humanity (Gen. 9:15) and promises to individual persons (Gen. 17:16; 18:10). But most of all God makes a covenant with the chosen people (Gen. 12:1-3; 17:1-14). In that covenant God not only makes a promise to the Jewish people, but a promise that all people will eventually be blessed through them. The faithfulness of God may therefore be known by the fulfillment of these promises. To someone steeped in the Hebrew Bible it would not be possible for God to fail on a promise. To say so would deny God. For many early Christians the Jesus movement must have appeared as the fulfillment of God's promise to all people. That fulfillment is a "new covenant." (The Greek *diatheke* is translated *testamentum* in the Latin, and therefore "new testament" in the KJV. The English word testament no longer carries the sense of covenant.)

In contrasting the new covenant with the old covenant we are not to suppose the old was set aside and a new promise formed. The Greek word for new (*kainos*) does not necessarily mean brand-new, but new for this situation (as a secondhand car can be a "new" car for a family). So the Christian covenant is not a new promise, but a new understanding of how the fulfillment will occur. That new way, the way of the heart, had already been noticed by the prophet Jeremiah (Jer. 31:31-33). The covenant was not to be a burden, a yoke, but a joy and satisfaction (Matt. 11:28-30), especially for people for whom a covenant with God was a new thing.

Like the breaking of the bread, the drinking of the cup is also done as a participative, dramatic recall of Jesus and his passion. In v. 26 the tradition states the *anamnesis* clearly: in the act of breaking the bread and sharing the cup, the faith community repeatedly announces to itself and the world the saving passion of Jesus. The breaking of the bread and the drinking of the cup are dramatic and participative statements of the Christian faith.

11:27-34 Paul returns to the love feast or Agape. He has reminded the Corinthian Christians of the eucharist tradition in order to deal with the disorder at the Lord's Supper. In essence, if people think they are simply eating and drinking, they are badly mistaken. They are involved in a recall of the passion of Jesus; they are proclaiming by their action the kerygma (see summary essay,   250); and they are forming the community of the new covenant. For divisions to occur in the faith community during that dramatic recall makes of the kerygma a mockery and a denial of the redemptive act itself.

The key word is discernment (v. 31). Obviously a person at the Lord's table who does not discern that he or she is involved in the death and resurrection of Jesus will fail to act accordingly. That was Paul's concern in vv. 17-22. But vv. 27-34 raise yet another element of discernment. Each person should discern how he or she relates to the body. The act of eating and drinking at the Lord's table has also a reconciling effect. Each person should be prepared to accept that continuing effect of the death of Jesus (v. 31).

In the body language of the early church, death often refers to the utter alienation of a person from the community (see Acts 5:1-11). Illness and alienation cannot be easily distinguished (Mk. 3:1-6). Using the body metaphor Paul can say some are sick, even dying (v. 30). Failing to discern the body and its central act of formation signals the deepest level of alienation. One supposes the metaphor also has a literal meaning: some people are indeed sick, and some are dying.

Paul concludes with the obvious advice: if you cannot participate in the Lord's Supper and eucharist with faith discernment, then you had better stay home (v.33). The argument of chapters 8–11 has now gone full circle. Yes, there is no reality to an idol. But eating meat offered to idols in front of other sisters or brothers implies a failure to discern the body (8:11). That results in the failure to discern the power of a religious act; the failure to discern the nature of the faith community; the failure to discern the influence of an individual act on the life of the whole; the failure to discern the nature of empathic love. Such lack of discernment amounts to death (11:29).

THE TEXT IN ITS BIBLICAL CONTEXT

In verses 11:27-32 Paul finally summarized the issue of chapters 8–11: it is critical for each member of the faith community to discern the nature and activity of the body of Christ. The ethic of the community lies in that discernment, not in regulations or norms. Discernment of the body will guide members of the faith community in such an issue as eating meat offered to idols. Yet without any regulations the faith community becomes vulnerable to destructive social practices (as happened with Israel, 10:1-13). The two problems in chapter 11 illustrate how the symbolic statements of the faith community can be quietly eroded by pressure from the social matrix and/or lack of discernment by members of the body. In the first case, the matter of a covering on the head, the faith community adapted styles of dress which denied who they were as the people of God. In the second case, that of divisions at the Lord's Supper, serious lack of perception appears in the practice of a religious act.

These issues have always plagued the people of God. No doubt assimilation and accommodation have occurred in all walks of life. We can see that in the history of Israel.[16] The settling in Palestine was an accommodation to sedentary life never fully accepted by some of the Hebrew people (Jer. 35). The idea of a king over Israel met great resistance because monarchy seemed like assimilation of other Near Eastern political structures (1 Sam. 8:4-9). Even the building of the temple was considered incongruent with the history of Israel (2 Sam. 7:4-9). The vast majority of problems, however, dealt with religious practices. Material and property belonging to other cultures, and their customs, were declared forbidden, though Israel did not always obey (Joshua 6:15-7:15). Frequently foreign religious practices were blamed on foreign

---

[16]Norman Gottwald, *The Tribes of Yahweh: A Sociology of the Religion of Liberated Israel 1250–1050 B.C.E.* (Maryknoll NY: Orbis Books, 1979) 220-27.

women, such as the wives of Solomon (1 Kings 11:4). Eventually, according to the Chronicler, foreign wives were forbidden (Ezra 10:11).

Historically, the people of God have assimilated practices from their social matrix. In itself there is nothing to fear from assimilation. To the contrary, any dominant culture usefully adapts the practices of neighboring people. But religious practices are different. They define the relationship to God. In this chapter an early Christian community was shifting toward practices which denied who they were as sexual beings (the head covering), and which, in the case of the Lord's Supper, denied the very nature of the community of the new age. Such matters had to be addressed.

THE TEXT IN THE LIFE OF THE CHURCH

On the basis of 11:2-16 many Christian women have worn head coverings at worship. Many women have understood the head covering as a sign of submission to men or to their husbands. Many men have insisted on the practice and the traditional exegesis. A passage intended to increase discernment has become itself a law and a means of oppression.

For our time the text also warns against clericalism. In the early centuries of the church the leaders were not separated from the congregation. Not until the fourth century was the priest seen to be different from the church member. Paul in this passage speaks against a clericalism which makes a person something other than man/husband or woman/wife.

As to the relationship between male and female, the equality of man and woman does not obliterate sexual distinctions. Though "dress" does not commend one to God, it does, in this case, indicate an attitude expressed by both men and women leaders.

Likewise the passage on the eucharist has become the classic text for the church's practice of communion. Through the years the church has used these words to define the nature of the bread and the cup. For many Christians the body and blood of Jesus are really present in the bread and the cup. For many others the bread and the cup are symbols of the body and the blood. Over the centuries people have been excluded from the faith community because they did not believe appropriately about the bread and the wine. Paul spoke against such divisions. The act of breaking bread and the act of sharing the cup are intended to create a unity which transcends divisions and belief systems.

FIRST CORINTHIANS 12:1–15:58
REGARDING SPIRITUAL GIFTS

INTRODUCTION

In 12:1 we find the fourth question from the Corinthian Christians. We cannot be certain what form the question took, but if our analysis is correct it must have focused on the work of the Spirit in common worship (chapter 14). As with the unit chapters 8–11, we assume Paul here first reflects on the function of the Spirit in the Body of Christ (12:1-31), then adds an analogous illustration— this time a beautiful homily on love (13:1-13). Only then does he tackle the real question that perplexes the house churches: what order should guide the congregation as it is open to the leading of the Spirit (14:1-40). There is no question from the Corinthians about the resurrection. Chapter 15 stands parallel to chapter 11 as an analogous problem which Paul wished to address.

The unit follows the chapter divisions.

12:1-31 The Spirit Guides the Body
13:1-13 Love Above All Else
14:1-40 On Worship in Good Order
15:1-58 Resurrection Now

THE SPIRIT GUIDES THE BODY 12:1-31

PREVIEW

We turn again to a question raised by the house churches at Corinth. If we understand the problem as one posed by the Christ house church (see commentary on 2:12), then the passage parallels other sections (chapter 7; chapters 8–11). Does the presence of spiritual gifts imply the rejection of or allow neglect of human institutions? We have already seen how the faith does not negate sexual relationships, marriage, concern for persons in the faith community, sexual differences, unity of the body. Now we turn to another key issue. Do spiritual gifts negate institutional structures?

In 12:1-3 Paul hits the issue head on. Being led by the Spirit does not negate historical and institutional elements of the faith. In vv. 4-13 Paul shows how the Spirit acts to create the diverse gifts needed by the faith community, yet acts in such a way that unity is both preserved and created. The famous "members of the body" passage (vv. 14-26) illustrates by analogy how even the human body contains a necessary diversity of members, yet maintains unity. Finally, Paul assures the Corinthian house churches that the Spirit has created among them the various offices necessary for the appropriate functioning of the faith community (vv. 27-31).

• OUTLINE •

12:1-3 The Spirit Affirms Jesus
12:4-13 The Spirit Gives Diverse Gifts for the Unity of
the Body
12:14-26 The Human Body Serves as an Analogy
12:27-31 How the Spirit Organizes the Body of Christ

EXPLANATORY NOTES

12:1-3 This now is the fourth of the questions put to Paul and marked in the letter by the Greek phrase *peri de,* translated "now concerning." The first dealt with relationships between persons already married (7:1); the second with marriage and the single person (7:26); the third about meat offered to idols (8:1); and now we have spiritual gifts. In the other cases we suspected the issues arose because of the beliefs and practices of the Christ house church. Again it seems probable some group of people understands the activity of the Spirit in a way Paul had not anticipated. We do not have their position available. It appears to place the work of the Spirit beyond historical and human activity.

In all the previous issues Paul has answered by defending marriage, sexual differentiation, and compassion within the faith community. In this case he defends the organization of the body and historical activity of the Spirit. One suspects v. 2 reflects cynicism on the part of the Christ house church. That is, before they were Christians they were led astray by the "spirit" to worship worthless divinities. Paul acknowledges they were misled, but avoids the implication that there was a spiritual misunderstanding ("somehow or other," NIV).

Whatever the objection, Paul minces no words. No one who is speaking under the Spirit of God can deny Jesus or speak negatively (curse) about Jesus. It is extremely difficult to grasp the background of this statement. Who could possibly have said, "Jesus be damned"? First, we should note the use of some names for Jesus. By and large the word "Jesus" refers to the man from Nazareth. Normally, in the letters of the New Testament Jesus is connected with Christ or Lord or both. Without being rigid in our distinctions we can observe that usually the phrase "Jesus the Christ," or "Jesus Christ," as it came to be, marks the primary Christian confession of faith. It says we believe the promise of God for a coming kingdom was indeed fulfilled in and through Jesus the king, the Messiah. On the other hand, the term "Lord" refers to universal rulership. Popular religions of the time referred to their deity as *kurios,* Lord. Even the Roman emperor was lord. To say Jesus was Lord was to proclaim the universal authority of the Christian deity.

The spiritualists of the Corinthian church (the Christ house church?) must have rejected the historical Jesus. If the spiritualists were gnostic in their sympathies they would have quite reasonably rejected any idea of associating deity with a human. Perhaps that is enough to explain the exclamation "Jesus be damned." But one suspects more. By the year 54, when Paul wrote this letter, the oral tradition about Jesus had not yet reached gospel form. The actual schedule of that development cannot be determined, nor can the causes. But the early church must have already started collecting the words and actions of Jesus as its primary authority (see summary essay, 249). People who lived by the words of the risen Lord (Spirit?) would surely have opposed the formation of such a narrative ethic anchored in a historical person.

We may have here the visible tip of a deep conflict in the earliest church—those who thought they understood best the life of the new age rejected an authority (paradigm) from the old age. Jesus and his story are a part of life prior to the life of the Spirit. Paul tries to bridge the obvious gap. No one living in the Spirit can consign Jesus to the old age (history). And oppositely, anyone who can proclaim the historical Jesus as the Lord of history must be speaking in the Spirit. Having made that connection Paul goes on to show how the Spirit guides the life of the faith community.

12:4-13 There are two elements in the development of this chapter: diversity of function comes from the one Spirit, and the Spirit creates what the body needs. The first observation is stated in vv. 4-13, yet the second argument always lurks in the wings. Verses 4-6 state the case. Granted there is diversity, the faith community is held together by the triune God. Paul makes a remarkable statement: the diversity of gifts comes from one Spirit, the diversity of ministries comes from one Lord, and the diversity of works from the one God.

The statement in vv. 4-6 is very important. There are very few trinitarian statements in the New Testament. This one may not be definitive, but certainly instructive. The Spirit of God develops the functions of the body. To be sure, this is not a surprising observation. Modern sociologists have long noted how groups develop an identity which then guides individuals to assume certain necessary tasks. Long before sociology was a science Paul understood the Spirit of God as that power of God which created the various aspects of community.

The Lord (Son) rules the world, but primarily in ministry. So the ministry of the community is an extension of the lordship of Christ, while the nurturing of the faith community belongs to the gifts of the Spirit.

The works of God belong to the Creator (Father, in traditional theology). So the "mighty acts of God," such as the Exodus, or the return from exile, are the power of God at work in the world.

Paul may not be consistent in these distinctions, but we do feel some sense of the different functions of the trinity: nurture, ministry, and creation-maintenance. And all are of the one God. In v. 7 Paul returns then to the gifts of the Spirit given for the common good and working of the faith community. The gifts mentioned are used by the congregation; those who receive them facilitate the function of the faith community. We will look at each of these gifts separately. The first is "word of wisdom" (see commentary on 1:17). In chapter 1 (v. 17) the term had a negative connotation as something Paul would not use at Corinth. In that context we defined the *logos sophias* (word of wisdom) as a form of Hellenistic persuasion. Here it is a gift of the Spirit for the upbuilding of the congregation. Without pressing the issue too pointedly, we might suppose that persuasion used to convert leaves open the possibility of retrogression, while persuasion used for the nurture of the congregation serves to create unity.

The next gift (v. 8b) seems similar to the first. It is the *logos gnoseos* (word of knowledge). As we have seen Paul uses "knowledge" as knowing God or understanding ultimate matters (see commentary on 8:1-3). As the one gifted in the "word of wisdom" has the gift of persuasion, so the one with the gift of the "word of knowledge" can enable others to gain in faith perception.

In Pauline language faith (trust) must be a gift of God. One cannot trust another by simply willing it. Trust is always something given—especially trust or faith in God. The faith community depends on the gift of trust. Some persons have been given the skill of facilitating that trust (v.9).

We have already seen that failure to discern the body caused illness in the Corinthian church (see commentary on 11:27-32). The early church knew illness and alienation were closely related, if not identical. Jesus in Mark made that clear when he forgave and healed the paralytic (2:1-12). The gift of healing (v. 9) is directly described in the book of James. In 5:13-16 the elders so gifted receive the confession of the ill person, anoint her/him, and pray for restoration and health.

Works of power (v. 10) probably should be translated "miracles" (RSV), though that term has been badly misunderstood. Miracles have been interpreted as divine interference in the orderly system of this world. From a biblical standpoint God's creating overcomes, or gives meaning to a constantly present chaos. Human sin and cosmic chaos are in some way identical. In the new age God's creating power becomes evident once more. The Gospels note the approach of the new age with healings, raising of the dead, stilling of the storms. These powers are also present in the community of the new age. Some persons in the congregation are gifted by the Spirit to facilitate the miracle of the new age.

In the ancient world, prophecy (v. 10) described at least two types of activities. As an ecstatic condition, brought on by music, wine, or self-flagellation, prophecy was well known throughout the Mediterranean world (1 Sam. 10:5-6; Acts 8:9-24; 21:9?). Perhaps less known was the style more prevalent in the Hebrew Bible—a person called to speak for God. Isaiah, Jeremiah, and Ezekiel were such persons. We know already that women and men who spoke for God in the congregational worship were prophesying (11:4-5). Such "preaching" for the congregation was a gift of the Spirit. While it is difficult to determine just what discernment of the spirits would be (v. 10), we must suppose there were some false prophets in the congregations. In 14:29 Paul will speak of some who weigh or discern (same root word as in 12:10) what the prophets have said. Paul describes this critical ability as a gift of the Spirit.

In crosscultural situations throughout the Mediterranean area there were language barriers even though the common language was Koine Greek. This was especially true in cities where slaves, veterans, and merchants mingled with the local population. Christianity headed deliberately for these urban crosscultural situations. Indeed, a study of early Christianity might lead one to conclude the first Christians avoided monolithic, homogeneous areas, such as rural regions. In the context of these multicultural situations, the ability to communicate became very important. Some members of the body were granted the gift of languages (v. 10, NIV). Presumably such persons could facilitate communication by this gift. The coming of the Spirit in Acts 2:1-13 had made possible the return of the community to a new unity (Acts 2:6)— a unity which had been destroyed by the Tower of Babel incident (Genesis 11:9). Speaking in other languages could be divisive since not all could participate or appreciate what was happening. The one gifted with language created unity by including those who did not belong to the major language group. Either the same person or yet another needed to communicate with the majority group what had happened. That person had the gift of interpretation of languages (v. 10; see summary essay, 256).

While we learn much from this list of gifts or skills, Paul intends to assure the readers that these functions all come from the Spirit for the benefit of the faith community.

In order to clarify his understanding of the work of the Spirit Paul offers a well-known analogy: the relationship of an individual member to the body. In contrast to some other analogies (chapter 9), Paul leaves no doubt for the reader about this one. In v. 12 he says the relationship of parts of the body to the whole is like the relationship of members of the faith community to Christ. In v. 13 Paul makes quite clear his intent. The new faith community consists of persons from differing cultures (Jew and Greek) and persons from differing social strata (slave or free). All have been baptized into the faith community and therefore are under the guidance of the Holy Spirit. All have a function in the community. Paul wants to describe how persons of diverse backgrounds become one body. It is the function of the Spirit.

12:14 The body analogy needs reflection. At issue is the relationship between the one and the many, the individual and the corporate. Paul lived in a philosophical world that believed primarily in the uniqueness of the individual. We know the "many" only because we have met a number of individuals in that category (Aristotle). That is, categories like pots and pans, are known to us because we have experienced many pots and pans. We know what to call them. So the category "Christian" exists insofar as someone has encountered a number of Christians. Of course, such an individualistic view of life, particularly of persons, does not explain the power of a category to reproduce itself, or in the power of a corporate entity (the Spirit) to alter the identity of participating individuals.

The Stoic view of life (a popular philosophy at the time of Paul) was much more realistic. The Stoics believed the world was a harmony in which all individuals at best cooperated together for the benefit of the total. Needless to say our Western civilization has been much influenced by the Stoic view. Most of the common ventures of our civilization have been of a cooperative nature (in politics, music, sports, for example). The reader wonders if the body analogy in this chapter actually reflects the powerful thought world of Stoicism. Does Paul mean to say all members of a body must work together for the common good?

In Hebraic thought there tended to be an identity of the one with the many.[1] In biblical thought the individual represents the total. The total is not made up of parts, it is not the total sum of the individuals. Each person carries in her/himself the identity of the whole. How could someone be isolated from their formation? For that reason the disobedience of one member of a family or clan could result in the destruction of an entire group (Gen. 18:22-19:16; Josh. 7:24-26; Judges 19-21). During the history of Israel there was, from time to time, a move to break this understanding of the one and the many (e.g., Ezekiel 18:1-4). Paul, though, shows more of the corporate style of thinking. In this passage Paul wants to say that each part of the body takes its meaning from being a functional body member. A collection of arms, legs, and

---

[1] Aubrey Johnson, *The One and the Many in the Israelite Conception of God* (Cardiff: University of Wales Press, 1961) 1-13; Thorleif Boman, *Hebrew Thought Compared With Greek,* trans. Jules L. Moreau, Library of History and Doctrine (Philadelphia: Westminster Press, 1960) 69-73.

torsos does not create a body.

Two verses of the analogy strike us. In vv. 22-23 Paul says the weaker and less presentable parts of the body are treated with special honor or modesty. One wonders what Paul had in mind. What functional gifts of the congregation fit this analogy? Are administrative tasks less "spiritual." Paul gives no hint. In v. 26 the identity of the members with the total becomes self-evident. Whatever happens to the corporate happens to each individual.

12:27-31 In conclusion Paul speaks once more of the functions of the body which individuals might fulfill. The first three "offices" as enumerated are apostles, prophets, and teachers. The three roles are a package of some type. They are listed in Ephesians 4:11 (with apostles and prophets first, and teachers last). Apostles and prophets are listed as a pair in Ephesians 2:20, while prophets and teachers are found in Romans 12:8. Most readers have assumed apostles, prophets and teachers have something in common. Harnack proposed the three were traveling leaders.[2]

In most religions of the world there has been a leader, a series of leaders, or a period in leadership when wandering was the mark of the charismatic teacher. The reason for the wandering is fairly obvious. It would be nearly impossible to begin a new religious movement without leaving the original social matrix. Within the matrix only reformation or revolution is possible. A fresh start requires the suspension of values (see commentary on 7:29-31). In the Hebrew Bible the Exodus was not only a liberation from slavery, but also a forty year wandering. It was necessary to wash out the culture of Egypt (Num. 11:18-20). Jesus was also a wanderer. He called people to leave their jobs and their homes in order to follow him (Mark 1:16-20). In fact leaving the social matrix may have been the primary requirement for a disciple (Mark 10:21).

In the Didache (a second-century Christian document) traveling leaders are obviously a part of the church scene. Indeed the local congregation must be admonished to house the traveler only three days (Did. 10–15). In this remarkable description of early church life one can already see the shift from wandering, catholic leaders—apostles, prophets, and teachers—to trusted local leaders such as bishops or el-

---

[2]Adolf Harnack, *The Mission and Expansion of Christianity in the First Three Centuries*, vol. 1 (rpt. New York: Harper & Brothers, 1962) 319-68.

ders. Our historical interest in this passage uncovers its original intent. Paul admits there are important gifts of the Spirit just as there are exciting gifts. But these special spiritual gifts may come to just a few. The real gift of the Spirit comes to all. It lies at the heart of the faith and holds the body together. That gift is love—the more excellent way. Paul turns then to his justly famous reflection on the meaning of love.

THE TEXT IN ITS BIBLICAL CONTEXT

Chapter 12 and its equivalent in Romans 12:3-8 form the constitution for the Pauline church. Paul tries to convey to non-Jewish Christians how a social unit functions—in particular, the faith community. In terms of the Hebraic understanding of the one and the many, Paul understands how one can be different from the others yet represent all. How does he communicate that to people who have not been formed with that same Hebraic sense of corporate identity? He uses two elements which are not necessarily found in the Hebrew Bible. He speaks of the Spirit leading the entire community. In the Hebrew Bible the Spirit, or the Lord, did raise up leaders on needed occasions. We think especially of the so-called judges who responded to the call of the Spirit. But Paul goes farther. All find their role in the community by means of the Spirit. In fact, Paul stands over against the notion that the Spirit only calls leadership.

From the evidence we have, there is no reason to suppose the Jewish heritage understood the body as parts, or even the analogous body as made up of members. The body did not function as a unit made up of different pieces. The body in biblical thought represented different ways of knowing the psyche. For example, the eye was a window into the person (Matthew 6:22-23; 7:3-5); the hand was power—personal (1 Cor. 16:21), political (Mt. 27:24), and religious (James 4:8); the ear indicated the obedience of the psyche (Mt. 13:14-17). The analogy of a body composed of different members belongs to a Stoic worldview, like that of Seneca (*Epistles* 95.52) who spoke of us as members of a giant body.

Did Paul go too far with his analogy of the body? It was important for us to know that we are integral parts of one community. Perhaps something was lost, though, when we began to think of ourselves as parts instead of different representations of the whole. It would be a different world if we could think of ourselves not simply as female or male, black or white, parent or child, leader or follower, rich or poor, but that each of us in a specific way stands for the whole, be it a family, a society, a club or, most of all, a faith community.

First Corinthians 12 has become a constitutional chapter for Free Churches. It places self-conscious, voluntary membership in the body of Christ at the heart of the matter. The message of 1 Corinthians 12 needs to be stated clearly and forcefully. In the 1830s Alexis de Tocqueville, a French social philosopher, praised the American character in his study, *Democracy in America*.[3] His major reservation was what he then called a tendency toward "individualism." In an important recent study (*Habits of the Heart*[4]) a group of social scientists associated with Robert Bellah examined the depth to which self-reliance has become the basis for North American society. The average American is described by the team as one who must leave home and religion in order to find self-actualization. This means the average person must make basic decisions and interpret key events without the resources of community support and involvement. There may be no more serious fault in North American society than this.

Churches, which should proclaim the actuality of our common formation and necessity of a common life, have contributed to our malaise. Some speak of religion itself as a process of self-realization. Others preach a gospel of personal salvation. The biblical sense of belonging is not just another alternative which we might consider. It describes life in a way that must be acknowledged. We are primarily members of a body and our faith deals primarily with that fact.

LOVE— ABOVE ALL ELSE 13:1-13

PREVIEW

Paul set the stage for the love chapter by describing the work of the Spirit in forming community. What is it that marks such a community? Is it wisdom? Is it theological rectitude? Is it faithfulness? Is it an expectation of the end? Is it charismatic gifts? Is it intense spirituality? All of these are fine, even necessary, but it is a deep concern for each

---

[3]Alexis de Tocqueville, *Democracy in America* (New York: Vintage, 1956).

[4]Robert N. Bellah, Richard Madsen, William M. Sullivan, Ann Swidler, and Steven M. Tipton, *Habits of the Heart: Individualism and Commitment in American Life* (New York: Harper & Row Perennial Library, 1985) 142.

other—love—that actually marks the Christian community.

In the first three verses Paul compares love with other religious expressions primarily of a charismatic nature. In 13:4-7 he shifts to a beautiful positive statement about love. In vv. 8-13 Paul returns to the contrast, especially with prophecy, speaking in tongues and knowledge. This time, however, Paul stresses the lasting or ultimate nature of love.

Because of the great literary quality of this passage, a number of readers have suggested that Paul either borrowed it or wrote it on another occasion and inserted it here. It is true that one could move from 12:31 to 14:1 without noticing chapter 13 was missing. Yet, we should expect Paul to describe the more excellent way, and the thirteen verses hardly interrupt the flow. According to the pattern found in chapters 8–11 Paul moves from problem to analogy and finally solution. If the same pattern holds true here chapter 13 serves as the analogy. Like chapter 9 it appears to be an insert only if we do not understand Paul's style.

Furthermore, Paul did like to reflect on the trilogy of faith, hope, and love. In 1 Thessalonians (1:3) he prayerfully remembers their "work of faith and labor of love and steadfastness of hope in our Lord Jesus Christ." Again, in the opening prayer of the letter to Colossians (1:4-5), he says he has heard of their faith in Christ Jesus and of the love which they have for all the saints, because of the hope laid up for them in heaven. No doubt Paul had reflected homiletically on this triad. We are very fortunate to have the result included in this letter.

• OUTLINE •

13:1-3 Without Love
13:4-7 Love Is . . .
13:8-13 The Greatest Is Love

EXPLANATORY NOTES

13:1-3 In an incredible three verses Paul says that some of the most precious elements of the Christian faith have no value without love. In v. 1 it is the gift of ecstatic religious expression; in v. 2 it is the gift of articulate understanding of the faith; and in v. 3 it is self-giving already modeled by Jesus on the cross.

Paul first compares love with speaking in tongues. In commenting on the letter we have noted only briefly that "tongues" could be the gift of including everyone in a common language (see explanatory note on 12:10). At Corinth it must have also referred to ecstatic expression. In chapter 14 we will see that speaking in tongues played an important role among some of the house churches, presumably the Christ house church. Paul wishes to make a contrast between speaking with the tongues of angels (ecstatic) and speaking with the tongues of men. The apparently incoherent speech heard in glossolalia actually was the coherent speech of angels. Perhaps Paul thought of the heavenly language reflected in Revelation 14:2-3. The initial phrase should be translated "If I speak not only in human language, but also that of angels."

The hymn deals with *agape*. *Agape* has been considered by many the key word/concept of Christianity. Anders Nygren defines *agape* as "unrequited love," a love described by God's love in Christ on the cross.[5] *Agape* contrasts to *nomos*, the key word/concept for Judaism. *Nomos* (law) defines a religious structure in which obedience to God defines piety. *Agape* also contrasts with *eros*, a love defined as reciprocal (a love which is returned). Nygren tried to show that *eros* characterized Hellenistic society. Actually, it would be unfair to think of Judaism strictly in terms of law. The sense of covenant love or everlasting grace (*hesed*) marks the Hebrew Bible as much as *agape* marks the New Testament. Perhaps it would be better to say that Christianity rediscovered the Jewish sense of love. Compared to love even a charismatic expression like speaking in tongues will sound like that of an inanimate object (gong or cymbal). It is possible that more than an metallic object is meant. To be sure, the parallel statements in verses 2 and 3 speak of faith and martyrdom as nothing (inanimate?) without love. But the gong might be a Hellenistic religious instrument, so that speaking in tongues, without love, parallels a futile religious expression.

Verse 2 makes an even stronger statement. The gift of prophecy, understanding of mysteries, and even knowledge (*gnosis*) itself are nothing without love. We have already seen the importance of the prophet in early Christianity (see commentary on 12:28-89). Prophecy was a gift of the Spirit which approximated preaching in the worship of the early

---

[5]Anders Nygren, *Agape and Eros*, rev. ed., trans. Philip S. Watson (Philadelphia: Westminster Press, 1953) 105-253.

church (see commentary on 14:3-5). Mysteries are not to be taken as esoteric practices and ideas, but virtually as revelation itself. As in Daniel (2:28), when mysteries are made known to the faithful, it enables them to understand the course of history. Knowledge, or *gnosis,* may have been the primary concern of the Corinthian elite, especially the Christ house church. Knowledge should never be confused with information: in this context it comes closer to perceptive spirituality (see summary essay, **245**). Some readers suppose the hymn on love was written to counteract the power of *gnosis.* They have suggested the famous, last phrase of this chapter once actually read: So faith, hope, love, and *gnosis* abide, these four; but the greatest of these is *gnosis.* To declare these great gifts nothing without love was indeed a bold move.

While v. 2 dealt with spiritual gifts in the faith community, v. 3 moves into the kerygma or passion narrative itself. Jesus gave himself on the cross. For the powerful or autonomous Christian the model of self-giving has become identified with Christianity itself. To give up one's possessions to feed others (the poor, NIV) is a mandate for true discipleship (Mark 10:21). To surrender one's body approaches the cross itself. The text is confused at this point. Some manuscripts read "to be burned" while others read "to boast." At issue is only one Greek letter, an easy error for some copyist—*kauthesomai* (boast) or *kauchesomai* (burn). The best witnesses read "to boast," yet that reflects a later period when pride in martyrdom might have occurred. In light of our understanding of the passage, "to be burned" does seem more likely. To follow Jesus to the death for the sake of self-fulfillment (boasting) obviously would have little value, with or without love. None of the previous contrasts are that useless. Paul means simply that even following Jesus to death does not matter without love.

13:4-7 Why is love so important? Love genuinely seeks and rejoices in the satisfaction of others. No comment is needed on this famous list of characteristics. Essentially love does not seek its own (v.5); love does not rejoice in wrongs (done to others, v. 6); love is supportive of others (v. 7); love is trusting of others; it expresses hope for them and endures failures (v. 7). These three verses contain a blue ribbon list of adjectives which describe how and why love builds up the faith community.

13:8-13 Love never *falls* (normally translated "fails"), but Paul admits our knowledge (*gnosis*) and our proclamation are only partially complete. The time will come when we are complete ourselves and then we will no longer know and prophesy partially. In Corinthians Paul uses the Greek word *teleion* to mean mature. In 2:6 it refers to those who have grown wiser in the faith (in contrast to the infants of 3:1?). In 14:20 *teleion* contrasts with children or babies. Here the analogy also involves a child.

In v. 9 it looks like *gnosis* and prophecy themselves are incomplete. Only at the endtime will full knowledge be available. But the analogy of the child becoming an adult does not suppport that interpretation. As v. 12b indicates it is the individual's process of understanding which matures. The process of growing up in faith is analogous to first thinking and speaking like a child, then eventually thinking and speaking like an adult. We have here one of the few hints found in Paul's letters about human development. As children we think inwardly of ourselves and look outwardly only to see who we are. Being a child resembles looking in a mirror at ourselves. The child does not take into consideration the function of the community in creating self. As an adult the individual recognizes that being understood, or loved, is the key to understanding, and loving. The adult is open to others. Having *gnosis*, then, without being known can leave one childish and dilettante (see commentary on 8:3).

A great passage ends with a powerful conclusion. Paul refers often to the power of faith, hope, and love. To name love as the greatest required no little effort. According to Paul Christians are saved by faith (Rom. 1:16-17). Sin has been caused by the loss of faith or trust. Trusting cannot be done as an act of personal will. Trust can be restored only when the Christian accepts God's faith in her or him and experiences that trust in the faith community. We call the disciples of Jesus a "faith community" because those people assembled in the name of Jesus have been restored to trust despite ever-present suspicions and doubts. What makes such trust possible? It is hope. Hope is the consistent expectation that the promises of God can and will be realized (9:10; 2 Cor. 1:20; Rom. 5:5). The faith community depends on hope. One could speak just as well of a community of hope (Eph. 4:4). In its hope the community becomes a parable to the world where despair or pessimism often reigns (Heb. 10:23-25). The basis for such remarkable hope lies in the paradigm of Jesus' death and resurrection (Rom. 8:12-25).

Because of the centrality of faith and hope, the supremacy of love comes as something of a surprise. Yet many readers of early Christianity agree that love is its central motif. The centrality of love does not refer to an intensification of feelings. The radical nature of Christian love is found in its parameters (or lack of thereof). The Christian is asked to love enemies as well as friends (Mt. 5:43-48; Rom. 12:9-21). In terms of Pauline theology *agape* love is the love of God expressed to us while we are yet in unloving and unlovable sin (2 Cor. 5:21; Rom. 5:8). *Agape* love, as God's love, includes all, even the enemy, and seeks the redeeming reconciliation of everyone. Otherwise there is no fulfillment of the promises of God and no reason to yearn for the endtime. Love, therefore, must be the greatest of these.

THE TEXT IN ITS BIBLICAL CONTEXT

The assertion that love characterizes the New Testament while law represents the Hebrew Bible ought not go unchallenged. *Hesed,* or covenant love, lies at the heart of the Judeo-Christian faith. From early times the redemptive act of God in the Exodus was understood as an expression of God's *hesed* or everlasting love (Exodus 15:13; Hosea 11:1-4). While covenant love was particular and involved the sense of election, love was not to be limited. Attempts by the Israelites to love only the privileged met with fierce resistance by the prophets (Amos 8:4-6). Yahweh sought *hesed,* not religious exercises (Hosea 6:6). Such love, with its knowledge of God (Hosea 6:6; cf. 1 Cor. 8:3) would be an inclusive love, since God is Lord of all.

The *agape* love of the New Testament does not differ in quality from that of the Hebrew Bible. New Testament *agape* love does make clear what was intended from the beginning, however. Love of God was universal love. Jesus summarized the commandments as two: to love God with all your being and to love your neighbor as yourself (Mark: 12:29-31). Love of God with all your heart, personhood, mind, and strength (from Deut. 6:4-5) means to orient your total being toward the fulfillment of God's universal promise (Gen. 12:3). To love your neighbor as yourself means to love all persons, friend or foe, as you love the ambiguity in you own self. Just as society cannot exist without love of the unlovable, so a person cannot exist who cannot love the unlovable in his or her self. In Matthew 5:43-48 Jesus makes it clear that love of enemy reflects the divine being.[6]

---

[6]Victor Furnish, *The Love Command in the New Testament* (Nashville: Abingdon Press, 1972) 91-118.

In different language Paul says the same thing in 1 Corinthians 13, and John makes love the essence of his Gospel (John 3:16). The author of 1 John insists that God's love will be expressed in our love for each other (4:11) and that anyone who professes to love God and hates a brother or sister must be a liar (4:20-21).

Those who consider love the heart of the Christian faith are correct. It is the nature of God as revealed to us in the entire Bible.

THE TEXT IN THE LIFE OF THE CHURCH

The latter part of the twentieth century has been marked with a sharp return to religious fundamentalism. Throughout the world there are religious leaders who call believers to a literal adherence to rules and a violent opposition to those who disagree or those who believe in another way. As a result we have witnessed severe oppression of dissidents; loss of rights, especially for women; terrorism against other cultures; and a sharp loss in the ecumenical spirit. It is critical for the Judeo-Christian heritage to speak to this issue. To limit the world community only to those who agree is a fatal violation of the revealed God of love.

ON WORSHIP IN GOOD ORDER 14:1-40

PREVIEW

Answering the question about spiritual gifts (12:1), Paul continues his reflection. Paul discussed the function of the Spirit at work in the body of Christ (chapter 12), stressed the centrality of love (chapter 13), and now turns to what really concerns him—worship at the Christ house church. As in chapter 12, Paul affirms the action of the Spirit (vv. 1-5). Using three analogies Paul argues that building up the church in the Spirit means more than exhibiting ecstatic experiences such as speaking in tongues (vv. 6-12). Paul then applies his analogies to the worship at the Christ house church. He argues that the faith community could benefit more from instruction than from ecstatic expressions (vv. 13-19). Furthermore, according to Paul, ecstatic manifestations of the Spirit will not be significant to outsiders who might come to the worship. On the other hand, prophecy might be convincing to the non-believer (vv. 20-25). So for the sake of good order Paul describes an appropriate worship (vv. 26-33a). The role of women in the order of worship appears as an apparent addendum or interlude (vv. 33b-36).

Finally, Paul argues that anyone who does have a spiritual orientation will recognize what is being said and will conduct worship in good order (vv. 37-40).

• OUTLINE •

14:1-5 Spiritual Gifts for the Faith Community
14:6-12 Analogies to Speaking in Tongues
14:13-19 The Analogies Applied to Corporate Worship
14:20-25 Worship Should Benefit Visitors
14:26-33a A Helpful Order to Worship
14:33b-36 Women Should not Talk During Worship
14:37-40 Corporate Worship Should be Conducted Decently

EXPLANATORY NOTES

14:1-5 While Paul insists that love is central, nevertheless he wishes the Corinthian Christians to pursue spiritual gifts (here *pneumatika,* things of the Spirit rather than *charismata,* gifts, 12:4). Paul not only understands that the body of Christ will be directed by the Spirit (chapter 12), but that the life of the congregation arises from the action of the Spirit (note the fruit of the Spirit in Gal. 5:22-26). Congregational worship specifically comes from the presence of the Spirit in the faith community. If the congregation were of the flesh, it would follow its own self-interest, closed to all but its own accumulated insights. The presence of the Spirit opens up the congregation as well as the individual person.

For the individual person the presence of the Spirit may result in a form of speech that is not immediately understood by those who hear it (glossolalia; see summary essay,   256). In the formation of a person the first communication comes through actions (being held; being nursed; being hugged; being bathed). Shortly thereafter symbols also become a part of communication with the infant (bottle; light; mother; father; bed). Language arises later as a way of communicating with family and other children. Certain sounds produce specific results. Repetition of these sounds form language for the child. Language is a social institution which creates and binds together those who use it. While it is true that the feelings attached to first actions and symbols cannot be changed (love, fear, satisfaction), under pressure spoken language can be changed. Reformation of social institutions will likely require some adjustments in language (for example, the use of inclusive language). But revolution will require a new language (like Paul's use of conscience) or new meanings for old words (like Paul's use of righteousness). For such changes a break with the old language will need to occur. We call that break in institutionalized language "glossolalia."

Each person needs to be free of the old language. For brief times the individual may even be inarticulate (therefore, "speaking in tongues"). For a radical conversion such moments are almost necessary. It may occur in ecstatic moments, music (note v. 15), art, tears, laughter (see explanatory note on 7:30), or even more deeply in basic actions and symbols such as hugging, dancing, kissing, touching (16:20; Rom. 16:16; 2 Cor. 13:12; 1 Th. 5:26; 1 Pet. 5:14). Paul wants everyone to have such change moments (v. 5). But such ecstatic moments relate primarily to the individual and not to the group. Ecstatic language or glossolalia marks the individual's shift to a new community. On the other hand, the new language for the community comes through prophecy (see summary essay,   256). Or, to put it in modern terms, speaking in tongues is necessary for deconstruction of the old age, but prophecy is necessary for reconstruction (vv. 3, 4, 5, 12, 17) of the new.

In both the biblical world and the Hellenistic world there were ecstatic prophets. In the Bible we first note ecstatic prophets in the incident with Saul and the lost donkeys (1 Sam. 10:9-13). Similar prophets were found in other religions, such as the prophets of Baal (1 Kings 18:28). But the Jewish prophetic movement shifted more toward criticism of the Hebrew social structure and advice to the state (Micah, Amos, Hosea, Elijah, Elisha, Nathan, Isaiah, Jeremiah). Eventually it became clear radical changes in the Jewish faith were necessary. This necessity (the time of the exile, 587/6 BCE) created apocalyptic prophets who used new and nearly indecipherable language as a way of describing the coming new age (Ezekiel; Daniel; Enoch; Baruch). Christian prophets fit into this apocalyptic type, and their new language was a gift of the Spirit. For corporate worship Paul asks that prophecy with its new language, not speaking in tongues with its indecipherable language, become the central activity of the Spirit.

14:6-12 As so often before, Paul uses analogies to deal with the problem before he offers a solution. Here he uses a musical instrument, a battle trumpet, and language itself. What do these analogies have in common and what do they say about speaking in tongues? No criticism is made of the musical instrument, the bugle or the language. The notes of the flute or harp are not distinct; the sound of the bugle is not clear and the language is foreign (barbarian, in Greek). The point is: they cannot effect the corporate situation. The audience does not know what is being played by the musical instruments. The army does not know it is to charge. Foreigners do not understand what is being said.

14:13-19 After the analogies Paul moves to his conclusion. Persons may speak in tongues, but they should ask also for the gift of interpretation. The point was critical. The new Christian movement broke from Judaism and Hellenism by speaking in inarticulate language, using symbols and actions (see explanatory note on 2:2). But the new movement could not gain momentum without being articulate—not in the language of the old age, but in something new. Someone had to clarify in a new language the meaning of the break with the old ways and the direction of the new faith community. That gift is the gift of interpretation (v. 13). Any new movement, such as feminism in our own day, must first break with the old language. Then it must develop a new or resignified language. Those two stages can be clearly observed. The new Christian community at Corinth had reached that second stage—it needed public clarity.

In order to explain this, Paul uses his own spirit language in a somewhat different way. As we have seen, Paul almost never speaks of a personal spirit (see explanatory note on 5:3-5). Here in v. 14 he does not mean each person has a spirit, but that each person relates personally to the spirit of the faith community (my spirit means my part in the spirit). In the spirit of the community of the new age each person can pray, sing, and give thanks without being articulate. But the mind (*nous*) has not been used. As indicated above it is the mind which formulates articulate speech. Actions and symbols may be more visceral. Actually, Paul does not speak of the mind very often. In 1 Corinthians there are two other instances, both connected with the gifts of the Spirit. In 1:4-9 Paul gives thanks for the gifts of the Spirit among the faithful at Corinth, but he wishes they would be of the same mind (*nous*, v. 10). In 2:14-16 Paul claims the spiritual person cannot be judged by the unspiritual, for the spiritual have the mind (*nous*) of Christ. The mind expresses corporately the life of the Spirit. For the good of the total community Paul urges the Christ house church people to pray, sing, and give thanks also with their minds, that is, with intelligible or interpretive speech.

In the New Testament there are no descriptions of corporate worship. We must discern what occurred by allusions. Along with 14:26, Ephesians 5:19, and Colossians 3:16, passages like this give us some hints. As a part of corporate worship speaking in tongues must have been a form of prayer (v. 14a), that is, a direct approach to God. Music had always been a part of Jewish worship, so one expects at least the singing of psalms and hymns (2 Chron. 7:1-6). The singing of spiritual songs and melodies would have been something else. Informal Jewish music, much like modern American jazz, probably did not make a sharp distinction between composition and performance (note the spontaneous victory songs and dances of 1 Sam. 18:6; 2 Sam. 6:12-23). The earliest church must also have known spontaneous singing, or chanting, which had no preset form or specific words (Eph. 5:19). Likewise, prayers of thanksgiving included particular actions, such as lifting the head and raising the eyes (John 11:41). One can easily imagine the thanksgiving prayers of early Christians involved as much bodily stance as it did articulate words.

In contrast to our more formal worship, speaking in tongues, spontaneously chanting vowels, and standing in an attitude of prayer came easy for the earliest church. The difficulty was forming a new way to express the faith in rational language. Paul said he would rather speak five such "new" words than speak endlessly in indecipherable syllables.

14:20-25 Paul urges a more coherent system of communication for the sake of the congregation (v. 4). They will be edified and helped if they can state their faith in rational terms. While Paul was thinking of the congregation, he may have really had evangelism in mind. How can others consider becoming Christian, if the worship contains much that cannot be understood? Indeed they will consider the Christians crazy (v. 23). Paul's concern was not without warrant. Despite the popularity of the mystery cults in the ancient world, many people considered their adherents and their activities nothing short of madness. Followers of Isis might be baptized in the icy Tiber during the coldest part of winter. One author mentions the folly of going about naked in midwinter (Minucius Felix, *Octavius* 22.8). Even a Christian author would laugh at mystery initiates who went around with long hair and dirty fingernails (Clement, *Protrepticus* 10). Early Christians had to suffer under similar accusations. Even when Paul attempted to be coherent some Greeks laughed at him (Acts 17:32) and the Roman procurator Festus thought Paul's great learning had made him mad (Acts 26:24).

In contrast to speaking in tongues Paul once again holds up prophecy (or preaching) as the most useful form of communication for corporate worship (v. 24; see vv. 3, 6). And with that he turns to the appropriate ordering of congregational worship.

14:26-33a Having completed his argument Paul now turns directly to the congregation with his proposals. Paul consistently addresses congregations as "brethren." It is important to be reminded here that in Greek a plural masculine noun can refer to both male and female regardless of the ratio. A plural feminine noun refers only to female. So the Greek *adelphoi* should be translated brothers and sisters, while *adelphai* should be translated sisters. We would translate v. 26 in this way: "What (is to be done), then, brothers and sisters? Whenever you gather together (for worship), each one of you has a psalm, each has a teaching, each has a revelation, each has a tongue, each has an interpretation. Let everything be done for edification."

In terms of the democracy of worship, or the priesthood of all believers, obviously everyone present participated, or could participate. Even with the smallest estimated average number of a house church (see summary essay, 248), the amount of material to be shared could have been enormous, to say nothing of the potential confusion. Obviously the sharing by everyone was accomplished by two or three speaking at once (vv. 27, 30, 31, 33). Paul asks that these parts of the worship be done only by a few (two or three) and that they be done seriatim without interruption, rather than simultaneously.

Paul does not include here all aspects of worship. Prayers are not specifically mentioned. In v. 26 there is no mention of prophecy and v. 29 would lead us to believe only prophets would prophesy. Yet vv. 31-32 indicate that anyone could prophesy as long the spirit of prophecy was subject to those designated as prophets, or those who had the gift of discerning the spirit of prophecy. We have already discussed most of the worship elements mentioned. The hymn refers to a psalm (psalmos) or a traditional Christian hymn, such as Philippians 2:5-11. A teaching (*didache*) normally refers to proverbs, sayings, mandates, exhortations, and parables. Modern readers often distinguish between teaching materials, called the *didache,* and preaching materials, called the *kerygma.*

Many teaching materials can be seen in the Pauline letters. Some are formal. Didactic materials could be constructed from the sayings of Jesus. Paul's teaching on divorce would be an example (7:10-11). Much of Romans 12:9-21 relates closely to the sayings of Jesus. The sayings of Jesus had not yet been collected or written down, but were circulating in oral form. The mention of *didache* in v. 26 likely refers to this process of repeating the teachings of Jesus. It could be, however, that the teachings of Jesus were enveloped in local catechisms which must have been useful and popular among various congregations. We find some hint of such early teachings in 16:13-14.

If a *teaching* passed on the sayings of Jesus then a *revelation* passed on the narrative of God's saving action (gospel). At first this revelation must have been stories of the passion of Jesus. Eventually other stories, from the baptism to the triumphal entry, must have been added. We have no right to suppose every revelation or apocalypse was a story about Jesus. We do have a right to suppose the Gospels, while in oral stage, took form in the worship services of the faith community. Apparently every person present could recite a favorite gospel story. In addition to a hymn, a teaching, and a revelation, the service would include a speaking in tongues. The sermon, that is, the word of encouragement or direction, came from a prophet (v. 31). Whatever the prophets said could be evaluated (considered) by the others.

Since all could participate in the service, it must have seemed like chaos. Paul called for order (peace). The shift to order may have been a critical moment in the Pauline churches. Did this limitation of total participation lead to the development of a special clergy? Certainly in the later Pauline letters we find bishops and deacons are responsible for order in the faith community (1 Tim. 3:5).

14:33b-36 These three and one-half verses have caused as much difficulty as any verses in the New Testament. On the basis of this paragraph the church has frequently prevented women from participating in corporate worship. For today's reader there are three approaches possible: (1) to say it means what most have said; (2) to question its authenticity; or (3) to say it does not mean what many have supposed.

It is likely the passage does not belong here. Though no manuscript lacks these verses, a few well-known manuscripts place the verses after verse 40. At v. 33 these manuscripts would read as follows.

For God is not a God of confusion, but of peace, as in all the churches. Those who think they are prophets, or spiritual, should acknowledge that what I am writing to you is a command of the Lord.

Verses 34 and 35, starting with "Women should keep silent in the church," then appear at the end of chapter 14.

How could some manuscripts have the verses after v. 33b and others after v. 40? There are two plausible explanations. The first manuscripts may have been as we now have it, but some copyist(s) saw that v. 37 really ought to follow v. 33b. So they changed it. We have no known example of that happening elsewhere in the New Testament. It is also possible the three verses were not in the original. Someone inserted them at 33b, but other copyists, knowing there was nothing about women keeping silent in other manuscripts, placed the verses at the end of the chapter. There are examples of this in the New Testament. For example, all agree that the story of the woman taken in adultery does not belong in chapter 8 of the Gospel of John. Yet some manuscripts have the story there, while a few others have it in chapter 7, or at the end of the Gospel of John, or even in another gospel, after Luke 21:38. It seems more likely that confusion about the placement of a story or paragraph would arise only when it was not in the original. So there is fairly strong agreement about vv. 34-35. They must not have been a part of the original text.[7]

Furthermore, these two verses stand in direct conflict with what we already know. In chapter 11 we saw that women were not to prophesy and pray with their head uncovered. Obviously, women were not intended to be silent in the church. They prophesied and prayed. Our interpretation of 14:26 indicates the same thing: all men and women could participate. Verbal participation in the worship was not limited to clergy or to men. For these reasons it seems likely that the two verses were added at a later date by someone who shared the same concern about women exhibited in 1 Timothy 2:11-12. Because it was added, confusion arose about its proper place in the text.

If the reader prefers to think Paul wrote these verses, then some interpretation which does not directly contradict chapter 11 would be preferable. Most readers prefer to interpret the verb translated "speak"

---

[7]Gordon D. Fee, *The First Epistle to the Corinthians,* New International Commentary on the New Testament (Grand Rapids: Wm. B. Eerdmans, 1987) 699-710.

in some special sense. Some suggestions are "talk," "prattle," or the like. According to this interpretation some women talked in such a way as to disrupt the order, that is, by speaking simultaneously (see v. 27), by asking what has been said in tongues (vv. 27, 35), or perhaps even by excessively speaking in tongues (the silence requested in v. 28 is the same as in v. 34). We do not really know the nature of the disruption and we do not know why the admonition has been directed toward wives. Whatever the problem, Paul asks for order, but does not contradict himself by forbidding women to take an active part in worship.

This interpretation of vv. 33b-36 maintains integrity in Paul's writing, but otherwise leaves much to be desired. It explains the admonition to be silent and avoids the impossible conclusion that in all the churches of the saints women did not fully participate in worship. But it does not explain why in this instance Paul would say wives were to be subordinate to their husbands and in the privacy of their own homes were to ask the men what had happened. Nor does it give any hint what law (Torah?) forbade women to speak. Normally Paul tells us what law he means (v. 21). Some have supposed we have here a reference to Genesis 3:16-17. Women are to be subordinate to men because sin entered the world that one time when man (Adam) did listen to woman (Eve). If this is a law regarding public worship then it refers to an oral tradition we have lost.

It would be better to suppose vv. 34-35 are an addition from a later time when the church had to come to terms with a society in which women were not expected to speak in public assemblies.[8] The verses were added because the letter to the Corinthians in general and chapter 14 in particular (see explanatory note on v. 21) assumed women participated verbally and equally in the public gathering of the local faith community. The author of the pastoral epistles may have made this "correction."

14:37-40 Concluding his thoughts regarding public worship Paul applies an incredible argument.

> Every spiritual person will recognize that what I say is true. If they don't recognize that, then they are not spiritual and should not be

---

[8]Hans Conzelmann, *1 Corinthians. A Commentary on the First Epistle to the Corinthians*, trans. James W. Leitch, Hermeneia (Philadelphia: Fortress Press, 1975) 246.

allowed to speak!

To use an argument so self-serving indicates the gravity of the situation (like 5:3-5?).

THE TEXT IN ITS BIBLICAL CONTEXT

Our descriptions of corporate worship in the Hebrew Bible derive primarily from the great festivals, not the daily or even the Sabbath services. From such occasions we know there was some remembrance of the redemptive events of the Exodus, by song and by recitation, singing and dancing, sacrifices and a covenant meal (see Exodus 15:1-21; 18:10-12; Psalms 149 and 150). On such great occasions of celebration the order of worship apparently followed a fairly set progression. One such progression can be seen in Isaiah 6. The worship begins with a vision of the Lord (vv. 1-2) and continues with praise (vv. 3-4); confession (v. 5); absolution or forgiveness (vv. 6-7); and finally dedication (v. 8). This progression of worship has become the foundation for western, Judeo-Christian posture before God.

The destruction of Jerusalem in 587/6 BCE caused a dispersion of Jews throughout the world. Jews of the Diaspora formed small congregations called synagogues. Very likely they did not differ greatly from the Christian church of the first two centuries. Some synagogues met in fine buildings, like that of Capernaum, but others must have met in houses (Dura-Europos) or public halls, like the first Christians (see summary essay, 248). Unfortunately we cannot determine the order and style of synagogue worship at the time of Paul, but probably there was at least an antiphonal recitation of the Ten Commandments; an antiphonal recitation of the Shema (the creed found in Deut. 6:4-9); a series of blessings; a teaching from the Pentateuch, followed by a translation into Aramaic or Greek (usually also interpretative, like a pesher or midrash; see summary essay, 250); perhaps a reading from the prophets; singing; prayers; and sometimes an explanation or homily (note Luke 4:16-30; Acts 13:15).

So far as we know there is nothing comparable in Judaism to the intense democratization of worship as seen in 1 Corinthians 14. The Pauline churches depended on the action of the Spirit to guide the community in worship. There does not appear to be a predetermined leadership or a set format. We see in this chapter the limitations of such freedom. Chaos has set in. Paul must choose between the democratic action of the Spirit and enforced order. He moves a step in the latter direction. Some believe the leadership of each local house church arose as the owner of the house took charge of the covenant meal. In addition we could imagine that the sense of order sought by Paul eventually required a worship leader. Such leaders became the pastors and elders we know in the later New Testament period.

THE TEXT IN THE LIFE OF THE CHURCH

The situation today and the problem in 1 Corinthians 14 are not strictly identical. Most congregations need more of what Paul decried in this passage. Worship too often has become formal, sterile, and perfunctory. For all churches, but especially for congregational types, which depend on worship as the locus of community formation, a vital sense of corporate worship is essential. Returning to a worship led by the Spirit has at least three potential salutary advantages. A Spirit-led worship includes everyone. Many churches which have otherwise taken seriously the priesthood of all believers all too often have shifted to a clerical sense of leadership. To be led by the Spirit means more congregational participation. A Spirit-led worship draws the congregation and participants into a closer sense of divine presence. The presence of clergy who appropriately (or not) mediate the Word of God can create a sense of human institutionalization. Dependence on the Spirit gives a sense of God's immanence or presence. Finally, a Spirit-led worship often results in a sense of freedom, enthusiasm, and enjoyment. When we speak of the incredibly rapid expansion of Christianity in the first centuries, surely we must include some of these as the attractive characteristics of many house churches.

On the other hand, there is a sense in which many congregations need more order. Following something of a haphazard tradition, many styles of worship do not reflect the dynamic sense of worship found in Bible. There is an appropriate progression in worship, for example, it is difficult to sing of forgiveness before confession (as is often the case). We, like the church at Corinth, need a sense of appropriate order. But even more we need that openness to the Spirit which builds up the community of faith.

RESURRECTION NOW 15:1-58

PREVIEW

Though still dealing with the issue of spiritual gifts Paul has now shifted to a parallel problem, much like his treatment of the hair covering and the Lord's Supper in chapter 11. Through chapters 12–14 he has answered the specific question about the Spirit in worship (12:1), but now adds a complex theological reflection before moving to the fifth question (16:1). At issue is a serious faith problem. Christians do indeed live in a time of the Spirit. Nevertheless there was a beginning of the new age at the resurrection of Jesus and there is yet to be a final endtime victory over death. As we saw at the beginning of this section (see explanatory note on 12:1-3), apparently the Christ house church had lost some sense of historical reality. Jesus and his resurrection had become unnecessary. And the final resurrection played no particular part in their faith.

Paul counters with a strong statement about resurrection, as a present reality and as a coming victory. Paul reminds them first of the tradition which they received—how Jesus was raised from the dead and seen by many witnesses (vv. 1-11). If that tradition is not true, then the faith of Christians has little value (vv. 12-19). But Christ has been raised and death has been destroyed (vv. 20-28). Paul then gives two primary arguments for the resurrection. First, the moral life depends on an endtime resurrection (vv. 29-34). Then, in a second argument Paul uses the analogy of planting and growing. The spiritual body of the resurrection rises from the natural body which is planted (vv. 35-50). At the endtime this spiritual body will be victorious over the final enemy, death (vv. 51-58).

• OUTLINE •

15:1-11 The Account of Christ's Resurrection
15:12-19 If Christ Has Not Been Raised From the Dead
15:20-28 But Christ Has Been Raised From the Dead
15:29-34 Motivation Depends on the Resurrection
15:35-50 The Analogy of Sowing
15:51-58 Victory Over Death

EXPLANATORY NOTES

15:1-11 The resurrection is the heart of the Christian gospel. In this chapter Paul reminds the Corinthians of that fact. That gospel, which they received and in which they stand, makes them whole as a community.

The gospel of which Paul speaks comes in the form of a creedal type formulation. Normally the Bible does not offer creedal statements. The faith is carried by narratives like the paradigmatic stories of the Exodus or of the death and resurrection of Jesus Christ. Still there are from time to time short statements which summarize the narratives or make clear the ethical action intended. In the Hebrew Bible one thinks of the Shema: "Hear O Israel: The Lord our God is one Lord; and you shall love the Lord your God with all your heart, and with all your soul, and with all your might" (Deut. 6:4-5). A larger summary of ethics can be found in the Ten Commandments (Deut. 5:6-21; cf. Exod. 20:2-17).

In the New Testament we can see a short summary of the early Christian faith in Romans 8:34:

Christ Jesus,
who died,
who was raised from the dead,
who is at the right hand of God,
who indeed intercedes for us.

A somewhat larger summary can be found in 1 Timothy 3:16:

He was manifested in the flesh,
vindicated in the Spirit,
seen by angels,
preached among the nations,
believed on in the world,
taken up in glory.

The summary of 1 Corinthians 15:3b-4 has special significance. It was given to the Corinthians as a statement of the faith by which they had been made whole (v. 2). It is then an affirmation of the faith of the first Christians. It is likely the earliest of such affirmations. Paul wrote the letter to the Corinthians about 53 CE (see introduction, 7-8). This affirmation uses the Hebrew Bible as its authority (according to the Scriptures) and refers to Jesus as the Jewish Christ or Messiah. The confession was not simply for Gentiles; it originated in a time prior to Paul's mission.

The use of the affirmation actually represents a change in emphasis for Paul. His first New Testament letter was 1 Thessalonians. There is nothing in that letter, written from Corinth, which points specifically to the redeeming death and resurrection of Jesus (see 1 Thess. 1:9-10). Paul anticipates more the coming of the Lord Jesus Christ (1 Thess. 5:23). Sometime, while at Corinth, he began to emphasize more the death of Jesus on the cross (see commentary on 2:2), and his subsequent resurrection. Now an affirmation centered on the resurrection, as found in 15:3b-4, has become of primary importance (15:3 in RSV, NIV), though not necessarily the first faith Paul shared with the Corinthians (as in the KJV). Possibly this shift in Paul's thought has caused the Christ house church to misunderstand the nature of the resurrection.

The structure of the affirmation can be easily seen because of the "refrain," *according to the Scriptures*:

> Christ died for our sins
>   according to the scriptures,
> he was buried,
> he was raised on the third day
>   according to the scriptures.

It doesn't take much practice in literary analysis to see that "he was buried" breaks up the pattern. The original probably read,

> Christ died for our sins,
>   according to the scriptures;
> he was raised on the third day,
>   according to the scriptures.

What does the reference to the burial mean? It occurs in the gospel accounts (John 19:38-42; Mt. 27:57-61; Mk. 15:42-47; Lk. 23:50-56), but in the shorter affirmations only here and in Paul's sermon at Antioch of Pisidia (Acts 13:29).

Of all New Testament writers only Paul speaks of being buried with Christ in baptism (Rom. 6:3-4; and especially Col. 2:12). Most readers suppose the reference to burial was made to oppose those who thought the death and resurrection of Jesus only appeared to happen (Docetists). If so, the burial may speak to the Christ house church and spiritualists at Corinth who obviously have not given credence to the historical nature of the death and resurrection of Jesus. But the singular use of the burial imagery by Paul makes one suspect that the phrase "he was buried" not only came from the apostle himself, but carries metaphorical significance. For Paul the burial (in baptism) represents the shift from the old age to the new. The burial of Jesus must have represented the end of the old age and the beginning of the new age in Christ. It signifies the end of entrapment in a world of law, tradition, dependence, works righteousness, and religious customs. People of the old age go to the tomb, face their own death, and find the tomb empty. A new age has begun, an age in which there is no fear of "the powers" of this passing age. It seems likely Paul added the burial phrase to an already existent tradition in order to stress the transition from old to new.

Returning to the original confession, we begin with "Christ died for our sins." The statement has an incredible jarring affect. The Jewish Messiah was not to suffer at all, much less suffer for the sins of the people. The Messiah, or Christ, was the anointed king (see 1 Sam. 16:13; 2 Sam. 7). Texts of the Hebrew Bible which refer to the Messiah (such as Isaiah 11:1-5) describe the governing qualities of the king, but not the suffering (see summary essay, 229). The uniqueness of the Christian faith lies, in part, in this radical statement. The long-awaited king (Messiah) will free us from the old age through suffering, not by conquest. The kingdom of God is available through the cross, not through royal legions. The Messiah has been redefined, resignified. We can see these redefinitions at many places in the New Testament. In the Gospel of Mark Jesus reprimands Peter for calling him the Messiah (8:27-33). Instead he redefines his role as that of the suffering Son of Man (8:31). In Luke's Gospel the resurrected Jesus scans the entire Hebrew Bible in order to redefine for Cleopas and his comrade the intent of Jewish messianic expectations (24:21-27).

Although, according to the Gospel of Mark, Jesus refused the title Christ (8:27-33) and redefined himself (even the Messiah!, 14:62) as the Son of Man, very early the first church identified Jesus as Lord (see explanatory note on 16:22) and Messiah or Christ. The title Son of Man was dropped by the end of the first century. The first Christians understood themselves as a foretaste of the kingdom and the resurrected Jesus was their ruler (Lord, Christ, and Son of God). The Jewish Messiah had been radically redefined by Jesus, the cross, and the first synagogue of believers.

The Messiah died for our sins! The English "for" translates the Greek *huper,* a preposition considered by many to be the key word for redemption in New Testament affirmations. It occurs in the eucharistic formula: this is my body broken *huper* you (see commentary on 11:24; cf. Mk. 14:24; Lk. 22:19-20, NIV; footnote in RSV). In the Gospel of John *huper* is used in the primary statement of redemption: I will give over my person *huper* you (10:11,15; 13:37,38; 15:13; cf. 11:50-51). In Paul the term does occur most frequently in formulas which he probably received from others. It may occur in 1:13 as a way of mocking the Christ house church. The "for all" in 2 Cor. 5:14 sounds like a formula Paul quoted from elsewhere. The same is surely true of Romans 8:34 and Gal. 1:4, though Romans 8:32 might be Pauline. This is a way of saying that we cannot easily determine what Paul means by "for us," or "for our sins." It is not necessarily his language.

Apart from these affirmations of the early church, Paul seldom uses the plural word "sins." For Paul, Sin is a power of the old age, a power occasioned by the law, a power that causes death (15:56). He understands the redemptive action of Christ in terms of the power of Sin. He does not think in terms of Sin as immoral actions. Consequently he does not think of redemption as sorrow for wrongs and subsequent forgiveness. Rather, as seen in this chapter, redemption is the release from the power of Sin. Redemption frees persons and societies, otherwise trapped in the old age, to live in mutual enjoyment of each other. The death of Jesus has enabled us to be free of enslaving Sin. Paul can state this in various ways: legal (Col. 2:14-15); sacrificial (Rom. 3:25); liberation (1 Cor. 6:20); identification (2 Cor. 5:21).

The phrase "according to the scriptures" really means "according to the scriptures as we have understood them through Jesus Christ." There is no reference to a suffering Messiah in the Hebrew Bible. Just as Jesus redefined the meaning of Messiah, so also he reinterpreted the Hebrew Bible (so Luke 24:27). Reinterpretation of the scriptures lies at the heart of Jewish study of the sacred book. The Pentateuch or Torah is the sacred book, while the Prophets (history and prophets) are understood as reinterpretations. We can see this process quite easily. For example, in Hosea 2:14-15 the wilderness generation (time between the Exodus and the taking of Palestine) appears as a time of faithfulness and growth, while in the same work it is described as a time of unfaithfulness (Hos. 13:4-8). The prophet varies his interpretation of the wilderness according to the needs of his audience.

The discovery of the Dead Sea Scrolls (primarily during the 1950s) enabled us to see for ourselves the process of reinterpretation. A leader in the community of the scrolls, the Teacher of Righteouness, had the authority and skill to interpret the Hebrew Bible according to the needs and times of the Qumran community (see summary essay, 261). For example, in the *Pesher on Habakkuk,* the teacher understood the Baby-lonians of Habakkuk to be the Romans of his period (1QpHab 2.10-14). Jesus did much the same in the Sermon on the Mount when he said, "You have heard it was said (to people of the old age). But I say to you" (Mt. 5:21-48).

So we look in vain for proof texts. "According to the scriptures" refers to the way the first Christians understood God's intention as seen in Jesus Christ. Once this is understood, then we do see intimations of the death and resurrection in the Hebrew Bible. One favorite text was the servant song of Isaiah 52:13–53:12. Though the Isaianic songs did not refer to the king, they did indicate that one obedient to Yahweh would suffer for the sins of many (53:12). Strangely enough, Isaiah 53 hardly occurs in the gospels or on the lips of Jesus, but the episode with the Ethiopian eunuch in Acts 8 indicates the importance of reinter-preting Isaiah 53 for the early church. Or, in another text, Jesus may have been identified with the heavenly Son of Man because the Son of Man had already been reinterpreted as the suffering saints of the Most High (Dan. 7:21-22). So Jesus is the suffering Son of Man in Mark 8:31-37. Eventually it was understood that the kingdom of God does not come by conquering enemies, but by the gift of mutual freedom under the lordship of Jesus Christ.

The second part of the confession, "he was raised on the third day," applies more directly to the issue at Corinth. There is a misunderstand-ing about the resurrection itself. Perhaps it is a fortuitous misunder-standing or just a normal reaction. Whatever the reason, we can be pleased Paul wrote this passage to Corinth. We have learned much from it. As we have seen, the death and resurrection of Jesus stands in the center of our faith. To be sure some stress the cross more than the res-urrection. Paul himself resolved at Corinth to know nothing except Jesus Christ and him crucified (see commentary on 2:2). Except for the short notice in 6:14 the resurrection is mentioned only in this chapter. Some believe the faith of the author of 1 Peter, or even the Gospel of Mark, depends more on the cross than the empty tomb. Later some authors, like John, put more emphasis on the incarnation than the death and resurrection. But when Paul wrote, the death and resurrection were central, and they have remained so throughout Christian history.

For Paul the resurrection marks the beginning of the new age. The death and resurrection of Jesus also expresses his endtime hope in present terms. As we have seen, Paul's first faith was in the coming of the Lord, an endtime faith. We might diagram it like this:

OLD AGE │ ---------------------------------- │ NEW AGE

Paul's lasting contribution to the Christian faith is that he shifted his endtime hope to the present time. The death of Jesus was the end of the old age and the resurrection was the beginning of the new. We might diagram it like this:

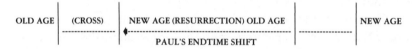

OLD AGE │ (CROSS) │ NEW AGE (RESURRECTION) OLD AGE │ │ NEW AGE
         ------------------ ◀-- ------------------
                            PAUL'S ENDTIME SHIFT

Because we believe in an endtime of peace, where the wolf and the lamb will feed together, we can be a part of that endtime now. That present endtime is the time of the resurrection. For Paul all are elements of the same faith: the coming endtime, the present resurrected life of the body of Christ, and the resurrection of Jesus at the time of Pontius Pilate. Somehow this unity has been broken at Corinth. Some, perhaps in the Christ house church, believe in the present resurrection, but have lost the attachment to the historical Jesus and the coming endtime.

Like many others the spiritualists at Corinth have misunderstood the resurrection. Some may have rejected a resurrection "of the flesh." That affirmation was not claimed until the fourth century. The New Testament speaks of "being raised," or "resurrection of the body," or "resurrection from among the dead ones." Though the Gospel of John especially is anxious to stress the real presence of Jesus, other writers make it clear that the resurrection body was something other than a resuscitated body. Paul makes that absolutely clear in 15:44.

Neither is the resurrection to be confused with immortality. Some in the Greco-Roman world believed a soul (*psuche*) resided in our human body until death. At death the soul would pass on to another world, for another type of life. Again the New Testament writers argued against such an understanding. The empty tomb and the appearances describe an event in our time and in our world, not at a later time or another space.

In a sense, most of the problems with the resurrection stem from a desire for an individual afterlife. The Jewish world from which Paul came did not think that way. It was understood that persons were formed in a community, and eventually, as adults, could perceive themselves as individuals. Such a perception however did not erase the constant function of communal formation. Indeed, the single person represents the whole in a way that involves the entire primary community. There are many striking examples of this in the Hebrew Bible. One thinks particularly of the story of Achan in Joshua 7. Everything pertaining to Achan was destroyed because of his disobedience. It was not a matter of vengeance, but an understanding that if one were disobedient to God, all would be.

Resurrection for Paul is communal. Death also then is a communal loss. Death causes a separation from the formation process, both for the one who dies and the ones who continue to live. In the resurrected state the individual person continues, but, by the mercy of God, in a new way. Death ends community based on what is perishable or corruptible, and begins a formation which is not perishable or corruptible (15:42-44). In other words, in the resurrection a person's bodiness (formation) continues, but now in ways which are not open to destructive, sin-oriented tendencies. There is good news, gospel, hope even in death. Death has lost its power. The New Testament teaching on resurrection, like its teaching about life, views the afterlife of the individual as a participation in the ongoing community. It can hardly be otherwise.

Paul is writing to an audience that does not understand these things. He has a difficult task. He must explain the heart of the faith to people who almost surely will not understand. And he must write in such a way that not only convinces groups like the Christ house church, but also satisfies the other factions or house churches. Little wonder, then, that he starts at a point held in common: the confession of vv. 3b-4. After three days Jesus was raised, according to the scriptures. Like the reference to Christ dying for our sins, this is a general reference to the will of God as understood through the Hebrew Bible. There are no specific resurrection texts related to the Messiah (with its free style of interpretation [pesher] the early church used Jonah 1:17 and the ensuing psalm of "death and resurrection").

Following his reiteration of the early tradition, Paul turns next to the resurrection appearances. Even though we find no other such order of the resurrection appearances (vv. 5-8), it does not seem likely that this section comes totally from Paul. Yet it does not have a rhythmic structure, like other traditional confessions. Perhaps it is best explained as a summary of early narratives. According to some tradition the resurrected Jesus first appeared to Peter. In the Gospel of Mark he does not appear to anyone, though the women first saw the empty tomb. In the ending added at a later date (16:9-20) Jesus appears first to Mary Magdalene. In the Fourth Gospel Jesus likewise first appears to Mary (20:11-18) after she becomes the first to see the empty tomb (20:1-2). In the Gospel of Matthew the women first see the empty tomb, and then Jesus appears to them as they rush to tell the brethren (28:9). In the Gospel of Luke Jesus "first" appears to Cleopas and his friend as they walked disconsolately to Emmaus (Luke 24:13-31). But when they tell the others they are told he had appeared to Simon (Peter). So actually only Luke agrees with the Petrine priority.

It is difficult to determine why this summary speaks of Peter first, when most accounts say the women saw Jesus first. One could argue that this is just another example of the early church suppression of women (see commentary on 14:34-36). One does need to note, however, that this summary in vv. 5-8 precedes any written Gospel by at least twelve years or more. Even if only the passion narrative had already taken final form in the oral tradition, these contradictions would have been apparent to everyone. Apparently the narrative was still fluid.

The Petrine priority is more than a historical statement. When one compares Peter with the beloved disciple in the Gospel of John (1:35-42; 13:23-24; 18:15-16; 19:26-27; 20:3-5; 21:7), it becomes clear that Peter represents that tradition in which faith depends on eyewitness accounts of the resurrection and other saving events (Acts 1:22). In the Gospel of John faith depends more on one who has received fully the incarnate Word (the beloved disciple, 21:23-24; and probably Mary, 12:1-8). The narrative of the women and the tomb also belongs to a faith tradition other than the Petrine eyewitness account. Their faith story comes from a sense of freedom from death or slavery (the empty tomb), rather than a church based on the resurrection (appearance of Jesus). In this case, because of the antihistorical bias of the Christ house church, Paul chooses to emphasize the Petrine tradition—an eyewitness account of the saving events.

According to the summary, Jesus next appeared to the twelve. Presumably "the twelve" refers to the primary disciples around Jesus—the brethren of Matthew 28:10, the disciples of Mark 16:7, the eleven of Luke 24:33, the disciples in John 20:19-23, and the apostles of Acts 1:2. Who are the twelve and what do they represent? We are accustomed to speak of the Twelve Apostles (see summary essay, 222). Obviously that will not do here. In v. 7 the Lord appears to all the apostles—a group not identical with the Twelve. Most agree that the Twelve represents the new Israel with its twelve tribes. So the Twelve can be found primarily where the church wishes to identify itself as the continuation of the promises of God to the Jews. This is especially true in Acts 1-6. In Acts 1 the names of the Twelve seem quite certain, but a survey of the lists (Mt. 10:1-4; Mark 3:13-19; Luke 6:12-16) shows that the number twelve is far more consistent than the names of twelve men.

Other than this passage, nothing is known of the appearance to five hundred brethren, or even of the appearance to James (vv. 6-7). The appearance to all the (other?) apostles indicates the flexibility of the term "apostle" (see summary essay, 222). Because of this flexibility Paul can include his own vision of the Lord as a resurrection appearance (9:1; Acts 9:1-9; Gal. 1:16). Still, that appearance must have been disputed and Paul's apostleship cast in doubt (2 Cor. 10-13). Paul recognizes the peculiar character of his experience by listing it as the last appearance to one who arrived on the scene at the wrong time. His feeling of being last only intensifies his sense of God's grace (vv. 10-11).

This summary of the resurrection appearances makes several things clear. The resurrection appearances describe the real presence of Jesus. It was not "just a memory" or "a good idea." The function of the real presence of Jesus was to form the community, beginning with the chief apostle, Peter, moving on to the new Israel, and then to the larger community. In turn these people (of Jerusalem) became the witnesses or apostles who carried the new community to others.

The resurrection of Jesus does not differ in kind from present resurrection or the endtime. The resurrection of Jesus created the new age, the body of Christ. Our burial with Christ in baptism also brings us into the new age, the resurrected body of Christ. When we die we may be raised into the body of Christ in yet a new incorruptible way. At the end we may all participate in the final kingdom. Yet the resurrection of Jesus has a unique function. It has become the historical paradigm of our faith. The resurrection of Jesus becomes the heart of our faith because of two limitations: time and space. The resurrection of Jesus is the first fruit (15:20) of the new age. The first in a line of types becomes the definition of all the rest. So it is with the resurrection of Jesus. Jesus was raised at the time of Pontius Pilate. Granted that Jesus is a real presence with us even today, still the formation of the faith community started at a specific time in history. That first real presence of Jesus in the faith community is spoken of as resurrection appearances.

Another less-obvious limitation is also at work. The appearances, with the possible exception of the untimely vision of Paul, occurred in the vicinity of Jerusalem. (The Galilee appearances form the ascension narrative and the final commission to the disciples: Mt. 28:16-20; Acts 1:6-11; John 21:22.) The resurrection of Jesus shifted the task of Israel to the new Israel, the faith community. That shift first occurred in the holy city. The resurrected Jesus begins a new age, at a specific time, and yet continues the promises of God to Israel, a specific place. Paul begins this famous chapter with a strong affirmation of that truth.

15:12-19 In his first reflection on this early Christian confession, Paul insists on the unity of the future endtime resurrection, our present experience of new life, and the resurrection of Jesus. Denial of one means denial of all. In vv. 12-14 Paul stresses the validity of the Christian message (preaching), of which vv. 3b-8 is an example. There is a double implication in this starting point. One is the matter of truth. If early Christian evangelists say Christ was raised from the dead according to God's promise ("according to the scriptures" in vv. 3b-4), then, if Christ were not raised, the early Christians have totally misunderstood and mistakenly proclaimed the nature and intent of God.

The second resides in the nature of preaching itself. The act of preaching the good news is itself good news. The death and resurrection of Jesus occurs again and again as it is proclaimed and becomes a part of faith experience. For the prophets of Israel, word and the event were intimately connected. Indeed, the prophets of the Hebrew Bible often spoke in the past tense when they gave the Word of God. So in the early church the preaching of the death and resurrection created hope in the endtime and offered freedom to participate in the new age. If Christ were not raised from the dead, then all of that "goes down the drain." Of course, it works in a circle. If you do not have an endtime hope in the resurrection of the dead, then the resurrection of Christ is a useless affirmation, only an interesting historical oddity (v. 16). And if Christ has not been raised, as the first in a line, then present experience of the new age, with its new life, has not occurred (v. 17). The three affirmations are an indissoluble unity.

The famous statement of v. 19 makes the case, but unfortunately we are not certain how. The Greek text could be taken, for example, in the following ways.

> If we are only hoping for this life in Christ,
> we are of all people most miserable.

> If in this life only are we hoping in Christ,
> we are of all people most miserable (cf. RSV footnote; NRSV, NIV, KJV).

> If in this life we in Christ are only hoping,
> we are of all people most miserable (cf. RSV).

In the first instance skeptics are addressed. If the life of the new age is only a hope, not a reality, then we are in miserable condition. In the second instance our hope as Christians is only for this life. In the third instance, somewhat like the first, we Christians are only hoping: we lack the certainty of Christ's resurrection. Assuming those addressed are the spiritualists of the Christ house church, we would opt for the second reading: the hope of that group deals only with present experience.

15:20-28 Paul has used a negative possibility to demonstrate what would happen if we did not believe in the resurrection of Christ. Now he turns to the positive side of his discussion: Christ was indeed raised from the dead (v. 20). Christ is the first to be resurrected. The meaning of "first" is complex and important. Because the resurrection of Jesus is the paradigm for our faith, it must be the first for all of us, the beginning of the new age. From vv. 22-23 we see there is more than chronology involved. Paul starts a comparison with Adam which he will complete in vv. 42-50. Here we need to understand why such a comparison should be made.

In biblical (or primal) thought one does not easily distinguish between the one and the total (many). For example, the tribes of Israel (such as Judah, Benjamin) simultaneously are persons and large numbers of related people. Many who write in biblical studies speak of this as "corporate personality," the use of one person to represent all. The primary "corporate personality" of the Hebrew Bible was Adam. Adam represented all humanity. Adam and Eve represented humanity as man and woman. What happened to Adam in the Garden is what happens to all people. What Adam did was what we all do.[9] Eve, following the suggestive inquiry of the serpent, placed her own well-being above that of the primal couple, Eve and Adam. Humanity (Adam) fell because persons preferred their own personal identity to the identity of the corporate body (by taking of the tree of knowledge of good and evil). This has become the model of the old age. As we come of age, we all prefer our own person to the formation of which we are a part. In this way we Sin and eventually die (extreme individuation or extreme subordination). Christ is the first fruits of the new age. He did not choose his own identity over the corporate (the cross). Therefore he brought life to the new age (the resurrection). Jesus Christ is the "corporate personality" of the new age, the firstfruits. Once this is understood, much of Paul's thought in this chapter easily falls into place.

The life of the new age occurs in an expansive order. First the corporate person, Christ, is raised. This announces the beginning of the new age, though one cannot place a chronological date on its appearance. It is a condition of life, not strictly an event in time. New life is available now for those who belong to Christ. But eventually there will be an end. By that we (Pauline Christians) mean we know that all the enemies of God can and will be defeated. Belief in the endtime does not entail belief in some specific time when the world will end. Belief in the end is a strong faith that God is in charge, that all things will be subject to God. It is a belief that such victory is imminent. It enables us in the faith community to live victoriously even though victory is not immediately apparent. Constant belief in the coming of the end creates a continuing, powerful hope (permanent eschatology).[10]

The endtime comes not only for the faith community, but for all people. What is true for those who follow Christ is actually true overall. The faith community understands the limited nature of the present reign of Christ, but assumes its eventual universal nature. All things are now subject to Christ, eventually even death itself. When all things are sub-

---

[9]Eugene Roop, *Genesis* (Scottdale PA: Herald Press, 1987) 39-40, 311, 321-24.

[10]John Dominic Crossan, *In Parables: The Challenge of the Historical Jesus* (New York: Harper & Row, 1973) 26.

ject to Christ then Christ will be subject to God (the end will have arrived). Then what is true of the faith community will be true everywhere.

15:29-34 There are many difficult passages in the letters of Paul, but v. 29 may be the worst. One could safely say that no reader has ever come up with a satisfactory explanation. Actually the Greek text as we have it reads fairly clearly. It would translate as follows.

> Otherwise, what are they doing who baptize on behalf of the dead persons? If dead persons are not actually raised, why even baptize on their behalf?

As it stands, apparently some Corinthian Christians baptized surrogates for persons already dead. If that is true then why has the church never practiced baptism for the dead, as modern Mormons do? Why is this the only mention of such a thing either in the New Testament or in all of church history? The normal resolution is to suppose there is an error in punctuation (Otherwise, what are those who baptize doing? Is it only for the dead?), or an error in understanding. This may be true. But it is also possible we later Western Christians have not fully understood society at the time of Paul.

In most societies the dead do not leave the family. They remain a part of the extended family. This was true in the Greco-Roman society of that time. The dead were buried in family burial homes (mausoleums), or, at least, in places accessible to the family. On set occasions, such as birthdays, or death days, the family enjoyed the company of those no longer present as living persons. The dead partook in the meals (normally by pipes extending into the grave) and entered the conversation. The dead were not ubiquitous. Their *daimon* (presence) stayed within a few feet of the burial place (see commentary on 10:20). Of course, if there were many family dead, these corporate meals were fairly frequent. Our accounts from ancient times speak of the meals as pleasant moments at the outdoor, suburban, family house of the dead. To these Greco-Roman families Paul's teaching on resurrection must have seemed somewhat curious. The dead had not left. They were only in a different stage of relationship. And surely this caused some of the misunderstanding which Paul now addresses.

But what of the baptism? When a family converted to Christianity, who was included? The issue has been much debated. Obviously there must have been many instances when individuals left family to "follow

Jesus." The call of the disciples reads that way (Mark 1:16-20). The story about Jesus and his family makes no sense unless he and other early Christians had left their homes (Mark 3:31-35; 10:28-31). Yet even then, the families of the disciples apparently were present in the company of new Christians. Peter's mother-in-law entertained the group (Mark 1:29-31); according to Matthew, the mother of James and John had access to Jesus; according to Paul, everyone but he and Barnabas took families with them on their missionary travels (see commentary on 9:5).

We have seen how Jewish families acted as a unit. Even the Greco-Roman family was more corporate than our highly individualized western models. Society was then what sociologists would call dyadic or interdependent. A split from the family, for whatever reasons, would have been traumatic. It surely did occur in early Christianity. But likewise there must have been many more instances when the entire family converted. That is, when the parent(s) shifted, so did the entire household. There is no other explanation for the many references to a convert's household (Acts 10:2; 11:14; 16:15; 16:31; 18:8; 1 Cor. 1:16 and 16:15). When a household was baptized, some were baptized, others not. Again we cannot say for certain who would have been baptized—only the father? the father and mother? all adults? There is no reason to suppose any children were baptized. Nor can we speak confidently of such adult servants or slaves who automatically accompanied the household.[11] Unless one argues that every person was baptized, and that is nearly impossible, then it must be argued that some people entered the Christian community on the basis of another's baptism. Whether they were baptized later (e.g., at adulthood, or when freed from slavery; note Phil. 16) cannot be ascertained.

For those families who included the dead in their extended system, baptism must have brought for them the whole family into the new faith. Most readers agree that Paul does not include himself among those who would baptize for the dead. Those who do so are "they," not "we." If we are correct about this situation, v. 29 has little significance. Those who included the dead in their own conversion to Christianity did so because of their understanding of the family, not because of any hope in the resurrection. They would have been puzzled by the contention of

---

[11]Bartchy, ΜΑΛΛΟΝ ΧΡΗΣΑΙ, 59.

v. 29. Paul's argument was simply abortive, perhaps even irritating rhetoric. Everyone knew it was an irritated aside, so it was never used or mentioned again.

In v. 30 Paul turns to the real argument: unless there is a resurrection, there is no ethical motivation. At first glance this may not appear to be an obvious assumption. For a morally concerned people an emphasis on this present life can be very motivating. The Jewish people before the exile did not have an extensive belief in an afterlife, yet they held to a strong ethical tradition. Life depended on one's everyday relationship to the neighbor since all of life was sandwiched into a present lifetime. In contrast, those who lived in a more dualistic world viewed life as evil or simply as transitory. At best, life in this world prepared one for the next. At worst, life was meaningless. For many others the only motivation for ethical behavior would be obedience to principles. For this reason there were many philosophical schools, such as Stoics, Epicureans, and Cynics, which taught basic principles to those who were interested. Paul quotes one of these in v. 32.

The ethic of Paul depends much on the Jewish type. But he does has altered that ethic in two major respects: (1) the family of God has become universal and (2) the end of life is the beginning of a new opportunity. The Jewish ethic dealt primarily with relationships within the tribal system. Christianity stretched that family to all humanity. Such a radical expansion entailed risk. And ethically speaking the resurrection makes such a risk possible. Without the resurrection anyone would be inclined to protect the status quo. Those who believe in the resurrection know the end of the status quo does not signify the end of God's action. Indeed, we can so anticipate God's resurrection action that we begin to live as if the resurrection had already occurred. Paul can so act as to die everyday (v. 30), because he knows there is a resurrection. That doesn't mean he knows there are rewards in another life. But he does know he can risk life, because the future does not depend on his own self-preservation.

As an example, he refers to fighting the beasts at Ephesus. The reference has been of more than passing interest to readers of the New Testament. After Paul left Corinth he eventually resided in Ephesus from perhaps autumn of 53 to about the summer of 56. During this time he must have written the Corinthian correspondence (see introduction, 7-8).   Was he also incarcerated? Was he sentenced to face beasts in a Roman-style spectacle? Some believe this imprisonment would have been the occasion for the letters of Philemon and Colossians (near to Ephesus) as well as Philippians and Ephesians (the so-called captivity epistles). On the other hand, the reference to beasts may be no more than a vivid metaphorical description of his many adversaries in Ephesus (16:9; 2 Cor. 1:8-9).

For Paul ethics will dissolve without a hope in the resurrection. As an example of such ethical bankruptcy Paul first quotes Isaiah 22:13, "Let us eat and drink, for tomorrow we die," apparently used by Jews as a cynical way to mimic Epicureans (a philosophical school). Gentiles, without the resurrection, lack a sense of present corporate responsibility. They tend to stress individual ethical responsibilities, with, perhaps, an eye on the common good. Using a quote from a Greek comic writer, Menander (342–292 BCE), Paul warns his readers that association with those who have no resurrection faith will eventually affect their own moral fiber.

15:35-50 Paul anticipates that some will ask about the nature of the resurrection. The "foolish person who asks" is someone about to receive a revelation or some kind of knowledge. It was common in Hellenistic literature to belittle the one about to receive a new understanding (the author of the Johannine epistles uses "little children"). In order to field the question he offers a series of analogies. The basic analogy involves the process of sowing. Not all of his analogies are immediately apparent (we still feel foolish) and even the analogy of sowing goes well beyond the simple task of planting and reaping (see summary essay, 220).

The sowing analogy contains two elements appropriate to the resurrection. Obviously, death and resurrection seem like putting a seed in the ground in anticipation of new life. There are limitations. For example, the seed does not actually die. That did not stop the early church from using it as analogy. In fact, the author of the Gospel of John, also speaking specifically to Gentiles (John 12:20-26), used the planting of a seed to explain the Christian understanding of death and new life. A second part of the analogy also applies. The seed goes into the earth alone, but it comes up greatly multiplied. It is planted a single (naked, in v. 37) kernel, but returns as a head of grain. Paul speaks of the new life as the corporate body God has chosen (v. 38). The author of John refers to the germination as an increase (John 12:24). When Paul speaks of the body yet to be (vv. 37-38), he does not mean a kernel of wheat is planted and a plant comes up. He means that the single seed comes back to life with a new corporate existence.

Paul makes that more apparent in v. 44. The persons die as individuals (isolated from their corporate body and living only out of their own *psuche*). The *psuchikoi*, as Paul calls such persons (translated "physical" in the NRSV, "natural" in the NIV), are defined simply as people without the Spirit (see explanatory note on 2:14; Jude 19). In sharp contrast those resurrected enter a spiritual body, that is, life in a corporate body led by the Spirit. Paul consistently speaks of the corporate life of the new faith community as *pneumatikos* or spiritual (see explanatory note on 12:1), and his evangelistic task is to sow in the churches such a spiritual life (9:11). With limitations the much-used analogy of sowing works well. Human or natural existence characterizes life before the new age, while spiritual existence characterizes life in the new age. The same is true of death and resurrection.

The two analogies in vv. 39-41 confuse us because Paul shifts from the form of the resurrection (corporate spiritual body) to the nature of flesh and glory. Paul only wishes to shake the rigid mind of his "foolish person." Words and categories have different meanings. He is not speaking theologically here. Flesh (*sarx*) has many forms and the various celestial bodies give off different levels of brightness (*doxa*). He apparently chose these two analogies because the readers would have known that he uses *sarx* in quite a different sense (as personal identity; see explanatory note on 5:5), and he uses *doxa* to describe the presence of God (see explanatory note on 11:7). As words differ according to context, so the reader is not to suppose the resurrection body is the same as the human body. Having made his point about the variety of meanings, Paul now speaks of the resurrection in a way that does not match the sowing analogy. The primary word pair he uses is perishable—imperishable. We might picture it as follows.

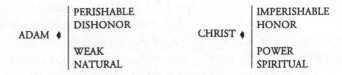

	PERISHABLE		IMPERISHABLE
	DISHONOR		HONOR
ADAM ◆		CHRIST ◆	
	WEAK		POWER
	NATURAL		SPIRITUAL

In this life the individual's relationship to the corporate body is perishable, that is, open to misunderstanding, alienation, malformation, sin and death. In Romans 7 Paul will spell out how difficult it is for the individual person to act toward others in love and openness. But in the new age or, better yet, in the resurrection, the communal relationship is not susceptible to the kinds of problems found in the old age. In the resurrection, or spiritual body, each person has an ongoing positive participation in the body of Christ.

Paul speaks of these two conditions in terms of two corporate images: Adam or the first Adam, and Christ or the last Adam (v. 45). As mentioned above, Paul, and other Jewish writers, would use individuals to describe larger units (see commentary on 15:22). Abraham incorporates all Semites, Moses all Jews, Jesus all Christians, but Adam incorporates all humanity (see summary essay, 220). Created humanity, Adam, is a living being (the Greek word translated "being" in v. 45 is translated, as an adjective, "physical" in vv. 44, 46, NRSV). But redeemed humanity, the *last* Adam, is a life-giving spirit. Created humanity will individualize, will sin, and will die. Redeemed humanity will be guided, corporately, by the Spirit and will live in life creating community. First Adam was of the earth, from dust, that is, of creation. The second Adam is a gift of God (heaven). We all have lived in the image of the first Adam, but we may also live in the image of the second Adam, Christ (man from heaven, v. 49). These figures simply repeat in various ways the sense of a corporate created humanity and a corporate redeemed humanity, a life in the old age and a life in the new.

All of this presents many issues for life. What is the relationship of the redeemed life to the created life? Is it necessary to go through some change? Does maturation as a human being depend on a "conversion"? Can the once-born person know the life of the Spirit? As far as Paul is concerned, apparently not. Flesh and blood, that is, created humanity and its continuing tradition (family, race, history; cf. John 1:13) cannot inherit or enter the reign of God (see summary essay, 234). How could that which is eventually headed for self-destruction suddenly become, without any alteration, something that cannot die? Paul then turns to the mystery of change.

15:51-58 In no other passage does the apocalyptic nature of Paul's thought become so self-evident as here. The movement from created person to redeemed requires an end to the old age and the beginning of the new. That is the mystery, a term used in much apocalyptic literature (see summary essay, 261) to describe the seemingly unfathomable way God works (see commentary on 2:7). Paul signals his use of apocalyptic imagery with a reference to the sound of a trumpet. One could plausibly argue that the trumpet signals a cultic action, the blowing of the *shophar* (ram's horn) by the priests (1 Chron. 15:28; 16:6), but more likely the trumpet signals the advances of troops in a holy war. We note them (blown by the priests!) in the conquest of Jericho (Joshua 6; see also 2 Chron. 20:20-28). In the apocalyptic War Scroll (Dead Sea Scroll document from about 100 BCE), specific instructions are given regarding the kind of sound (staccato, trill, blast) to signal types of attack (1QM 8.1–9.9, 16.2-9). In other apocalyptic scenes God, or the angels, may blow the victory signal (Isa. 27:13; Rev. 8-9).

The final trumpet is the last signal necessary, for it marks God's ultimate victory (1QM 18.3-4). That victory comes over the greatest enemy of the covenant relationship—even death itself. It marks the beginning of relationships which are no longer susceptible to failure (now to be imperishable) and death (the inadvisable translation "immortality"—NRSV, NIV—places the emphasis on individual survival after death rather than the inviolable nature of our new corporate existence).

Paul has reached the heart of his faith. As so often when he touches faith-life deeply he bursts into a rapturous exclamation (see Romans 8:15, 31-39; 1 Cor. 16:22). Here his song of victory in Christ comes from two powerful texts in the Hebrew Bible: Isaiah 25:8 and Hosea 13:14. The quote from Isaiah reflects the quality of the new age where there will be no more tears (Rev. 21:4) and where even death itself will have been swallowed up by the new life. In the quote from Hosea the prophet marvels at the grace of God which extends even unto Sheol, death itself.

Verses 56-57 summarize the Pauline argument yet to be made so forcefully in Romans 5-7. The progression to death moves from law through Sin. The law is good and just, but it raises our individual consciousness. As conscious adults we are so aware of the limits established by law that we may rebel. As such we often prefer our individual identity to the joy and love of our formational community. Paul defines Sin as such an attitude or condition of self-concern. Evil deeds or sins result from the condition of Sin. In fact, Sin at this level usually results in omissions. We find ourselves unable to do what we want (Romans 3:20; 7:18b; 8:7). Or, to the contrary, we find ourselves meeting expectations (obeying the law) in order to receive approval (Gal. 3:10-11). In either case we enter the condition called Sin because we have sought our own identity at the expense of mutual relationships.

Though Paul does not mention it here, whenever we seek our own identity alone then other persons can appear to want to deprive us of our freedom. They appear to force us into enslaving relationships. Or they appear to make us think we can win approval if we just try harder. In either case other persons become satanic to us (2 Cor. 11:14).

When we cannot do what we wish to do, and when persons around us appear to be against us, then we can no longer act acceptably. Either we become so negative we start doing things we don't want to do in order to assert our identity (Romans 7:15), or we try even harder to please others (Gal. 1:10; 3:1-2). In any case we die because we have lost a useful, vital relationship to our formative community. While Paul here speaks primarily of faith-death, physical death also severs our relationship to our formative community. In the final analysis Paul does not distinguish between physical and faith death. Victory is the same in either case: we have been freed to be ourselves in community with others. Death has lost its power. Victory came from God through Jesus Christ (v. 57).

Because of that victory the faith community can live with steadfast lives. They know the moral life is not in vain.

THE TEXT IN ITS BIBLICAL CONTEXT

In the Hebrew Bible there are few intimations of a resurrection from the dead. Most readers would notice Daniel 12:2: "And many of those who sleep in the dust of the earth shall awake." Daniel spoke of a resurrection which is simultaneous with the deliverance of the people of God, and the beginning of the endtime. Some people think the idea of a resurrection came to the Jews while they were in the exile. Influenced by dualism from the Middle East (Persia), the Jews were able to think of the person as made of physical and spiritual components. With the death of the physical the spiritual lived on. But that is not the meaning of the resurrection in biblical thought. The resurrection simply expresses apocalypticism in other words: the end of life offers a new opportunity.

Among the Jews at the time of Jesus the idea of the resurrection took two forms. The Zealots were the strong apocalyptic types. They believed the end was at hand, that the legions of God were poised to drive the Romans out of Palestine. Their sense of resurrection was not so much a faith in new life after death as it was that death of the oppressor would usher in the new age. Much of the New Testament needs to be understood in light of this difference. It is so easy to shift from death and resurrection to killing and resurrection. Many of the disciples of Jesus were Zealot-like, or expressed revolutionary sympathies. Peter himself carried a knife (John 18:10). The disciples had two swords among them (Luke 22:38). The two brothers, James and John, were called sons of thunder (Mark 3:17). Some think the second name of Judas, Iscariot (Mark 3:19), means knife man. And one of the disciples was called Simon the Zealot (Luke 6:15). Many of the disciples apparently expected a conflict between the followers of Jesus and the Roman armies. They thought of Jesus as a victorious Messiah. They did not expect his ignominious death (Luke 24:21). They resisted his self-understanding as a suffering Son of Man (Mark 8:32). At the end it was still difficult to distinguish between those who killed in order to bring the new age and those who thought a new age could arise after death occurred.

The Pharisees were not at all Zealots, but they too believed in the resurrection. In fact, belief in resurrection was a major difference between the two leading parties of the Jews, the Sadducees and the Pharisees. It was the Sadducees who tried to trap the apocalyptic Jesus with their trick question about the woman and seven husbands (Luke 20:27-33). Paul was able to use the conflict to his own advantage when called before the Sanhedrin (Acts 23:6-10). The Sadducees were conservative. They believed only in the Pentateuch (first five books of the Hebrew Bible). They did not apply their faith to the present day. It was the Pharisees who adapted the Law (Pentateuch) to the present and considered authoritative the continuing history of the Jews as found in the writings and the prophets. While their belief in the resurrection was not identical with that of Christians (see commentary on 15:3-4), nevertheless their belief in new resurrected life enabled them to adapt their faith to different contexts and new times. Faith in the resurrection produced flexibility for the Pharisees much as it freed the first Christians from slavery to the old age.

THE TEXT IN THE LIFE OF THE CHURCH

Paul's insists on the centrality of the resurrection of Christ. He was right. Little, if anything, takes precedence. The radical nature of the Christian faith depends on the resurrection. There are a variety of ways to take the resurrection. Some see it as a way of understanding the ongoing faith community. Some see it as a basis for individual hope. I

Corinthians 15 has been understood both ways (see summary essay, 253).

The resurrection addresses those who insist on protection and security of the individual, institutions, and country. Such persons set up mechanisms of defense along economic, racial, and national lines. Paul calls it living for the flesh. People who seek security and self-preservation may then speak of themselves as immortal. The doctrine of immortality extends the security of the individual into eternity. Used that way, hope for immortality can become Sin to the nth degree.

In sharp contrast, the life of the Spirit, with its hope in the resurrection, does not, indeed, cannot, dwell on preservation of the flesh (personhood, institutions, nations). Rather the corporate life of the Christian becomes one of risk. A Christian hospital can accept more welfare patients than economically advisable because it knows God's love for the poor does not depend on its continued existence. A faith community can witness to true discipleship in threatening times because it knows God can raise up even stones as a witness. Christians can call for total disarmament in the midst of a cold war because they know the future of the world does not depend on the survival of their nation. A Christian can risk his or her life because a Christian knows this life is not the end.

There are many stories of persons who have "died" and yet lived for another day. Such people often say they have no fear of death. They are willing to take risks the rest of us cannot fathom. They have nothing to lose because they have already died once. Christians have already died once. They have been buried with Christ in his death (baptism, Rom. 6:3-4). Death has lost its sting.

FIRST CORINTHIANS 16:1-24
CHRISTIAN MUTUALITY

INTRODUCTION

The final chapter does not contain any of the confrontations found in chapters 1–15. There are a number of items which reflect the way the faith community was formed and how it functions. The first section does begin with the Greek formula *peri de*, "now concerning," which indicates a question from the Corinthians. This one was an inquiry about the financial contributions for the community at Jerusalem. Paul clarifies the process (vv. 1-4). In vv. 5-12, presumably answering a final question, Paul mentions prospective visits by himself, Timothy and Apollos. Paul closes the letter (vv. 15-24) with words of advice and greetings.

• OUTLINE •

16:1-4 The Collection for the Saints
16:5-12 Christian Hospitality
16:13-24 Concluding Remarks

EXPLANATORY NOTES

16:1-4 The Collection for the Saints in Jerusalem. Scholars have suggested a number of reasons for the collection: the famine mentioned in Acts 11:27-30; a community of goods which exhausted resources in Jerusalem (Acts 2:44-45; 4:32; 6:1); or a Christian temple tax (Mt. 17:24-27?). If there were a specific cause, we probably cannot determine it. More important for understanding the text is the way the collection functions in and among the churches. In this passage Paul speaks of the collection as a *logeia,* but elsewhere (Rom. 15:26; 2 Cor. 9:13) he speaks of it as a *koinonia,* the same word used for fellowship or community (Acts 2:42); and for communion, the action of breaking bread and drinking the cup together (1 Cor. 10:16; translated participation in the RSV, NIV; sharing, NRSV). In Romans 12:13 Paul admonishes the Roman Christians to have in common with (contribute to, NRSV) the saints and to practice hospitality.

The collection must have functioned as a form of mutuality among the churches. Indeed, Paul explains the collection to the Roman Christians as a reasonable mutual sharing: spiritual blessings from Jerusalem in return for material blessings from the Gentiles (Rom. 15:27). One way of building community among the congregations was to share in financial resources. The motivation for the giving was not simply a specific need in Jerusalem, but the mutuality created by the offering.

Christians already were meeting on the first day of the week.[1] It is not quite certain when Christians broke with the Sabbath in order to move to the day of the resurrection (John 20:19), though this early witness in v. 2 receives corroboration from other texts closer to 80 or 90 (Acts 20:7 and Rev. 1:10). We have already examined some elements of the Sunday service (see on 14:13-19). No mention was made of the offering in that context. As shown above, the offering of one's resources was a mark of mutuality. It needs to be stressed that the offering or oblation was the giving of one's self as a gift of service to God (see Romans 12:1). The sacrifice is not God's self offering for us, nor is it a means of gaining favor with God (much less appeasing an angry God). So the first Christians shared their resources as a major way of creating the faith community (Acts 2:44). This particular collection does seem strange, however. As it reads, each Christian is to put aside something each week until Paul arrives. One would have supposed each Christian would make an offering each Sunday and the house church would save it for Paul. Was there no treasury in the Corinthian house churches?

16:5-12 The early church was known for its hospitality. The first communities entertained the apostles and traveling leaders (Acts 11:26). We know that church hospitality continued through the first century and into the second. Readers of the Didache are advised to entertain trav-

---

[1]Willi Rordorf, *Sunday: The History of the Day of Rest and Worship in the Earliest Centuries of the Christian Church* (Philadelphia: Westminster Press, 1968).

eling leaders for three days. After that leaders are to work or move on. Though we do not consider this issue the major problem of 1 Corinthians 9:3-7, we can see there some hints of the practice (note also Philemon 22). On the other side of the coin, local leaders should be selected from among those who could and would show hospitality (1 Tim. 5:10; Shepherd of Hermas, Sim. 9.27). The hospitality of the presbyter or bishop eventually formed the medieval practice of sanctuary.

Paul mentions three occasions which call for hospitality by the Corinthians. First Paul intends to visit them in the fall and perhaps even stay the winter. He doesn't intend to leave Ephesus until midsummer. This visit will be Paul's second visit to Corinth. After the first visit, in 51 CE, he moved on to Ephesus (Acts 18:1-19). We know very little about the second visit (see introduction, 13). There is no mention of it in Acts. We know there was such a visit because he writes later of his upcoming third visit (2 Cor. 13:1). The second visit obviously did not go well, for it was painful to Paul and the Corinthian Christians (2 Cor. 2:1-2).

Prior to the painful visit Paul sent to Corinth his beloved companion Timothy (4:17). The tension between Paul and some Christians at Corinth could not be hidden. Timothy was to remind the Corinthians of what Paul had taught them, for Timothy indeed travels among them as Paul himself (v. 10). Knowing the tension between himself and the church, Paul appeals for a hospitable treatment of his surrogate, Timothy. They are to take care of him and send him on the way in shalom (covenantal peace, v. 11).

In v. 12 we come to the final *peri de*, "now concerning," of this letter (see above, 11). We assume, as in the other cases, this refers to a question in the letter from the Corinthians. Their last question concerned Apollos. What had they asked? From the context it would appear they were asking Paul to send Apollos back with the three brethren mentioned in v. 17. Paul's answer may surprise us. We have come to know Paul as a scrapper for Jesus Christ. In the eyes of the Corinthians we know there is some type of competition between Apollos and Paul (1:12; 3:4-6, 22; 4:6). How could Paul the fighter permit Apollos to interfere at this crucial moment in Corinth? Paul genuinely wants the gospel preached, people to respond, and the church to grow. In a similar situation he tells the Christians at Philippi of people who actually do street preaching in front of his jail in order to endanger him (Phil. 1:15-18). Nevertheless, he is pleased that the gospel is preached.

In somewhat the same manner, he urges Apollos to respond favorably to the request of the Corinthian house churches.

16:13-24 A letter of the Greco-Roman period normally ended with some occasional remarks, specific greetings and a final salutation. Paul follows the usual procedure. In this letter he offers just a minimum of advice (v. 13). Normally, Paul reflects on specific issues facing the churches. As the readers enter into his narrative world, they will see life as Paul sees it and they will act accordingly. Consequently, there is little need for extensive mandates or advice. Still, at the end of many letters Paul will write some general advice. In his first letter he penned some admonitions which sound much like the Sermon on the Mount (1 Thess. 5:12-22). A similar series occurs later, in the letter to the Romans (12:9-21). In his letter to the Galatians Paul uses yet another style common in early Christianity. The Two Way system, as we know it, was a common way of encouraging people to act in a certain manner (Mt. 6:24; 7:13-14). The advice usually began "There are two ways: the way of life and the way of death." There followed lists of virtues and lists of vices. Paul does the same thing in Galatians 5:16-24 with works of the flesh and fruit of the Spirit. In 1 Corinthians we find yet another style.

The very earliest church used a short catechism adapted from Judaism. It reflected the endtime expectation of the earliest synagogue type church. The principle parts of the catechism were

1. Set aside the life of the old age (e.g. 2 Cor. 7:1).
2. Be subject to appropriate persons (e.g., 1 Cor. 16:15-16).
3. Watch for the age to come (e.g., 1 Cor. 16:13).
4. Stand firm in your faith (e.g., 1 Cor. 15:58).

We find this catechism primarily in early Christian letters like 1 Peter and 1 Thessalonians though evidently Paul still had it in mind when he wrote 1 Corinthians.[2] As we have indicated, 1 Corinthians was written at a time when Paul stressed a life based on the coming new age. The first Christian catechism called for a Christian lifestyle which rejected the values of the old age, pointed toward the new, yet did not call for a deliberate break with local laws and customs. Little wonder it appears here in v. 13 as Paul's final set of admonitions. As in chapter

---

[2]E. G. Selwyn, *The First Epistle of St. Peter* (London: Macmillan, 1952) 388.

13 Paul can summarize his catechism with the call to love (v. 14). Some of the people of Corinth are mentioned in vv. 15-18. We know Stephanas only from the baptism of his household in 1:16. Slave owners of the Greco-Roman period normally named their slaves according to various virtues. And in contrast to the two- or three-name system of their owners, slaves had only one name. We can be fairly certain Fortunatus ("fortunate") was either a slave or a freedman. He is not known otherwise. Achaicus might also be a slave with a place name (Achaia). The three men apparently brought the letter from Corinth for which we find the answers in 1 Corinthians 7–16.

From Ephesus Paul also sends the greetings of Aquila and Prisca. This early husband-and-wife team ministry has fascinated historians of the early church. We first meet them at Corinth (Acts 18:2). They had been exiled from Rome by the emperor Claudius during a disruption involving the Jews. Many think the disturbance was caused by the introduction of Christianity into Rome. At least the Roman historian Suetonius refers to the riots *impulsore chresto* (instigated by Chrestus or Christ?; see introduction, 6-7). So about a year before Paul arrived in Corinth, Priscilla (Prisca) and Aquila may have already introduced the new faith to the Greek city. When Paul left Corinth Priscilla and Aquila accompanied him to Ephesus, from where Paul sends back their greeting (16:19). While at Ephesus it was Priscilla and Aquila who instructed the great Apollos in the proper faith (Acts 18:26). At Ephesus Aquila and Priscilla also hosted a house church. Assuming house churches must have served about forty persons (see summary essay, 248), owners of house churches must have possessed considerable means. By the time the letter to the Romans was written (ca. 56), Priscilla and Aquila had returned to Rome where once again they hosted a house church (Rom. 16:3-5). In Romans 16 Paul gives a moving and unusual tribute to this couple who had risked their lives for him and had been instrumental in the Gentile mission.

The Corinthians are to greet each other with a holy kiss. Four other letters end with the same request (1 Thess., 2 Cor., Romans, and 1 Peter). Later the holy kiss became a formal part of the liturgy.[3] Justin

---

[3]The liturgical use of the kiss became more than a familial act. See Nicolas James Perella, *The Kiss Sacred and Profane: An Interpretive History of Kiss Symbolism and Related Religio-Erotic Themes* (Berkeley: University of California Press, 1969) 12-50.

Martyr (ca. 150) said they kissed each other after the prayers and before the eucharist (Apology 65). There is no reason to suppose these final greetings are liturgical. Families would kiss each other as a greeting (Gen. 50:1; Tobit 7:6-7). Hosts would also greet guests (Luke 7:45). Presumably Paul simply calls on members of each house church to greet each other as the family of God).

Paul writes the final greeting with his own hand. This means the letter up to this point was dictated by Paul to a scribe, presumably the Sosthenes of 1:1. At the end of another letter Paul emphasized his authority by signing with large letters (Gal. 6:11). There may be a hint here of that same intent. Indeed, as in the letter to the Galatians (1:8-9), Paul places a curse on those who do not respect the Lord of the faith community, that is, those who shift from the faith in which they first believed.

Then without warning Paul utters the earliest known prayer of the church: *maranatha*. The prayer or utterance comes from that short period when the church still spoke Aramaic, the common language of Palestine. The Aramaic term for Lord, *mara*, would mean "Our Lord" as *marana*. The term *tha* could be an imperative, Come! So we could best translate the phrase "Our Lord, come!" Once again this very early liturigcal cry reflects that same endtime expectancy we have associated with this letter.

THE TEXT IN ITS BIBLICAL CONTEXT

We cannot see in the Hebrew Bible the strategy for incorporating a new group. Such incorporations surely did occur. The twelve tribes were once distinct groups joined together by a common story—the Pentateuch. We can see the links or sutures between the tribes, links which sometimes were painfully torn apart (1 Kings 12:16). But we cannot see the way in which the tribes were joined together. As the story of the Jewish people developed there was no reason for taking in another group. They become more and more exclusive, with less and less opportunity for conversion to Judaism. The new covenant in Christ changes all that. Paul particularly received a lifetime commission to bring the Gentiles into the new form of Judaism (Christianity). The collection was a key way of uniting the Gentile Christians with the Jewish Christians. Paul did not allow the Gentiles to become dependent on the Jerusalem church. He empowered the Gentiles to become equal partners.

Hospitality plays a very significant role in the Hebrew Bible. A host would rather perish than violate hospitality. After Lot accepted into his home the two angels, he would have rather given the men of Sodom his daughters than endanger his guests. Likewise, when an old man of Gibeah invited a Levite into his home, he would rather sacrifice his daughter than let the men of Gibeah harm his guest. For the violation of hospitality at Sodom the city was buried forever. The penalty for Gibeah was death for the men of Gibeah and their tribe, Benjamin. The Hebrew people thought of God as one who gave ultimate hospitality:

> Thou preparest a table before me
> in the presence of my enemies;
> thou anointest my head with oil,
> my cup overflows.

In the New Testament hospitality reflects more the availability of the house church as a caring support unit. Among the characteristics of early leaders we find hospitableness high on the list (1 Tim. 3:2, 5:10; Titus 1:8). But even beyond the hosts of house churches, Christians are urged to practice hospitality (Rom. 12:13; 1 Pet. 4:9). Many associate the practice of hospitality with the rapid growth of the church. We probably see that form of evangelism in the admonition to show hospitality even to strangers (Heb. 13:2).

THE TEXT IN THE LIFE OF THE CHURCH

Free churches have stressed service to others. In our times it has become evident that the impulse to serve others can also create dependency. As one considers the evils of welfare systems, racism, sexism, and economic imperialism, it can be said that dependency is the common thread. Any system is evil if it makes one person or one group dependent on another. For the Christian the death and resurrection of Jesus Christ creates mutuality or *koinonia* rather than dependency. Continuing the power of the crucifixion, Christians seek to empower those who find themselves weak or peripheral. Paul empowered the Gentiles to be a part of the universal Christian *koinonia*.

We often think of stewardship as service to others, but actually stewardship offers to every person the joy of equal membership. Within the church all persons should be empowered to share responsibility for the work of the faith community. The work of the faith community dare not be limited to a few. In the world at large we of the faith community work for systems which do not make one dependent on another. So, for example, we prefer to dig wells in the Sudan rather than indefinitely furnish food for those starving. One creates dependence, the other *koinonia*.

Though the Apostle Paul may not have intended to associate the collection with hospitality, we must note that hospitality also develops a sense of mutuality as the church grows. Consequently the congregational type churches are more inclined to invite people to small groups than to organize mass evangelism. Like the house church of New Testament times, the Christian home today becomes a place where one group treats another group with mutual caring.

SUMMARY ESSAYS

ADAM

More than any other thinker of his time, Paul used the figure of Adam to clarify his faith perspective. Adam is the Hebrew name for the first person, the one created by God (Gen. 1:27; 2:7). The name derives from the Hebrew term *'adamah,* earth (Gen. 2:7). The person Adam represents all people much as Abraham represents all believers (Rom. 4:16), or Moses represents all Jews (1 Cor. 10:1-2). What happened to Adam happens to all of us. Or as Paul puts it, all of us sinned in Adam (Rom. 5:12). Adam did not infect the race with a fault, but as a type (Rom. 5:14) describes what life is like for all of us.

Adam has been translated *anthropos* in Greek and both have been translated "man" in English. While one cannot easily fault these translations, considerable confusion has risen because of them. In both Genesis 1 and 2 Adam consisted of two parts, male and female. But because in English the term man refers to a male being, the reader can wrongly assume the first Adam was a male human being. To add to the confusion even the Hebrew text keeps the term *'adam* (Gen. 4:1) for the male even after, in 2:23, they have been formed as male (*ish*) and woman (*ish-shah*). This confusion between male and female in Adam creates some of the problems we find in 1 Corinthians 11:2-16—especially the statement that the man is the source (head) of the woman (11:2).

While Adam represents all of mankind, Paul can shift that corporate representation to the old age. When that occurs Christ becomes the corporate person for the new age (15:45-49).

ANALOGY

Strictly speaking the term "analogy" does not appear in the English Bible. That may be a problem of translation more than an observation about the text itself. The Hebrew term *mashal* means primarily a "means of comparison." It is used for wisdom sayings and proverbs (1 Sam 10:12) or other kinds of sayings that compare (Ezek. 17:2). The word *mashal* comes into the New Testament as parable (Greek, *parabole*), a term used only in the Gospels (Mark 4:11). But a parallel term, *paroimia*, in the Gospel of John, refers to the way in which earthly things reflect spiritual truths (John 10:6; 16:25; 16:29).

Paul does not use either term, though he clearly uses many analogies in his letters. In 1 Corinthians 2:13 Paul says he does not teach by human wisdom, but by the spirit, comparing spiritual things with the spiritual. When does Paul use an analogy? The inability to discern analogy in Paul has caused considerable trouble in Christian history.[1] Some readers take literally what Paul meant as analogy. In that way they seriously alter the meaning of both the text and Paul's message. For example, in 1 Corinthians 7:14 Paul uses the formation of Christian children as an analogy to marriage between Christian and non-Christian, but some parents believe they have failed if their child is not formed as a Christian.

Sometimes Paul signals to us that an analogy is coming. Occasionally he uses the Greek word *hos*, "like," to introduce a comparison. In 3:10 he says being a leader is like an architect; in 4:9 an apostle is like a condemned criminal. But more often there is no signal. He does not warn us when he compares the church to a planted field (3:6-9); or a temple (3:16-17; 6:19); or a body (12:12-31; 6:15-20). We are not told that the muzzled ox, the plowman, the thresher are all analogies of ministry (9:8-11). We can miss the use of a race as an analogy of Christian growth and development (9:24-27).

Even when we have determined we are in an analogy our problems are not all solved. Parables can be realistic, or not. Sowing seeds on the road, or among the thorns is not true to life. Jesus teaches us with that parable because it we find it incredible. The Kingdom itself is incredible. But analogies are not like that. The listener or reader must agree with the example given. In literary analysis we speak of the example as the "vehicle": it carries the meaning. The meaning itself is called the "tenor." When a writer uses an analogy the "vehicle" must appear true to the "tenor." A former professor once said that marriage was like a bath: it was not so hot after you had been in it a while. The bath is the

---

vehicle. Is it true that a bath is not so hot after a while? Most would agree. The tenor refers to marriage. Is it true that marriage, too, cools off after a while? Some might agree, while others would not. You might disagree with the "tenor" of the analogy even if you agree with the vehicle, but the whole thing is useless if you disagree with the "vehicle" itself.

Do you agree that one person plants, another waters, but God gives the growth? If you agree with this vehicle, you may also agree that Paul planted, Apollos watered, but God caused the church to grow (3:5-9). Do you agree that a human body has many parts or members and they all work together to make the whole function? If you agree with this vehicle, you might then accept the tenor that the body of Christ, the church, consists of many varied members who work together as one unit (12:27).

Analogies go wrong when they are not recognized. Because the "vehicle" must be true to life, then the vehicle itself sometimes becomes the message. So many readers of the New Testament suppose the Corinthian Christians were having trouble with prostitution (i.e., the vehicle; 6:12-20), when actually the trouble was failing to live in the new age (the tenor). Analogies also go astray when the tenor is difficult to determine. When we read about the race and competitors in 9:24-27 we may be tempted to say that being a Christian requires winning, while actually the Paul who advocates freedom only says freedom also requires submission to discipline. In any case a good reading of Paul's letter requires close attention to the meaning (tenor) of analogies.

APOSTLE

In 1 Corinthians 1:1 Paul identifies himself as an apostle. He makes the same claim at the beginning of 2 Corinthians, Galatians, Ephesians, Colossians, as well as all three Pastorals. The importance of apostleship can hardly be overestimated, but the meaning and function of the term becomes more difficult to understand. As a noun or a title the word "apostle" does not occur often in Jewish or Greek literature. Many have compared the function of an apostle with the Jewish emissary who could represent the synagogue in a variety of ways. Because of the unique nature of the apostle in the New Testament and Christian history, other origins have, without significant success, been offered. Paul's emphasis on experience has caused some to suspect the apostles understood themselves to be emissaries of the Godhead who brought *gnosis* to willing recipients. While these theories may not be feasible, neither is the later development of the office of apostle true to the original.

In the letters of Paul, the first writings of the New Testament, there seems to be no clear limit to apostleship. In 1 Corinthians 9:6 Paul considers Barnabas an apostle who also has rights to a salary. In 15:5 Paul speaks of Christ appearing to the twelve and then, in v. 7, to all the apostles. If the five hundred of v. 6 were also apostles (taking the "all" of v. 7 to mean "the rest of"), then Paul likely defined apostles as those who had seen the resurrected Lord.

Not long after the writing of 1 Corinthians the gospel tradition began to identify the apostles with the twelve. While the first Gospel, Mark, did not speak of the twelve as apostles (3:13-19), Matthew (10:2-4) and Luke (6:13-16) did. Though the identification of the twelve varies from place to place, the concept has not. Later writers spoke of the twelve apostles as the foundation of the church. At a much later date early Christian leaders, such as bishops, would be compared to the apostles as foremost leaders of the church and as those who would safeguard the tradition. But the gospel tradition only wishes to establish the time of the first community. For the faith community the canon refers to the primacy of the first response to Jesus the Christ. The variety of responses make up what we call the New Testament. That first community is the time of the apostles. The reference to the twelve solidifies the source of that first community—it is the community of the new Israel with its twelve tribes. Any attempt to shift the twelve apostles into a hierarchy appointed by Jesus will miss the point.

AUTHORITY

The issue of authority permeates the entire letter of 1 Corinthians. The reader notices almost immediately that Paul does not exercise authority over the Corinthian Christians. He appeals constantly to the faith community itself. Even in the case of the man living with his stepmother Paul does not suggest his opinion must be obeyed. Rather, when the house church does come together for decision making, he wants his position to be noted (5:1-5). Throughout the letter we see Paul giving his advice, but never ordering. In the letter to Philemon Paul said he could order Philemon to take back Onesimus (v.8), but in 1 Corinthians we lack any such veiled threat. In the earliest period of the church the faith community was itself the final authority. According to Matthew, Jesus said that whatever the community agreed to on earth was also agreed upon in heaven. Where two of the community agreed it would be done in heaven (Mt. 18:18-20).

Paul himself cannot excommunicate, depose leaders, settle disputes, establish procedures in worship, demand financial support, insist on gifts for Jerusalem, deny anyone a second marriage, or establish dietary practices. To be sure, Paul's advice has been sought, but finally he is only one among the total community. At one time it was supposed Paul defined the order of church hierarchy in 12:27-31. And it may be Paul does distinguish between more itinerant leaders like the apostles, prophets and teachers and those who functioned in the local church. But Paul wrote to show that *all* leadership roles were a function of the community guided by the Spirit (12:11). No one stands outside the life of the community. There are leaders, but there is no hierarchy. A close reading of chapter 12 leaves one with the impression Paul wrote that section precisely to counteract those who were beginning to act as if they were outside the community process. In regard to the Lord's Supper he notes that some have become more genuine than others (11:19). Are not these the ones who have tried to shift the function of leadership to the authority of office?

Paul uses the following analogies for leadership: a faith expert (3:1); a servant (3:5); a farmer (3:6-9); an architect/builder (3:10-15); steward (4:2); criminal (4:9); father (4:14-15); and workman (9:1). Only once does Paul appeal to the familial example of the father's authority, and only once does he refer to his superior knowledge and experience (4:16). Otherwise his analogies of leadership refer to facilitation of community growth and functional edification.

If the early Pauline faith community was a Spirit led relational unit, then we must understand leadership as mutual development. Paul's answers to the questions from the Corinthians invariably center on mutuality: good sexual relationships; awareness of different levels of conscience; helpful order in worship; concern for each other in a variety of social, economic, and gender levels. Because of this mutuality the body in chapter 12 has no head— neither Christ nor any type of leader. Indeed, the body is Christ. Just as members of the body develop each other, so also the body develops Christ and Christ the body.[2] While oc-

---

[2]For the corporate nature of Christ/Christa see Rita Brock, *Journeys by Heart: A Christology of Erotic Power* (New York: Crossroad, 1988) 52-53.

casionally we find the words of Jesus used as authority (7:10-11), for the most part we find Paul and the Corinthians reaching for words and narratives which eventually formed our synoptic gospels (7:25-26 to Luke 20:27-33; 8:13 to Mark 9:42).

Some readers believe the earliest church was organized like the synagogue; others like Hellenistic town councils. The earliest Pauline church, as exemplified by the house churches at Corinth, broke with all contemporary modes of organization. The first Christians sensed a "cognitive dissonance" with their society.[3] Paul, and others, called such persons into communities with a rather free floating charismatic relationship. It was not simply Jesus or Paul who were charismatic (led by the Spirit), but all were charismatic. Authority was granted by this charismatic faith community to various people for specific functions. Paul was no exception.

BAPTISM

Some aspects of early Christianity defy analysis. The origin and function of Christian baptism will likely always be one of those. Several origins have been proposed, but no explanation even approaches satisfaction. Some have suggested Christian baptism simply replaces Jewish circumcision. Circumcision was performed on Jewish boys as a sign of their birth into the people of God. It cannot be construed as creating membership in the local synagogue, nor can anyone explain how the surgical act of circumcising could have shifted to a washing act of baptizing. Following the same line of thinking, others have suggested there was a baptism or washing for those who converted to Judiasm. Evidence for such a Jewish practice cannot be fully substantiated.

Most readers assume the actual precedent must have been the baptism of John the Baptist. Certainly the Gospels leave us with that impression, though they never say so explicitly. The baptism of John had nothing to do with joining or membership. All the people who responded to John were already Jews. It is true there was a John the Baptist group in the first century (Acts 19:3), but we have no hint that John

---

[3]On the social effect of cognitive dissonance see Peter Berger and Thomas Luckmann, *The Social Construction of Reality: A Treatise in the Sociology of Knowledge* (Garden City NY: Doubleday, 1967) 116-26; and John Gager, *Kingdom and Community: The Social World of Early Christianity* (Englewood Cliffs NJ: Prentice-Hall, 1975) 39.

formed the group or that his baptism had become a means of joining. John's baptism, according to the Gospels, was an endtime preparation. Expecting an end to this age, John invited Jews to prepare for the new age by a cleansing action. John the Baptist surely did belong to some apocalyptic Jewish group, perhaps even the Essenes of Qumran. The numerous cleansing pools found at the community of Qumran would indicate the importance of such washings (see 1 QS III, 4-12). We cannot say whether Jesus' disciples continued the baptism of John. John 4:1-2 leaves us in a bit of a quandry. Apparently the Jesus group did baptize, though the author reminds us that Jesus, the teacher-prophet, was not the one. Other than that only Matthew, in the Great Commission, speaks of the baptizing activity of the disciples (28:19).

Apparently the origin of Christian baptism lies in the formation of the endtime community. The earliest (Pauline?) communities understood the cross as a sign of the end of the old age, and the resurrection, with its resurrected body of Christ, as a sign of the beginning of the new age. Baptism was an act of leaving the old age (dying to it) and entering the company of the new age (rising to it). Paul says it plainly in Romans: "We were buried therefore with him by baptism into death, so that as Christ was raised from the dead by the glory of the Father, we too might walk in newness of life" (6:4).

This makes sense of John's statement in Mark 1:8, the Jesus saying in Acts 11:16, and the story in Acts 19:1-7. John did baptize for repentance before the endtime. But he did not immerse persons into the fellowship of the new age, the people of the Spirit. In contrast to the teaching of John the Baptist, Paul and his followers saw repentance and conversion as one redemptive motion which included reconciliation in the faith community. Some twenty to thirty years after the writing of Romans, baptism was identified with membership in the church. In Acts (written about the year 85) the disciples could call on people to repent and be baptized. In this way many were added to the church (Acts 2:38, 41, 47).

While baptism was an experience of faith community formation, nevertheless baptism occurred only for adults. Often the faith community must have incorporated persons separated from their families (Mk. 3:35; Mt. 19:29). At other times whole families must have shifted to the faith community (Acts 16:33). Paul himself admits baptizing the household of Stephanas (1:16). That probably means he baptized Stephanas, while the family and servants of Stephanas converted as a matter of course. In the cities of the Roman Empire the rapid growth of the early church was due to the incorporation of many slaves and displaced persons into a new family network.

Since baptism was an action of incorporation into the community of the new age, then baptism was a function of the local community. There was no particular reason for apostles or evangelists to baptize anyone. They would not remain in the community or participate in the house church. That is exactly why there should be no Paul groups or Peter groups in Corinth (1:14).

BODY

In the New Testament the Greek word *soma* always is translated body (possible exceptions are Rev. 18:3 and Col. 2:17), but, as in English, in the Greek there are primary meanings and extended meanings. In 1 Corinthians the Greek term *soma* occurs far more often than in any other book (44 times). In 9:27 it is the physical body that is pommeled, and in 13:3 it is a physical body that may be burned. In one extended meaning *soma* refers to a planet or some other part of the universe (15:40). In the other instances *soma* either refers to human community, the faith community (body of Christ), or occurs in an analogy where both physical (the vehicle) and extended meanings (the tenor, see summary essay, 220) are implied (e.g., the body in chapter 12).

In the case of *soma,* as with several biblical terms based on biblical Hebrew, the primary meaning itself does not correspond to our English. Granted the several instances where the reference is to a physical body, normally body refers to that which defines who we are. Hence, it refers to the primary human community. While we Westerners often think of ourselves as individual bodies with a mind (*nous*) and a soul (*psuche*), in the biblical culture (and many others) persons belong to a corporate body (*soma*) and express their individuality as a person (*psuche*). While we think of ourselves as bodies, they thought of themselves as persons. In the Hebrew Bible the term for person or *pysche* is *nephesh* (Gen. 12:5), not at all to be understood in the western sense as a soul which could be separated from the body.

Understanding the biblical use of body is essential for understanding 1 Corinthians. Only with a corporate concept of body do we understand how Paul was present with the Corinthian Christians (5:3); how Christians are members of the body (6:12-20; 12:12-26); how the body of Christians is the temple of the Holy Spirit (6:19); how husband and wife form the body identity of each other (7:4); how divorce cannot actually separate husband and wife (7:10-11); how the person of the husband or wife can alter the person of the spouse or even a child (7:12-16); how one member of the body is responsible for the formation of others (8:11); how the breaking of bread creates the body of Christ (11:24); how the death of the physical body does not preclude a new life in the resurrected body of Christ (chapter 15).

BURIAL OF THE DEAD

All too often we depend on written, especially literary, documents to help us understand ancient cultures. Those of us who read the New Testament are especially vulnerable. For the most part we use Greek philosophy and literature as a source for understanding the people to whom Paul wrote. However, there are other sources. Since the latter part of the nineteenth archaeologists have uncovered a mass of material and have perfected methods of interpreting what they have found.

Archaeological data comes from houses, public buildings, towns, and above all cemeteries. In many ancient cultures our primary knowledge of them comes from the contents of their tombs. We see how the burial occurred (inhumation or cremation, placement of the family, placement of the cemetery in relationship to the city or village); how they decorated the tomb (inscriptions, art, symbols); and what they placed in the tomb itself (food, dress, weapons, reasons for death).

In the Greco-Roman world, burials were of a fairly uniform type. Family members were buried together in a mausoleum or family plot. The mausoleums were decorated with symbols of religious significance and human friendship. This is especially true of sarcophagi (stone caskets). The placing of the burials in family groups offers us considerable information. First, there is no room here for the idea of the body being simply a storehouse or even a prison for a divine, eternal soul. Death simply is another state of being. The dead are still with the living, though in another mode. The living talk with the dead, eat with the dead, consult their wisdom, and sometimes seek their favor or intervention.

The arrangement of the tombs often demonstrate how the dead lived in houses and on special days "entertained" the living in those houses. We refer to these occasions as meals for the dead on their death day (*refrigeria*).

Second, we know that there were special dead among the burials.[4] These were either mothers and fathers of the family or local heroes. The placing of the tombs indicates that these special dead were surrounded by other dead who wished to be close by. We assume the dead communed with each other; we assume the special dead inhabited a small area near their grave (the presence of such a dead person was called a *daimon* in Greek); and we assume the living could communicate with the special dead when they came to that designated area.

If this picture is correct, and most agree it is, then we can be sure some of the new Christians at Corinth were deeply involved with their family ancestors. Others may have associated with significant dead (heroes) of Corinth. It would have been difficult for this important fact of life not to have impacted the Corinthian Christians and this letter from Paul. It seems likely that a part of Paul's concern about meat offered to idols actually was a reference to eating with the dead. Paul recognized that a person's ancestors could hold him or her in the old age. Is that why he spoke sharply about Christians participating in other cultic meals (10:1-22)? He says there that such tables are the tables of *daimons* (in Greek).

Even more intriguing is the reference to baptism for the dead (15:29). Is it possible Paul gave up trying to isolate the dead of the old age and recognized that those present in a different way (dead family) could also participate in the new age through baptism?

Whatever the truth about Corinth we do know the church eventually adapted the burial practices of the Greco-Roman world. By 155 the remains of Christian leaders were saved so that followers could continue to eat with them (The Martyrdom of Polycarp, 18). By the year 180 burials close to significant Christian martyrs was common. Around the the year 300 a calendar for eating with martyrs was underway.

CHRISTOLOGY

Basic elements of our faith perform certain functions. These faith statements are not doctrines to be believed simply because one is Christian. They are formulations to guide us in key issues of our life. God language speaks of our ultimate values. Christ language ordinarily speaks of reconciliation. In order to understand the Christology of Paul in this

[4]Peter Brown, *The Cult of the Saints: Its Rise and Function in Latin Christianity* (Chicago: The University of Chicago Press, 1981) 5.

letter we need to ask what questions were being asked.

The term Christ is a Greek word, *christos,* meaning "anointed." It translates a Hebrew term *meshiah* with the same meaning, anointed. Used in the context of faith the term refers to the act of selecting persons for divine purposes. Prophets, priests, and kings were all God's anointed. Eventually, however, the term "anointed" referred primarily to the king. Before or at their enthronement kings of Israel were anointed as sons of God. "The anointed one" then tends to refer to the intended or coming king. By the Hellenistic period (320–367 BCE) the term Messiah was reserved for the expected king of the apocalyptic endtime, the kingdom of God.

This expectation of a king of the new age deeply effected Judaism at the time of Jesus. Radical groups hoped for the coming Messiah. Indeed, sometimes they found him. The Jewish historian Josephus occasionally mentions such groups and their dismal failures. Such Messiahs invariably utilized violence and came to tragic endings. They called for the death of the old age under Roman rule and the birth of a new age marked by Jewish freedom. Apparently a number of Jesus' disciples thought he was such a Messiah (Mark 8:29-30; Mt. 20:20-28). But they were mistaken, as Judas so tragically discovered.

Intense expectation of a Messiah altered the nature of Jewish society. Some severed all relationships with the temple, its worship and its administration (especially revolutionaries and Qumranites; see the Temple Scroll). Apparently many persons who sought the company of Jesus were out of touch with the temple (unclean, "people of the land," tax collectors and prostitutes). The speech of Stephen in Acts 7 picked up many of these sentiments (7:48).

Theologically some of these messianists also reread the Hebrew scriptures with an eye for the coming Son of God, or Messiah. They found in Isaiah 7 and 9, for example, not only references to a new king in Israel, but the coming king (Messiah) of the new age. In addition to the intense expectation of a new kingdom, there developed a pattern of texts, taken from the Greek version of the Hebrew Bible, which described the Messiah. We see these primarily in the Gospel of Matthew. They are often introduced by the words "to fulfill what was said by the prophet." We know the pattern well: conceived of a virgin, born in Bethlehem, a voice crying in the wilderness, came from Galilee, misunderstood, marched on Jerusalem, to name a few.

Jesus preached the coming of the kingdom of God (Mark 1:15). He did not speak of a coming Christ, nor, if we take Mark 8:27-33 rather literally, did he identify himself as the Christ. Jesus did not fit the Messianic expectation of the Jewish radicals. He spoke more of the Son of Man as the one who would bring the kingdom. How is it then that Jesus was known so quickly as the Christ? The first Christians identified Jesus with the coming king (1 Thess. 1:9-10). To be sure he did not match the pattern of Messianic expectations developed in Judaism, but the first Christians found new texts (like Isa. 53) and adapted existing ones. For the most part the richness of Christology comes from texts, narratives and analogies describing how Jesus of Nazareth became the Christ of the coming Kingdom.

In 1 Corinthians we see several ways Paul can describe how Jesus the Christ saved us from the old age and delivered us into the new. Though we can hardly say it was Paul who first spoke of the death and resurrection of Jesus as the key story of salvation, it is central to his faith. The cross brought an end to the old age and its sin. The resurrection ushered us, as the body of Christ, into the new age (15:24-25). But there are other ways. In 5:7 Jesus is called the Passover lamb—the lamb killed to commemorate the exodus from slavery in Egypt to freedom in the promised land. In 6:20 Paul says that those of us enmeshed in the old age have been liberated from that servitude by a price paid. Though Paul does not describe the price, it likely was the cross (8:11). For the more Jewish types Paul speaks of the old age as the realm of Adam, while the new life comes in the realm of Christ (15:22-23). Not only was Jesus the Passover lamb, but he was also the support system in the exodus (the Rock, 10:4).

How does Christ reconcile? By freeing us from enmeshment in the old age and/or our spirit of rebellion. By bringing us into the new age where those enmeshed are free to be themselves and those in rebellion have found a community of love and respect.

CHURCH

In the Hebrew Bible images of Israel invariably reflect a corporate entity. From the beginning Israel was known as the people of God (Exodus 3:7) or people of Israel (Exodus 19:3). In the pivotal covenant ceremony between God and Israel, the people are called a kingdom and a nation (Exodus 19:6). Other images stress the corporate nature of Israel: a vineyard (Isaiah 5:7); a flock (Psalm 23:1-2); or a family (Hosea

11:1-2).

As in the Hebrew Bible, in the New Testament metaphors of the church also reflect corporate images, though individual conscious membership appears much more often. As the people of God were holy, or chosen for God's purpose, so individual members are called "holy ones" or "saints." The term does not stress heroic virtuosity, but marks participation in the chosen people who serve to fulfill God's promise. For the most part Paul simply refers to members of the faith community as saints (1 Cor. 16:1), but occasionally he identifies them by means of apposition: God's beloved (Rom. 1:7); those sanctified (1 Cor. 1:2); and churches of the saints (1 Cor. 14:33).

Likewise the image of family continues in the New Testament. Paul does not often speak of the church as a family or household (Gal. 6:10; 2:19), but he calls members of the church brothers (1 Cor. 1:10) or sisters (1 Cor. 7:15), and all siblings are children of God (Rom. 8:16-21; 9:8!).

The term "member" itself (Greek *melos*) refers to participation in another major corporate image for church, the body (Greek *soma*). The metaphor of the body occurs primarily in the letters of Paul, especially 1 Corinthians. We find it particularly in chapter 12 (cf. Rom. 12:3-5), but also in the analogy of 6:15-20 (cf. Rom. 6:19). The metaphors of people and family have remained very important in Christian history, but none have played so prominent a role as body—the body of Christ. The new age began with the resurrection of Jesus, and the church was known as his body. At the heart of church formation was (and still is) the eating together of bread and wine, the body and blood. The church understands itself as Christ's body broken for the world, yet also one for the world.

Readers have often asked if Jesus founded the church. Some suppose Jesus chose leaders to become the basis for the universal church (the apostles). Others believe Jesus did not intend a formal organization, so the formation of any church at all was contrary to the intention of Jesus. Others suppose the failure of the end to come resulted in an organization created by the disappointed, but determined followers. Some believe Jesus was part of a Jewish group which itself became the basis for the first Christian communuity. Attempts to separate Jesus (identify the historical Jesus and his intentions) from the church ignores the corporate nature of the faith community. The Jesus of the Gospels cannot be distinguished from the people, the family, his body, the faith community. When the faith community reads the Gospels, it reads of it-self.

CONSCIENCE

The term "conscience," so important in Christian history, first oc-curs in 1 Corinthians 8:7. In the discussion about eating meat offered to idols Paul refers to Christians whose conscience is weak and who would be defiled if they saw Christians with stronger consciences eating the meat in question. The root meaning of the Greek term *suneidesis* means to "know with," the same as its Latin (and therefore English) transla-tion. Originally it could refer to awareness of something or someone, such as awareness of God (1 Pet. 2:19). But more often it refers to that commonly accepted moral awareness found in every individual. Fre-quently the writers of the New Testament refer to the satisfaction of a good conscience (Heb. 13:18; 1 Pet. 3:16), a condition which must have been akin to *shalom* in the Hebrew Bible (Isa. 32:17-18). Less fre-quently they also speak of a bad conscience (Heb. 10:22), a condition similar to the lack of peace so often noted by the prophets (Jer. 8:9-15).

Later in Christian history some understand the conscience to be a God-given guide based on a universal, divine ethical standard. More recently the conscience has been understood as that which leads one to repentance (Luther),[5] or creates in us crippling guilt (Freud).[6]

A closer look at biblical anthropology indicates both later devel-opments have led us astray. The conscience marks that formation mo-ment which occurs between our awareness of individuality (*psuche*) and our dependence on our primary network (*soma*). Because we are all cre-ated by our primary network, we all have the sensation of conscience. But, because every network has a different sense of what is required for "peace," the content of conscience will differ from group to group. Vi-olation of the expectations of the primary network will create the pain of conscience. Many of those norms are not moral by the usual defini-tion. They could be social graces, customs, and group or peer practices. Though often misguided in terms of universal practice, the conscience,

[5]Krister Stendahl, "The Apostle Paul and the Introspective Conscience of the West," *Harvard Theological Review* 56 (1963): 199-215.

[6]Donald E. Miller, *The Wing-footed Wanderer. Conscience and Transcendence* (Nashville: Abingdon, 1977).

nevertheless, is our most powerful social force. The free church depends on the power of conscience rather than the force of state and national religion.

But when one shifts from one primary group to another (conversion) how is the conscience redeveloped? That was the problem facing Paul in Corinth—or in any of the Hellenistic churches. Paul always calls for patience. When the expectations of conscience have been changed, it takes time for persons to be sure that they will find *shalom* as individuals. For example, when a person has been formed to find acceptance through law, then grace or love, as a basis of acceptance, becomes very difficult (see Phil. 3:3-11; Mark 10:17-22).

For those who believe no force in religion should be used, freedom of conscience must be upheld. However, the slogan "freedom of conscience" can be easily misunderstood or abused. It does not mean there can be a variety of interpretations of the divine law. Rather, it means we recognize a variety of formations, and, like Paul, we accept the importance of each person's development (Rom. 14:1-23).[7] At the same time we also recognize that the formation of a new network takes considerable time and patience. Christians should not be impatient or judgmental, since our goal for everyone is God's *shalom* for the community and personal strength for every member (Rom. 14:19).

CONVERSION

Conversion has so often been associated with Paul that some word about the concept needs to be mentioned. Our English word "repentance" translates a Greek word, *metanoia,* which means a change of mind. Though there is little sense of guilt implied by the term *metanoia,* a change of mind often would be accompanied by dissatisfaction with one's prior decisions (Mt. 27:3). During the time of Jesus the Greek term *epistrepho* became synonymous with *metanoeo.* In the Greek Old Testament it translated the great word *shub,* used so often by the prophets to call for Israel to "turn around" and go a different way. These terms, "change of mind" and "turn around" occur fairly often in the New Testament, but seldom in Paul.

---

[7]Robert Jewett, *Christian Tolerance: Paul's Message to the Modern Church* (Philadelphia: Westminster Press, 1982) 134-37.

There is no place in Paul for a personal conviction of sin, regrets, and for a personal decision to believe in Christ (in our sense of the term). The nonbeliever, who lives in the old age, has been granted the possibility of a life of faith in the new age. That possibility is a gift of God, not, strictly speaking, a personal decision. The basic paradigm for the shift comes in the death and resurrection of Jesus Christ (Rom. 5:6-11). The cross and the empty tomb symbolize leaving the old age and entering the new. We reenact that death and resurrection when we are baptized (Rom. 6:1-4). Paul can use other images to signify the change, such as liberation from slavery (to sin; Rom. 6:6; 1 Cor. 6:20). Occasionally that act of freeing is also expressed in Jewish liturgical terms, e.g., in Romans 3:24-26 the cross reflects the sacrificial system.

Conversion then is not so much the personal decision, but the acceptance of the shift offered by God through Christ. Paul warns about slipping back to the old age (Gal. 3:1-5; 4:9). One may live in the ambiguity of the two ages, but to accept the values of the old age while presuming to live in the new certainly can confuse the people of the new covenant. That is why Paul wants the man living with his stepmother removed from the community of the new age (1 Cor. 5:5).

COVENANT

The term "covenant" describes the ways in which people relate to each other. When a person or a group of persons wish to align themselves to a superior person, we call it a suzerainty covenant. The superior is willing to be bound to certain stipulations in order to secure the loyalty and support of a vassal. Though no example or text of such a covenant appears in the Bible, it is everywhere apparent. Ezekiel 17:11-21 refers to a covenant between the king of Babylon and a prince of Jerusalem. When persons who are more or less equal bind together we speak of it as a parity covenant. Such covenants occur between two people, like the one between Jacob and Laban in Gen. 31:44-50, or between larger peoples, like the one between Israel and the Gibeonites (Josh. 9:3-27).

Readers of the Bible are more aware of the covenant, *berith* (Heb.) or *diatheke* (Greek), as a metaphor of the relationship between Israel and God. The paradigm covenant occurs in Genesis 15 (and 17) where God agrees to certain benefits for Abraham and his descendents if they agree to a vassal relationship. The covenant was established by an ancient ceremony involving the halves of sacrificed animals. The Hebrew people lived out of their self-awareness as God's covenant people. The document describing the odyssey of the covenant people is itself the covenant (called by many Christians the Old Testament).

The covenant establishes an intentional network, though its intentional nature wanes as continuing generations take their covenant for granted (as have the Jewish people through the centuries). In the covenant relationship a particular style of life formation is developed (Deut. 6:6-9, 20-24); the limits of social relationships are described (Deut. 5:12-21); appropriate behavior with God is made known (Deut. 5:7-11; 6:4-5). Normally the content of the covenant is made known to the next generation through stories, tabletalk, and action (ethical as well as liturgical). Eventually, though, covenant can become simply habit and pro forma affirmations. The original paradigm can become an event which formed the people rather than a defintion of the human network. The vibrant quality of life lived in a supportive, progressive community may shift to a contractual organization based on law.[8] The prophets were aware of these problems. They not only chastized the Jews for acting contrary to their own covenant (Hosea 6:7), but they spoke of a day when the original sense of covenant would return to the Jewish people (Jer. 31:31-34). Christianity is one result of that hope.

Jesus called for a renewal of the original sense of covenant when he said, "You have heard it said, but I say . . . " (Mt. 5:21-48). More importantly, the synoptic Gospels and Paul, in their account of the Last Supper, understand the meal as the ceremonial establishment (like Genesis 15) of the new covenant (1 Cor. 11:25; Mk. 14:24; Mt. 26:28; Lk. 22:20). In the letter to the Galatians Paul picks up more of the prophetic hope for a new covenant. In one of the few allegories of the New Testament Paul compares the old covenant with the child of the slave Hagar and the new covenant with the child of the free woman Sarah (Gal. 4:21-31). In a slightly different vein Paul says the covenant cannot be passed on through law, but only through promise (Gal 3:15-18). Centuries before modern sociology the apostle Paul saw that covenants may be permanent, but they must be constantly renewed. The faith community cannot exist from generation to generation on the basis of

[8]Victor Turner, *The Ritual Process: Structure and Antistructure* (Ithaca: Cornell University Press, 1969) 132; Ernst Troeltsch, *The Social Teaching of the Christian Churches*, 2 vols., trans. Olive Wyon (London: George Allen & Unwin, 1950) 1:43-51.

contractual law.

Like its predecessor, Judaism, Christianity also lost its sense of a community based on love and freedom. Eventually, in the 4th century, Christianity became the dominant religion of the Roman Empire. By then it stressed faith as assent to doctrine, and kept a cohesive Christian society intact by means of law and imperial force. The Roman hegemony was broken up by the Reformation, but it took the Left Wing of the Reformation to return Christianity to a covenant sense of faith shared by adults.

ENDTIME

The term "endtime" is used as a synonym for eschatology (Greek *eschaton*, last). Eschatology, properly speaking, refers to a study of or consideration of the end. The adjective eschatological, "endtime" in this commentary, refers not only to the consideration of the end, but the effect of the approaching end on our lives today. Besides clarity, one advantage of the term "endtime" is that it can also refer to the nature of the end or eschaton.

Judeo-Christians have always looked at life from an endtime perspective. Biblical faith depends on a movement from promise to fulfillment. The fulfillment of a promise, and our movement toward it, is rightly understood as endtime orientation. At first the Jews thought only of the time when God's purposes for the world would be realized. But during the monarchy, as serious injustices appeared, the prophets began to speak of that endtime as a day of judgment—a day when people would be held accountable for failing to live the life of the promise. It was known simply as "that day." Eventually, after the exile, the coming of the day of promise (and judgment) was understood to be in the hands of God rather than the Jewish people. This understanding of the endtime can be found in the book of Daniel and apocalyptic literature of the period before the New Testament.

When the prophets first began to speak of "that day" they meant it as a statement of judgment about the Jews (or other nations) of that time. Eventually those prophets more involved in apocalypticism began to use the endtime expectation as a means of exhortation. When the people were lax and acting contrary to the covenant community, prophets spoke of immediacy of the endtime—the day is at hand (Zeph. 1:7-9; cf. Mk. 1:15). When the people were discouraged and the Lord's promises seemed far away, the prophets said the endtime was delayed—

wait for it (Hab. 2:3; cf. Heb. 10:37-38). The first Christians came from the more radical Jewish endtime groups. Like the intertestamental apocalypticists, the early Christians spoke of an immediate endtime (Mk. 13:35-37). Yet they too encouraged the new believers to stand firm until the end would come (Mk. 13:7). By the time of Paul they spoke of the new faith community as the first fruits of the coming kingdom. Through the resurrection the anticipated kingdom had already come. As the first Christians waited for the final end they sought direction for their everyday life. From this need for guidance arose the Gospels. The life and teachings of Jesus became the guidelines for the early faith communities. Therefore the first Christians also understood that the kingdom began with the baptism of Jesus (Mark) or birth (Matthew, Luke) of Jesus (see Mk. 1:11; Luke 1:30-33). As they developed the sense of Jesus as the sovereign of the kingdom, they spoke of the kingdom as already present in him. So among the early Christians there grew a sense of the kingdom present, a sense not found in apocalyptic Judaism. This sense of the present kingdom has been called "realized eschatology" by many students of the New Testament.[9] We find this sense of realized eschatology in a number of sayings of Jesus (Luke 4:21; Mt. 11:4-6).

So in early Christianity we find a sense of the endtime at hand, a sense of it delayed, and a sense of it already partially present. Later some Christians thought the expectation of an end was a literal chronological expectation rather than a way of exhorting the faithful. When they literalized the endtime, they then supposed Jesus was mistaken about the end. To correct the problem the early Christians proposed Jesus was delayed (note John 21:22-23) for what would be a long time (2 Peter 3:8-9). Since endtime thinking has functioned to alter behavior since the time of the Exile (ca. 580 BCE), it would be futile to speak of the endtime message of Jesus as something unique, or as a mistake. There is no more of a literal delay in the teaching of Jesus than in Habakkuk.

Christians, like Jews, understand that one always lives in anticipation of the fulfillment of God's promises. Such hope is an essential mark of the Christian (1 Cor. 13:13). For that reason we speak of the

---

[9]C. H. Dodd, *The Parables of the Kingdom* (London: James Nisbet & Co., 1935ff.) 51; rev. ed. (New York: Scribner's, 1961) 35.

New Testament presenting a permanent eschatology.[10] To be Christian is to be always at the edge of the endtime.

EUCHARIST

The term "eucharist" derives from the Greek word *eucharisto*, I give thanks. It comes from the opening thanksgiving prayer of a Jewish religious meal, often associated with the cup of wine (Mk. 14:23; Mt. 26:27; Lk. 22:17; though note 22:19). For reasons difficult to determine, there were two forms of the eucharist in the early church. After we examine the texts and the history, it would appear that the first eucharist was an adaptation of a Jewish religious meal, perhaps the Passover. That meal consisted of a prayer of thanksgiving, a cup of wine, a prayer of blessing and then a rather set meal, including bread. The Jewish meal was one of expectation, with the participants looking forward to the fulfillment of God's promises.

The first eucharist, spoken of as the breaking of bread in Acts 2:42, 46, celebrated the unity of the faith congregation (*koinonia*, being in common or communion). The cup was drunk first (1 Cor. 10:16) and then the one bread shared (1 Cor. 10:17). The meal celebrated the unity of the community in the present and in the age to come. Once we understand this form of the eucharist, we can see its rich history in Christian tradition. We can suspect it became the *agape* or love feast we have seen in 1 Corinthians 11:17-22. We also suspect it coalesced with the popular meal for the dead (see summary essay, 228). Whatever happened, the only eucharist portrayed in early Christian art shows about seven people sitting at a table with fish, seven or twelve baskets of bread and a cup of wine.[11] According to the art we possess, the common meal of the early Christians through, perhaps, seven centuries, was a breaking of the one loaf as a sign of unity. The meal is described in the gospel stories of the feeding of the five thousand. There Jesus had compassion (love?), accepted the offering of a boy, prayed, blessed the bread, broke the bread, fed the multitude bread and fish, and still had seven or twelve baskets left over. In the early church the remaining (intentional) food was given to the poor (as, perhaps, earlier in Jerusalem, Acts 6:1).

---

[10]The rubric was used by Dominic Crossan in his *In Parables: The Challenge of the Historical Jesus* (New York: Harper & Row, 1973) 26.

[11]Snyder, *Ante Pacem*, 64-65.

This form of the fellowship eucharist can first be seen in an early Christian document called now the Didache. In it the prayers refer to the one loaf on the mountain shared by the faithful (9:4). It ends with the prayer for the endtime to come (*maranatha,* 10:6). Some elements of the meal can be seen in the worship materials saved for us by the church father Hippolytus. We do know that by the third century people like Hippolytus had organized a strong segment of the church around the fellowship meal, the power of saints, and large cemetery fellowships.

There was a second form of the eucharist. As the Passover redramatized the exodus from Egypt, so the eucharist redramatized the death and resurrection of Jesus. The primary event of liberation for the Jews was the escape from Egypt and the entrance into the promised land. Every year, to this day, they reenact that saving event. According to the synoptic Gospels, Jesus took the celebration of the Passover and shifted it to his own death and resurrection. That death and resurrection liberated a person from the old age and brought them to the edge of the new. Consequently a eucharist developed which reenacted the cross and the resurrection of the new body of Christ. That reenactment began, as it should, with the breaking of the bread, the body. After the believers reenact the cross by breaking the bread, they then drink of the cup. In that way they reenact the spilling of the blood which marks the beginning of the new covenant (as the blood of the Passover lamb marked the liberation from the Egyptians, Ex. 12:21-27; cf. also Gen. 15:7-11 for the Old Covenant). In Paul's tradition of the Last Supper this reenacting of the redemptive event is called the *anamnesis*. In 1 Corinthians 11:24 he said to do (act out) this breaking of bread (the body on cross) in remembrance of me (the *anamnesis*). The "remembrance" tradition can be found in the accounts of the Last Supper in the Synoptics, in 1 Corinthians 11:23-26, and in Justin Martyr, *Apologia* 65-66.

The two eucharists are very important. One celebrates and actualizes the endtime unity of the faith community. The other reenacts the liberating event which released us from the old age and brought us to the new. Historically the church has attempted to celebrate both, though with varying success and in vastly different ways. One obvious way has been to combine the two. Some churches today celebrate both a fellowship meal (*agape*) and an *anamnesis* (most notably the Church of the Brethren). Less formally, potlucks may replace the ancient *agape*. In the fourth and fifth centuries the church did try to combine the two. Under the leadership of Augustine and Ambrose the church forced the fellowship meal of the cemetery into the newly built city churches. Bones of the saints taken from the cemetery churches were placed under the altar of these churches (heretofore there were only house churches; see summary essay, 248). In this way both the *anamnesis* and the fellowship meal with the saints could be celebrated as one liturgy—the mass of the medieval church. This mass, an amalgam of this *agape* and *anamnesis,* became the primary sacrament of the Roman church.

As a sacrament the elements of the eucharist became salvific for those receiving them. During the middle ages, then, the bread of eucharist became actually the body of Christ. The "this" of 1 Corinthians 11:24 was understood to be the bread itself rather than the act of breaking the bread. The Reformation tried to break with the medieval understanding of the eucharist. Some insisted that the sacramental value of the bread and wine depended on the receptivity of the communicant. But others, of the so-called Left Wing of the Reformation, tried to return to the original sense of communion. They believed the miracle was in the creation of the community of the new age.

FORM, FORMULAS, AND SLOGANS

Any letter written today would have a set form. A personal letter would begin with a date of writing and the greeting "Dear . . . ." A business letter would begin with the date written, the return address of the sender, the full address of the receiver and the greeting "Dear . . . ." Most of us would recognize the type of letter simply by looking at the form.

The same was true in biblical times. Letters were often written by scribes and they followed a set form learned from their teacher. A typical letter is this early Christian letter found in Egypt:

Irenaeus to Apollinarius his beloved brother, many greetings. I pray continually for your health, and I am well myself. I want you to know that I reached land on the 6th of the month Epeiph and we unloaded on the 18th of the same month. I went up to Rome on the 25th of the same month, and the placed received us, as God willed, and every day we expect our dismissal, though up to now none of the corn fleet has been released. Many greetings to your wife, and Serenus, and all who love you, each by name.

Goodbye. Mesore 9

This typical letter illustrates the usual form of a private letter:

Address :	Irenaeus to Apollinarius
Greeting :	many greetings
Prayer (or Thanksgiving) :	I pray continually
Disclosure :	I want you to know
Request (lacking in this letter) :	I beseech you
Salutation :	many greetings
Date :	Mesore 9

1 Corinthians follows much the same pattern:

Address :	Paul to church at Corinth
Greeting :	Grace and peace
Prayer :	I give thanks
Disclosure :	Do you not know
Request :	I appeal to you, brethren
Salutation :	I, Paul, write this greeting

The readers of 1 Corinthians would have recognized Paul's letter as personal letter between friends. They would have recognized the phrases mentioned above as part of the normal letter. They also would have noted some differences. For example, the greeting of 1:3 included the Hebrew form (peace or, in Hebrew, *shalom*).

Letter writers used other phrases to guide us as we read. In 1 Corinthians there are not as many as formulas as in other Pauline letters. We do note some. Most obvious is the short phrase, *peri de* in Greek, which indicates a question from the letter written to Paul by the Corinthians (7:1; 7:25; 8:1; 12:1; 16:1; 12:1). Another formula, *gegraptai* in Greek, introduces a quotation from the Hebrew Scriptures (1:19; 1:31; 2:9; 3:19; 9:9; 10:7; 14:21; 15:45; cf. 6:16; 15:54). In one place (4:6) Paul even discusses the meaning of the formula "it is written." Twice Paul indicates that what he writes actually was a part of early Christian tradition (11:23; 15:3; note 15:1). He uses the formula "for I delivered what I received."

In addition to formulas, we find in 1 Corinthians some phrases which must have had a special meaning to both Paul and the Christians at Corinth. It is imperative that we take special note of these lest we misinterpret their meaning and function. We cannot be sure we have seen every slogan, but we can note some of the more obvious ones.

1:12 "I belong to . . . ." The Corinthian Christians indicated which house church was theirs by saying, "I belong to Paul," or "I belong to Apollos."

4:6 "According to the scriptures." Some of the Corinthian Christians must have insisted on warrants from the Hebrew Scriptures which differed from Paul's. He refers to their slogan in a sarcastic manner.

6:12 "All things are lawful." Paul must have described life in the new age as freedom from Jewish law. The Corinthians used the slogan to claim that freedom. It occurs again in 10:23.

6:13 "Food is meant for the stomach and the stomach for food." The freedom of 6:12 is buttressed by another slogan in 6:13. We do not know its origin, but Paul counters with a slogan of his own: "The body is for the Lord, and the Lord for the body."

7:1 "It is better for a man not to touch a woman." This slogan takes the form of a "better than" saying like those found in Proverbs and Ecclesiastes (Ecc. 2:24; 4:13). We suspect the Corinthians Christians took some of the slogans out of context. This would be a prime example. The comparison, introduced by "than," is missing. It surely said it would be better to give up sex altogether than to abuse it. But the spiritual types in Corinth took it to mean it was better never to have a sexual relationship.

7:9b "For it is better to marry than to be aflame with passion." If 7:1 was a "better than" saying, then it would be difficult to deny the same for 7:9b. But like 7:1 we know nothing about the use or origin of the saying. Presumably it was an exaggerated apocalyptic saying which said it was better to marry (again?) rather than do moral damage.

8:1 "All of us possess knowledge." Despite Paul's unhappiness with the gnostic types at Corinth, he also must have held spiritual knowledge in high regard. So this slogan likely came from the preaching of Paul himself. He does not deny the validity of the slogan, but places love over against it.

8:4 "An idol has no real existence." This slogan reflects Isaiah 46, but there is no precise quote. The ineffectiveness of idols must have been a strong element in Jewish teaching to the Gentiles. In 1 Thessalonians 1:9, a summary of Paul's preaching to the Gentiles, the object of Paul's mission was to turn people from dumb idols to the living God. The second slogan, "There is no God but one," could also reflect Isaiah 46:9, though it could also be a rephrasing of the great

Jewish confession (Shema) in Deut. 6:4-9.

12:3 "Jesus be cursed." Difficult as it may be to imagine, it would appear that this slogan arose with radical gnostic types. The church between the times was beginning to use Jesus as the basis for its day-to-day life. The more spiritual types found the guidance of the risen Lord more satisfactory. To combat the growing power of the gospel stories, they coined the slogan, "Jesus be cursed." As in several previous instances, Paul responds with another slogan, the early Christian proclamation, "Jesus is Lord."

GLORY

The term "glory" does not play as important a role for Paul as it does for John, yet even in 1 Corinthians it occurs in some important places (11:7; 15:40-43). The Greek word *doxa* translates a Hebrew word *kabod* which originally means heavy or heaviness (Job 28:25). A person can be heavy (Gen. 34:19?) or can be heavy by virtue of possessions (Psalm 49:16). In a world of limited goods possessions would naturally mark the fame or reputation of a person. Clothing, marriage arrangements, garments, military might can make a person or nation weighty. Though difficult to define in a precise way, some obvious synonyms for glory are: honor, reputation, fame, weightiness, visibility, power, brightness, praise, and even boasting.

The glory of God picks up most of these attributes. The divine glory normally is sensed by humans in terms of powerful presence. The divine presence appeared like a devouring fire on Mt. Sinai (Ex. 24.13-18). It hung as a cloud over the tabernacle, sometimes so powerfully it prevented even Moses from entering (Ex. 40:34-38). The glory continued to be present primarily at moments of worship. When Isaiah attended the enthronement of a new king he heard a song which described a whole world filled with the Lord's glory (presence, Isa. 6:3).

Paul uses the term *doxa* in many ways. He, too, can speak of the *kabod* of human beings, their fame and reputation. He told the Thessalonian Christians he was not seeking glory (2:6). Rather he works for the glory (fame?) of God (2 Cor. 8:19) and wishes all would do the same (1 Cor. 10:31). Like other biblical writers, for Paul glory remains primarily an ascription of God, and in the Lord we have access to that splendor (2 Cor. 3:12-18). Glory becomes more difficult to define when extended beyond the sense of powerful presence. In 1 Corinthians 11

Paul says man is the glory of God and woman is the glory of man. Apparently Paul means the male person is the fame or public presence of God, while the female person (in addition?) is the public presence of the family. The meaning seems clear, but the intent has escaped most readers, except to say that in public worship the man has some particular obligation to God, and woman has an additional social, public obligation as woman.

Paul can speak of degrees of *doxa* (2 Cor. 3:18) in God, and also can compare the *doxa* of one star with another or the *doxa* of the earth with that of the heavens (1 Cor. 15). Paul tries to build a case for the resurrection with these comparisons. While alive we may have a certain kind of glory, or even, to the contrary, dishonor, but in the resurrection that which is weak or lacking in honor has been given *doxa*. He apparently means the same thing when he says we are corruptible while alive, but incorruptible in the resurrection body. The promise of the resurrection is a new kind of *doxa,* or presence, in the body network.

GNOSTICISM

The discovery during 1945 of a storage jar filled with gnostic documents near the Egyptian village of Nag Hammadi has changed our understanding of the beginning of Christianity. These documents were the first large collection of materials written by the Christian gnostic groups themselves. [12] Heretofore we had depended heavily on the writings of the early Christian bishop, Irenaeus (ca. 180) for our knowledge of the gnostic groups. From Christian opponents we learned that gnostic Christians were contentious, libertine, used obscure language, and threatened the church. The documents themselves give us a much broader picture than what we have previously learned.

Actually we still have very little information about the gnostic movement, or about their way of life, though we do have much more information about their ideas. For the most part Christian gnostics quarreled with the Jewish understanding of Creation. When Adam and Eve ate of the forbidden fruit they knew (had *gnosis*); they were then ashamed of their previous ignorant existence and of the god who would make such persons (cf. Coptic gnostic tractate *On the Origin of the World*

---

[12] Gnostic and gnosticism are often capitalized. Here they appear lowercase, since gnosticism designates a rather anomalous, even amorphous philosophy and/or movement.

¶119). Their divinities were often obscure combinations of Jewish names for God, such as Yaldabaoth or Eleleth. Their alteration of the Jewish creation narrative often led to a denigration of the created order and an emphasis on spiritual life and truth. It is revealing that the most famous gnostic document, the very early *Gospel of Thomas*, contains many sayings of Jesus, but few narratives or stories.

Very likely the accusations about libertinism and sexual licence were overstated, though a disregard for creation can lead to its abuse. Some scholars believe the gnostic groups expressed more equality of the sexes than the male dominated mainline church, and that among gnostics congregational democracy prevailed even after the orthodox churches had adapted hierarchical power structures.

What then is gnosticism? Probably there is no answer. Obviously, as its name implies, it is a movement or attitude which stresses spiritual knowledge. As an attitude gnosticism is always present. Every congregation at any time always has some persons who thirst for a deeper understanding of the spiritual life. They read certain books (which might use language obscure to some); they attend special retreats on spiritual life and they develop certain spiritual disciplines. That gnosticism is always present. But the gnosticism of the Nag Hammadi documents apparently comes from Judaism itself. It represents a struggle with the earthiness of the Jewish faith. It found in early Christianity a spiritual home. Yet there was in the whole Greco-Roman world an attitude of disdain for the earthy. Movements like Neoplatonism could speak of the body as the prison of the soul. Other documents spoke of a divine spark in some people which needed to be free of the material world. A savior or revelator was expected, one who could free us from material things and allow us to live in or with the divine fullness (pleroma).

We may suspect the Christ party at Corinth was a gnostic house church. To be sure, we have no indication of a Jewish basis for this early Christian gnosticism. Yet we cannot ignore the facts: any city like Corinth would have fostered spiritual types (including Jewish). Some of these probably became Christians and formed a group that separated itself from the others.

HONOR AND SHAME

For some cultures the demand of the law or the pressure of rectitude creates guilt when the individual cannot measure up to the demand or the pressure. Most of us in the western world understand redemption in terms of guilt. For that reason we often speak of Jesus Christ dying for our sins. A price must be paid for the guilt we have incurred. In most societies such guilt would not be the basic problem; indeed, it may not even exist. The real problem could be described as one of honor. In most cultures the sense of individuality derives from a group consciousness. Acceptance and respect from the primary group (honor) overshadows all other considerations. To be rejected by the primary group would be death, worse than physical death. In such cultures the individual will go to any length to protect and enhance group respect, or, vice versa, will do anything to avoid loss of face. The language to describe this translates into English as honor and shame.

Persons who somehow demonstrated incompatibility with the community were living in shame. We think of the woman with the flow of blood who crept up behind Jesus to touch him (Mk. 5:27), or the lepers who stood at a distance and pled for mercy (Lk. 17:12). Those who were accepted by the community and who possessed family and wealth were said to have honor. One thinks of the wealthy young man who could not sacrifice his honor to follow Jesus (Mk. 10:22), or Job, who epitomized what honor meant in the Hebrew Bible (Job 1:1-5; 29). For people to leave family, home, community, and possessions meant a serious loss of honor. Consequently we see the frequent affirmation that God will grant believers honor in the endtime, or better, will not be ashamed of them (Phil. 1:20; Mk. 8:38; 2 Tim. 2:15). Or to the contrary the recalcitrant believer may end up in unbearable shame (2 Thess. 3:14).

To boast is to be self-conscious of one's own honor and make others self-conscious of it. Of all the New Testament writers Paul especially is concerned about the dangers of self conscious honor. He argues that no one has the right to boast (1:29; 3:21). In fact, if one can boast it is only within the body of Christ, that is, to witness to what God has done in Christ (1:31). Actually, Paul raises the issue to a significant faith level. Honor is only possible as a gift of God. It does not come from family, network, social status, or wealth (the old age). In chapter 4 of 1 Corinthians Paul states his case. The person worthy of praise receives such honor from God (4:5). Since that honor is a gift, why do the members of the Christ house church continue to boast about their progress in the faith (4:7)? Why is it they seem to be held in honor while he, their mentor, still lives in shame (4:10-13).

Paul's conflict with the spiritualists might provide a clue to the new definition of honor. We all know Paul is the honored apostle, yet he still suffers like a condemned criminal (4:9). Honor comes from living with the faith community between the two ages, not from entering the new. As an individual, Paul, with some boasting, can claim honor as one who suffered for the Lord (2 Cor. 10-13), as one commended by the Lord (2 Cor. 10:18).

HOUSE CHURCH

From the beginning the Christians met in houses. According to Acts 2:46 and 5:42 they worshiped constantly in the temple and in their houses. One assumes the upper room of some house was often the location of their meetings (Acts 1:13; 20:8), as it was the place of the first Lord's Supper (Luke 22:12). Wherever they were, apparently, Ephesus (1 Cor. 16:19) or Rome (Rom. 16:3-5), Aquila and Priscilla entertained a church in their house. When Paul wrote to Philemon regarding his slave Onesimus, he also addressed the church which met at Philemon's house (Philem. 2). Only one time does Paul indicate his letter should be shared with another house church (Col. 4:15). Popular early Christian literature like the Apocryphal Acts constantly mentions Christian meetings in houses, though early patristic literature makes sparse reference to houses as the locus for Christian assembly. At the same time there is no indication that all the Christians of a city ever met in one place (Justin Martyr, *Apology* 67).

Much of the church language of the New Testament, and especially that of Paul, reflects a household or kinship network.[13] Especially obvious are the terms sister and brother, language not prominent in Judaism or in Hellenistic cults. The house church fellowship has become the new family for its members. Paul speaks sharply of himself as father (see explanatory notes on 4:14-15), and of the Corinthians as babies or children (3:1-2).

So the earliest churches were quite small groups. We cannot say for certain how large a house church could have been. Banks (pp. 41-42) estimates forty to forty-five at the most. That seems reasonable for a large apartment. A villa surely could have accommodated one hundred people in its peristyle (columnar section between the atrium and the triclinium). One suspects not many early Christians owned such a villa. The house church (*domus ecclesiae*) and its small congregation continued

---

[13]Robert Banks, *Paul's Idea of Community: The Early House Churches in Their Historical Setting* (Grand Rapids: Eerdmans, 1980) 33-42, 52-61.

as the only form of the Christian fellowship until about 250 CE. It must be said that surely the church had sufficient resources to build or purchase larger places of meeting. They did not. The small house church apparently was congruent with the nature of the Christian faith. The buildings in which house churches assembled may have survived the centuries, but we cannot identify them. About 250 CE Christians began to make alterations in the houses. Fortunately, we have an example in the Syrian city of Dura-Europos. Besides converting a closet to a baptistery, one wall was demolished to create a larger room. From about that time on we have remains of remodeled halls (*aula ecclesiae*) holding perhaps up to two hundred people. Only after 300 CE did the Christians build church edifices (S. Crisogono in Rome). After the fourth-century, public Christianity met in larger halls and basilicas, but through the centuries church groups have tended toward small congregations and meetings in houses.[14]

JESUS

The man Jesus was likely born about 6 BCE in Palestine. He began a ministry in the early thirties and then was crucified, under Pontius Pilate, as a Messianic pretender about 32 CE. We know precious little more about him except through those around him who repeated his words and stories of his deeds. There is no reason to suspect the veracity of these accounts, but we do understand that we have whatever was selected and interpreted in terms of the earliest church. The church, living between the time of the cross and the time of the end, called forth the synoptic Gospels for direction in its daily life, its worship, its preaching, its relationship to nonbelievers, and its own structure. It is through these materials that we know the man Jesus.

We can see in 1 Corinthians the beginning of that process of pulling from the tradition those materials needed for the church. The words of Jesus about marriage and divorce were used by Paul to buttress his own teaching on the subject (7:10-11). The story of the Last Supper was used to describe the eucharist of the Corinthian church (11:23-26). There are more subtle attachments to Jesus. The Passion narrative (cross) is used to guide Paul in his relationship to the Corinthians (2:2). The resur-

---

[14]Del Birkey, *The House Church: A Model for Renewing the Church* (Scottdale PA: Herald Press, 1988).

rection narrative guides the church toward the new age (15:4-5). Other issues, like food offered to idols or clothing worn during worship, apparently had no obvious connection with the Jesus tradition.

Since the story about Jesus, the Gospels, developed as a mutual interfacing between the needs of the church for guidance and the traditions about Jesus, it would be impossible to separate Jesus from the life of the church. So when we speak of Jesus we speak also of the early church. The quest for a so-called historical Jesus assumes there was, behind our Gospels, a man who had a certain independent self-consciousness and who intended certain things for his followers. For some, such a Jesus has an authority beyond the Jesus of our Gospels. That necessitates a Jesus not related to his community. To the contrary, the resurrected Lord formed and was formed by the early church.

About ten years after the writing of 1 Corinthians, a Gospel (Mark) appeared that stressed primarily the story about Jesus. That Jesus was firmly rooted in the history of Palestine about 30 CE. Another tradition also appeared which reported nearly nothing of the story of Jesus, but contained his sayings (closely identified with the Gospel of Thomas). The Gospels of Matthew and Luke, as we know them, contain both the sayings and the story of Jesus—a Jesus of history united with the life of the early church. Those who saved the sayings only became more and more spiritualistic, detached from their own history and detached from the Jesus of history. More and more they cared only for the ideas. We call them the early Christian gnostics, and we know them primarily through the recently found documents of Nag Hammadi.

KERYGMA

The reader of the New Testament can discern a pattern in the sermons and the traditional sections of the letters. That pattern has come to be called the *kerygma* of the New Testament. A *kerygma* was a proclamation. In fact, the *kerygma* normally consisted of the repetition of a set message. The proclaimer, a *kerux,* simply repeated the message for those who could not hear the original. In a sense the *kerux* was a human loudspeaker system.

The repeated proclamation in the New Testament looks like this:

The prophecies are fulfilled, and the new Age is inaugurated
by the coming of Christ.
He was born of the seed of David.

He died according to the Scriptures,
to deliver us out of the present evil age.
He was buried.
He rose on the third day according to the Scriptures.
He is exalted at the right hand of God,
as Son of God and Lord of quick and dead.
He will come again as Judge and Savior of men.[15]

The fullest examples of a *kerygma* can be found in the speeches of
Acts (2:14-39; 3:13-26; 10:36-43; 13:17-41). Shorter forms can be
found primarily in the letters of Paul (Rom. 1:1-3; 8:34). In 1 Corinthians we find a complete *kerygma* tradition only in 15:3-7, though there
are allusions elsewhere such as 2:2, 2:8 and 8:11. These pieces of the
kerygma obviously derive from a time prior to Paul's writing of 1 Corinthians (15:3) and much earlier than the writing of Acts. The terse
style of these short summaries and their presence in early letters assure
us of their antiquity. For this reason some believe the preaching (*kerygma*) came first and then shorter stories about Jesus were used to fill
in the details (creating gospels).

While it is true that the *kerygma* can hardly be an abbreviated form
of a Gospel, still it is difficult to believe there was no set narrative to
which the earliest *kerygma* referred. Actually the *kerygma* picks up very
ancient faith sentiments. Fulfillment of the prophets refers to the
movement from promise to fulfillment, a theme central to the entire
Bible. Events have meaning because they fulfill God's promise to all
humanity. That is especially true of the Christ event. The reference to
Jesus as the son of David refers to the ancient promise that there would
always be a son of David (2 Sam. 7:16). The death and resurrection itself closely parallels the psalm of lament so popular in the Hebrew
Scriptures.[16] Indeed the story of the crucifixion can hardly be separated
from Psalm 22!

The *kerygma* rests deeply in the narrative world of the Hebrew
Scriptures and Judaism. As the stories of Jesus developed, based on this
Hebrew narrative world, at the same time the early church affirmed a
summary of the way the early faith corresponded with Hebrew expec-

---

[15]C. H. Dodd, *The Apostolic Preaching and Its Developments* (London: Hodder & Stoughton,
rpt. 1951; 1936) 17.

[16]John Dominic Crossan, *The Cross That Spoke* (San Francisco: Harper & Row, 1988).

tations. That is essentially our *kerygma*.

PARTIES AT CORINTH

Attempts to identify the parties at Corinth have ranged far beyond whatever problems were to be found in Corinth. In 1831 a German professor, Ferdinand Christian Baur of the University of Tübingen in Germany wrote about the parties at Corinth mentioned in 1:12.[17] Baur was a follower of the philosopher Hegel who had tried to show that history moved as a series of reactions. Some people would move in one direction, then others would react in another direction. For example, in our day when pro-choice people push their cause too far (thesis) then some (pro-life people) will react in the other direction (antithesis). Eventually some compromise may be reached that embodies both directions. For example, a compromise (synthesis) in the case of abortion might be to say abortion is normally unacceptable, but might be done in the case of rape.

Baur believed that the earliest church preached a gospel of freedom from law—specifically the Jewish law, though also legalism in general. Jesus and Paul taught us to be free. Paul carried this message of freedom to the Gentiles, but eager Jews, or even Jewish apostles, following him on his missionary journeys, tried to lay the Jewish law on his new converts. We see this especially in 2 Corinthians 10-13, where Paul might be referring to the so-called Judaizers as super apostles. The same hecklers appear in the letter to the Galatians (1:7). So the primary problem in Corinth, or any other Christian community, was, according to Baur, the reaction of Jewish elements to the new Christian movement. In 1:12 Baur assumed the quarrel existed between the party of Paul which represented freedom and the party of Peter which represented a turn toward Jewish law.

Scholars after Baur have taken very seriously this understanding of the quarrel. So most introductions assume Paul was at first very oriented toward freedom (as in 1 and 2 Corinthians, Romans and Galatians), but eventually became more "Jewish" or legalistic (as in the Pastoral Epistles). They would say that the Book of Acts represents the

---

[17]Ferdinand Christian Baur, "Die Christuspartei in der korinthischen Gemeinde, der Gegensatz des petrinischen und paulinischen Christenthums in der ältesten Kirche der Apostel Petrus in Rom," *Tübinger Zeitschrift für Theologie* 4 (1831): 61-206.

compromise or synthesis. In it Peter and Paul are presented as equals who were responsible for the beginning of the church in two different areas, Peter for the Jews and Paul for the Gentiles.

About the time the gnostic library of Nag Hammadi was discovered (see summary essay, 245), scholars began to question the basic assumption of the Baur theory. Not only did they deny the Hegelian basis for Baur's thesis, but they also doubted that the problem at Corinth was caused by Judaizers. Some scholars began to write about gnosticism at Corinth.[18] Eventually some supposed the real problem at Corinth was not Judaism, legalism, or immorality, but intense spirituality. Those who see gnostic types, or spiritualists, as the problem at Corinth tend to find in the Christ house church a party of Christians in conflict with the other house churches.

RESURRECTION

The concept of an afterlife has taken many different forms. That is as true today as it was then. We have anything from the resurrection of the physical body to the rebirth of the soul in another form. So was it then, in biblical times. A review of some of the options makes the resurrection described by Paul somewhat clearer.

Hebrew/Jewish. Basically, before the exilic period the Jewish people had no real sense of an afterlife. They spoke of an existence in Sheol (Psalm 139:8), but not of an afterlife (1 Sam. 28:14 may be an exception). While for some the lack of an afterlife might create immorality (eat, drink, and be merry, for tomorrow we die), for the Jews the reverse was true. Since this was the only life in which to serve God, then its three-score-and-ten counted for everything. One's life took meaning from those years, and those only.

Greek intellectual. Based on a Platonic understanding of the world, many Greeks believed that the physical body (*soma*) was an earthen vessel that had no lasting value. The body held in it a soul (*psuche*) that, upon the death of the physical body, entered into an eternal existence. By the time of Paul, and later, many intellectuals considered the body evil, an earthly prison for the eternal soul. Those we call gnostic related to this position in a general way.

---

[18]Walther Schmithals, *Gnosticism in Corinth: An Investigation of the Letters to the Corinthians*, trans. John E. Steely (Nashville: Abingdon Press, 1971).

Popular Greco-Roman. While the philosophical position of the Greek world favored immortality of the soul, there is little evidence of that among the average folk. In everyday life death marked a transition into a new way of participating in family and community life. The dead were buried in family houses built in cities of the dead (*necropolis*) located outside cities and towns. The family continued to commune with the dead by eating with them and seeking their help.

Apocalyptic Judaism. During the intertestamental period, beginning about 200 BCE, Judaism underwent some radical changes. Some Jews began to suspect the Jewish people would not fulfill the promises of God. They saw God bringing an end to human history and beginning a new age under the rule of a divine figure (the Lord). There developed then an understanding that every person would, at the end of life, or the end of this age, be raised into a new life. In the canon of the Hebrew Bible we can see that sense of resurrection in Daniel 12:2. It occurs elsewhere in noncanonical literature and then in the New Testament (Lk. 20:27-38). The Pharisees believed in the resurrection. That belief is probably related to the apocalypticism.

Resurrection in Paul. One can immediately see that Paul's understanding of the resurrection fits best the apocalyptic style. In his earliest extant letter, 1 Thessalonians, he described the resurrection in terms almost identical with intertestamental apocalypticism (4:13-18). In Rom. 6:5-11 death and resurrection mark the end of slavery to self and the beginning of a new life in Christ. That happens in life at baptism, but it also happens at death.

In the early church the Pauline understanding of the resurrection probably linked with the Greco-Roman. Early Christians buried their relatives and families in Christ much as the non-Christians, except they stressed the primacy of martyrs and leaders. The resurrection was not physical. Attempts to stifle the first Christians by destroying their physical bodies had no effect whatsoever. The dead, even without physical bodies, were still present as part of the family and the community. The resurrection was understood as the shift of the living into a new way of relating to those left alive.

During the medieval period the Greek intellectual view gained ascendancy in Christendom. Then resurrection became the way the soul ascended to heaven. The combination of the Greek understanding of immortality with the resurrection brought such scenarios as Dante's description of hell, where bad souls were punished, or the Catholic doctrine of purgatory, where the dead entered a period of trial. Even though the Reformation in part came as a rejection of the Catholic view of purgatory and indulgences, still the Reformers kept a sense of individual immortality.

The Left Wing of the Reformation tended to reject the medieval picture of heaven and hell. The disciple follows Jesus regardless of awards and punishments. Being a disciple of Jesus means continuing with Jesus to the endtime. For such Christians Jesus and his disciples will eventually become the way for God to bless all the families on earth (Gen. 12:1-3), that is, a universal resurrection.[19]

SATAN

For many cultures there is a dualism between heaven and earth, God and creation, spirit and flesh. The Judeo-Christian culture does not share in the dualistic sense of evil. There is only one power, one reality, one God (Deut. 6:4). That God created the world by speaking (Gen. 1:3). The world does not have a separate existence, but constantly depends on the power of God's Word (John 1:1-3). Jews and Christians believe that the creation is good and that all people participate in that goodness. Children are born good as participants in the goodness of creation. Notions that children are evil do not derive from the biblical material (as in some interpretations of "original sin"). Since in a monistic system (one reality instead of two) evil cannot be caused by opposing forces of good and bad, it must arise from the process of formation. Of all New Testament writers Paul is most clear at this point.

Evil derives from our eagerness to seek our own self-fulfillment, our desire to be mature without going through the process of "growing up." The formation process becomes ruptured and people act toward each other in ways which are either unloving or destructive. Everyone does this (Adam and Eve in the garden, Gen. 3), though it happens in different ways in various contexts (often according to one's place in society).

Just as evil arises in the formation process, so does Satan. In the Hebrew Bible Satan was a prosecuting attorney, most famous for his accusations against Job. Satan was a member of the court of Yahweh (Job 1:6; Zech. 3:1). Because the function or role of Satan was that of pro-

---

[19]Troeltsch, *The Social Teaching of the Christian Churches*, 1:339

tecting the law and the community, Satan eventually "tempted" persons, broken in their formation with God, into destructive attitudes and behavior. When one is broken with God, the law and the community appear opposed to our own self-interest. So, when we are threatened with corporate power and law, we are tempted to protect ourselves with even more individualism (rebellion), or to curry favor with the community by meek submission (entrapment). In either case we rupture the formation process even more.

Just as Satan can appear as the tempter because of our brokenness with God, so other persons can become satanic to us because of ruptures in the formation process (Gen. 3; Rom. 7). Some persons always appear to be defending the status quo either by enforcing the regulations or rewarding those who remain subservient. Such persons will become satanic, and we can no longer act as we would like (Rom. 7:7-25). They are not really evil, but they will appear that way to some persons. When the formation process is dysfunctional, a parent often will appear satanic to a child. The same will be true of local and national leaders. Such corporate persons always appear to be a threat to the individuality of some people. Therefore they become the source of that temptation which leads to aberrant behavior. Because evil arises from ruptures in the formation process, Christians are very concerned about the development of family and community. The faith community is one in which the rupture has been healed by Christ, where neither God nor others can appear satanic (Rom. 8:1-17).

SPIRIT

Central to the Judeo-Christian faith is the belief that God has made certain promises that eventually will surely be fulfilled. The power of the ethical life lies in the certainty that some day the wolf and the lamb will feed together, the lion will eat straw like the ox (Isa. 65:25), death will be no more, and neither shall there be mourning or crying or pain (Rev. 21:4). Because we believe this day will come to pass we give our lives to peace, justice, and love. We say that God is acting in history to fulfill these promises.

How does God act in history? We are accustomed to say that the churches are the hands and feet of God. That is true. The Bible is the narrative of God using persons to fulfill the promise. But how do such persons act on God's behalf? What guides them? In the Bible we call that guidance the activity of the Spirit. The Spirit is God's power to guide the human community toward the endtime.

Every group of persons is led by some spirit. We can easily observe that. At a sports event, at a political rally, in a riot, in a battle, people do things they would not ordinarily do as individuals. A group has its own life and its own dynamics, which can override the judgments, restrictions, and limitations set by the single person. What we call spirit is that energy of a group that can guide or even control the members. When we discern that Spirit is of God, we call it the Holy Spirit (see 1 Cor. 14:29-32).

The activity of the Spirit of the Lord is quite apparent in the Hebrew Bible. Under threatening circumstances the Spirit would raise up leaders who liberated the Hebrew people (Judges 6:34; 11:29). At other times the effect of the Spirit seemed much like that of surrounding cultures. For example, in the presence of other prophets Saul received the Spirit of God and apparently could divine in the same way they could (1 Sam. 10:9-13).

The New Testament understanding of Spirit follows fairly closely that of the Hebrew Bible. The Spirit empowers the people of God. There are a variety of ways this can happen. These ways overlap, but some are more distinctive in certain authors than in others. Three styles are most apparent: the Spirit and the life of the church; the Spirit and the mission of the church; the Spirit and the adaptation of the church.

The Spirit and the life of the church can be seen most clearly in the letters of Paul. Paul describes the life of the Spirit over against the life of the flesh. Flesh or *sarx* represents the attempt of every person to live for one's self, for one's individual self identity. To live by the Spirit is to know that one's self fulfillment comes through covenant relationships and openness to the faith community. According to Paul the fruits of the Spirit are things like love, joy, and peace, while among the fruits of the flesh are immorality, impurity, anger, dissension, and jealousy (Gal. 5:16-24). Besides greatly effecting the quality of life for every person, the Spirit also causes persons to take responsibility for corporate life. In 1 Corinthians 12 and Romans 12:3-8 Paul described how the Spirit worked in the congregation to create those roles necessary for the proper functioning of the faith community. The Spirit not only raised up prophets, teachers and helpers, but also administrators and interpreters. In short, for Paul the Spirit organizes the faith community for its God-given tasks and simultaneously grants those endtime kinds of personal satisfactions exemplified by peace, love, and joy.

In contrast to Paul's writings we find in Luke-Acts the Spirit actively guiding the church in its mission to fulfill God's promise. It was the Spirit that convinced Peter of the validity of a Gentile mission (Acts 10:19, 47). It was the Spirit that determined the direction of the mission of Paul in Asia Minor (Acts 16:6-10). It was *lack* of the Spirit that distinguished the wandering disciples of John from early Christians (Acts 19:1-7). Like the Spirit in the church at Corinth the Spirit in Acts caused ecstatic states (Acts 19:7), and probably divination (Acts 21:9). And, as in Paul, the Spirit also guided the life of the faith community. The sin of Ananias and Sapphira was to lie to the Holy Spirit about their financial assets (Acts 5:1-11). It was reception of the Holy Spirit which caused Saul turned Paul to regain his sight and to enter the Damascus faith community (Acts 9:17-19). But primarily the Spirit in Luke-Acts directs the faith community in its mission. "But you shall receive power when the Holy Spirit has come upon you; and you shall be my witnesses in Jerusalem and in all Judea and Samaria and to the end of the earth." (Acts 1:8)

In the Gospel of John the Spirit performs yet another function. The Spirit will lead the Christians into all truth (John 16:12-13), and will create in later Christians even greater works than those done by Jesus (John 14:12-14). The Spirit or Comforter continues in new and greater ways the Word-become-flesh (John 1:14). Here the Spirit is the powerful impact of Jesus the Incarnate on later generations. The impact is so powerful it can continue to influence the world to our day and can guide the church in new times. To a lesser extent we can speak of the spirit of George Washington, Abraham Lincoln, or Martin Luther King, Jr., as the continuing influence of these great leaders. The ultimate power on all later generations is that of Jesus Christ as expressed through the Holy Spirit.

VIRGIN

The Greek term *parthenos,* virgin, occurs in Paul's writings in the passage 1 Cor. 7:25-38, and once more in 2 Cor. 11:2 as a metaphor of the Corinthian church (translated "pure bride" in the RSV). In 1 Cor. 7:25-38 most persons translate *parthenos* as unmarried. As can be seen in the commentary on that passage, "unmarried" seems to be the appropriate translation, since the demarried, or previously married, are addressed in 7:1-9. But because the *parthenos* who delays her marriage can better serve the Lord, one might ask if other meanings lie underneath Paul's thought. It is clear that *parthenos* ought not be defined strictly as a woman who has not had sexual intercourse. The term also carries with it a religious or even covenantal overtone. Well known are the arguments that the term "virgin," as applied to Mary, the mother of Jesus, refers primarily to her willingness to accept the role given her by God and to submit to God's will. The Septuagint (Greek) translator of Isaiah 7:14 (see Mt. 1:23) probably used the term *parthenos* for the Hebrew *'almah* in order to describe the expected character of the messiah's mother.

Paul also thinks of these characteristics or else he would not have spoken of the church as a *parthenos* for Christ. By the turn of the century the religious use of the term became clear. Ignatius, bishop of Antioch around the year 114, wrote to the church at Smyrna and asked them to greet the *parthenous* (virgins), who are called widows (*Epistle to the Smyrnaeans* 13.1). In the ninth parable of the Hermas (ca. 140 CE) there are twelve maidens (*parthenoi*) who are carrying the large stones which build the church (*Shepherd of Hermas,* Sim. 9). Apparently a group of women has developed that are central to the life of the church and are called *parthenoi* (virgins) even though they may actually be widows. Knowing this, the call of Paul to widows and widowers to remain unmarried now appears as much an appeal to serve the church community as it was to remain true to one's original vows.

Even by the third or fourth century there was not yet in Christianity an order of women who had never had intercourse, as there had been in the Roman society (vestal virgins). Not only was the term "virgin" given to widows who now served the Lord, but it was applied to women and men who had only married once. In an early undated inscription from Rome we find reference to a certain virgin, Sabina, who lived with her husband three years and twenty-five days (SICV #136).[20] In an early fourth-century inscription, Elia Vincentia is buried by her *virginium* (virgin husband) to whom she had been married 364 days (SICV #283).[21] As in 1 Cor. 7, the concern was not so much celibacy or virginity as it was faithfulness to the Lord, to the immediate faith community, and to spouse.

---

[20]Snyder, *Ante Pacem,* 131.

[21]Snyder, *Ante Pacem,* 132.

WIDOWS

The role of women in the earliest church has been much discussed. It is apparent a particular type of woman was present in the churches of the Gentile world. We note the importance of Lydia, a businesswoman of Thyatira (Acts 16:14), or Phoebe, a minister from Cenchreae who supported many in the Corinth area and probably intended to bankroll Paul's trip to Spain (Rom. 16:1-2). We know nothing about Chloe except the little we are told in 1:11, but we may suppose she also was a successful businesswoman from Corinth.

We have assumed there were any number of persons in the ancient world who wished to be attached to the Jewish faith. For various reasons some of these people could not become Jews. For some men, conversion to Judaism may have entailed financial ruin, social ostracization, or political suicide. On the other hand, women, in addition to the usual problems, could not become Jews without the conversion of their husbands. Women whose husbands would not convert, or whose husbands were dead, or who were not married, had little opportunity to becomes Jewesses. They must have comprised much of that group known to us as God-fearers, persons who wished to be Jews, but could not. We know of the type as a description of Cornelius (Acts 10:2), Lydia (Acts 16:14), and Titius Justus (Acts 18:7). Outside the New Testament the category is scarcely known. Inscriptions recently found in the Asia Minor city of Aphrodisias list among people associated with the local synagogue about ninety citizens known as God-fearers.[22]

We cannot estimate the composition of God-fearers from city to city, but we can reasonably assume a number were women, like Chloe and Lydia, who apparently had no husband, yet ran businesses on their own. During the second century these women appear to have grown in power among local congregations. According to early Christian literature, men held primary leadership in the churches, but, according to the apocryphal acts (e.g., Acts of Paul, Acts of Thomas, Acts of Peter) women were the most visible representatives of the church. Their dedication and heroic stances went beyond what men were willing to do.[23]

---

[22]Kenan T. Erim, *Aphrodisias: City of Venus Aphrodite* (New York: Facts on File Publications, 1986) 131.

[23]Stevan L. Davies, *The Revolt of the Widows: The Social World of the Apocryphal Acts* (Carbondale: Southern Illinois University Press, 1980).

WISDOM

In Hebrew history, as in all familial- or tribal-type organizations, the wise man (Job 29) or wise woman (2 Sam. 14:1-24; 20:16-22; Jer. 9:17) played a very important role. The wise person gave advice (Job 29:21); inspired confidence among the people (Job 29:24); and made judgments which protected the marginal (Job 29:10-17). These wise people functioned in the local village or town.

But in the court of the king there was another type of wise person. This group could discern signs and give political advice (2 Sam. 16:23). Some of the most famous wise men of the Hebrew Bible were Jews serving in a foreign court. Even though the advisors of Jewish kings were often mocked by the prophets, that mockery can hardly compare with the cynicism expressed for conventional royal advisors. Joseph was a Hebrew wise man who put to shame the magicians and wise men of Egypt (Gen. 41:1-45). Moses grew up in the court of Pharaoh. When he returned to seek the liberation of the Jewish people, he dueled, in a grisly fashion, the wise men of the court (Ex. 7-12). They matched him plague for plague until the gnats (8:18), but from that point to the death of the firstborn they had to concede defeat.

Even more instructive is the story of Daniel. Called to the court of Nebuchadnezzar, Daniel and his friends kept the Jewish dietary and religious laws. In contrast to the well-fed wise men of the royal court, Daniel was not only able to interpret dreams, but he could divine or make known the dream itself (Dan. 2:27-30).

For Joseph and Daniel dreams were revelations about historical and political directions. In Daniel these revelations were called mysteries (*razim*). In essence they represented the Jewish perspective on life and history. The wisdom of which Paul writes in 1 Corinthians 1–2 has much in common with that of Joseph and Daniel. He sees in Christ and the cross a wisdom that appears to be folly to nonbelievers. He speaks of this revelation as a wisdom hidden from others, a mystery or *mysterion* (Greek translation of the Hebrew *raz*, 1 Cor. 2:7). And like Joseph and Daniel, Paul reflects that the rulers do not know this wisdom, this interpretation of history (1 Cor. 2:8).

Primarily, then, wisdom for Paul is an apocalyptic understanding of history and life—a dying to the old age and being raised to the new. The cross is the symbol and paradigm for that divine wisdom. For this reason, Christ, himself, is the wisdom of God (1 Cor. 1:24). In the Hebrew Bible and in intertestamental literature, wisdom could be personified. We find examples of wisdom as a person in Job 28, Proverbs 7–8, Ecclesiasticus 24, and Wisdom of Solomon 7–8. Paul shifts this personification to Jesus whose death on the cross became the content of the revelation.

The prophets criticized the wise men for acting on behalf of themselves. They sought their own glory (Jer. 8:8-9). Paul keeps the same criticism of conventional wisdom, though in 1 Corinthians 1–2 applies it to the Greeks (1 Cor. 1:19-20, from Isaiah 29:14). Those who are wise in Christ will be wise for the glory of God.

BIBLIOGRAPHY

Albright, William Foxwell. *From the Stone Age to Christianity: Monotheism and the Historical Process*. 2nd ed. Garden City NY: Doubleday Anchor Books, 1957; [1]1940.

Banks, Robert. *Paul's Idea of Community: The Early House Churches in Their Historical Setting*. Grand Rapids: Eerdmans, 1980.

Barré, M. L. "To Marry or to Burn: *Pyrousthai* in 1 Cor 7:9." *Catholic Biblical Quarterly* 6 (1974): 193-202.

Barrett, C. K. *A Commentary on the First Epistle to the Corinthians*. Harper's New Testament Commentaries. New York: Harper & Row, 1968. In Great Britain: Black's New Testament Commentaries. London: Adam & Charles Black, 1968; [1]1957.

_____. "Christianity at Corinth." *Bulletin of John Rylands Library* 46 (1964): 269-97.

_____. "Cephas and Corinth." In *Essays on Paul*, 28-34. Philadelphia: Westminster Press, 1982.

Bartchy, S. Scott. *MALLON XPHSAI: First-century Slavery and the Interpretation of 1 Corinthians 7:21*. Society of Biblical Literature Dissertation Series. Missoula MT: University of Montana, 1973.

Bassler, Jouette. "1 Cor 12:3 Curse and Confession in Context." *Journal of Biblical Literature* 101 (1982): 415-18.

Bellah, Robert N., Richard Madsen, William M. Sullivan, Ann Swidler, and Steven M. Tipton. *Habits of the Heart: Individualism and Commitment in American Life*. New York: Harper & Row Perennial Library, 1985.

Berger, Peter L., and Thomas Luckmann. *The Social Construction of Reality: A Treatise in the Sociology of Knowledge*. Garden City NY: Doubleday/Anchor, 1967.

Birkey, Del. *The House Church: A Model for Renewing the Church*. Scottdale PA: Herald Press, 1988.

Brock, Rita Nakashima. *Journeys by Heart: A Christology of Erotic Power*. New York: Crossroad, 1988.

Broneer, O. "Corinth: Center of St. Paul's Missionary Work in Greece." *Biblical Archaeologist* 14 (1951): 78-96.

Brown, Peter. *The Cult of the Saints: Its Rise and Function in Latin Christianity*. The Haskell Lectures on History of Religion, New Series. Chicago: The University of Chicago Press, 1981.

Bruce, F. F. *1 and 2 Corinthians*. New Century Bible. Greenwood SC: The Attic Press, 1976; [1]1971.

Caird, G. B. *Principalities and Powers: A Study in Pauline Theology*. Oxford: Clarendon Press, 1956.

Conzelmann, Hans. *1 Corinthians. A Commentary on the First Epistle to the Corinthians*. Hermeneia. Trans. James W. Leitch. Philadelphia: Fortress Press, 1975.

Crossan, John Dominic. *In Parables: The Challenge of the Historical Jesus*. New York: Harper & Row, 1973.

Dahl, Nils Alstrup. "Paul and the Church at Corinth according to 1 Corinthians 1:10–4:21." In *Studies in Paul*, 40-61. Minneapolis: Augsburg, 1977; [1]1967.

Dodd, C. H. *The Apostolic Preaching and Its Developments*. London: Hodder & Stoughton, 1951; [1]1936. New York: Harper & Row, 1964; [1]1937.

Ellis, E. Earle. "Traditions in 1 Corinthians." *New Testament Studies* 32 (1986): 481-502.

Fee, Gordon D. *The First Epistle to the Corinthians*. The New International Commentary on the New Testament. Grand Rapids: Wm. B. Eerdmans, 1987.

Furnish, Victor P. *The Love Command in the New Testament*. Nashville: Abingdon Press, 1972.

Gager, John C. *Kingdom and Community: The Social World of Early Christianity*. Prentice-Hall Studies in Religion Series. Englewood Cliffs NJ: Prentice-Hall, 1975.

Gottwald, Norman. *The Tribes of Yahweh: A Sociology of the Religion of Liberated Israel 1250–1050 B.C.E.* Maryknoll NY: Orbis Books, 1979.

Green, Garrett. *Imagining God: Theology and the Religious Imagination*. San Francisco: Harper & Row, 1989.

Groff, Warren F. *Christ the Hope of the Future: Signals of a Promised Humanity*. Grand Rapids: Wm. B. Eerdmans, 1971.

Hays, Richard B. *Echoes of Scripture in the Letters of Paul*. New Haven CT: Yale Univers_ity Press, 1989.

Héring, Jean. *The First Epistle of Saint Paul to the Corinthians*. Trans. A. W. Heathcote and P. J. Allcock. London: The Epworth Press, 1962.

Holmberg, Bengt. *Paul and Power: The Structure of Authority in the Primitive Church as Reflected in the Pauline Epistles*. Philadelphia: Fortress Press, 1980; [1]1978.

Hooker, Morna D. "Authority on Her Head: An Examination of 1 Cor. xi 10." *New Testament Studies* 10 (1964): 410-16.

Hurd, John C. *The Origin of I Corinthians*. New York: Seabury Press; London: SPCK, 1965. Corr. rpt. (with new preface): Macon GA: Mercer University Press, 1983.

Jewett, Robert. *Paul's Anthropological Terms: A Study of Their Use in Conflict Settings*. Leiden: E. J. Brill, 1971.

—————. *A Chronology of Paul's Life*. Philadelphia: Fortress Press, 1979.

—————. *Christian Tolerance: Paul's Message to the Modern Church*. Biblical Perspectives on Current Issues. Philadelphia: Westminster Press, 1982.

Jordan, Clarence. *The Cotton Patch Version of Paul's Epistles*. New York: Association Press, A Koinonia Publication, 1968.

Juster, Jean. *Les Juifs dan l'empire romain: leur condition juridique, économique et sociale*. Paris: Librarie Paul Geuthner, 1914.

Kelber, Werner H. *The Oral and Written Gospel: The Hermeneutics of Speaking and Writing in the Synoptic Tradition, Mark, Paul, and Q*. Philadelphia: Fortress Press, 1983.

Kennedy, C. A. "The Cult of the Dead at Corinth." In *Love and Death in the Ancient Near East*. Guilford CT: Four Quarters Publishing, 1987.

Klassen, William. *The Forgiving Community*. Philadelphia: Westminster Press, 1966.

Laeuchli, Samuel, ed. *Mithraism in Ostia: Mystery Religion and Christianity in Ancient Port of Rome*. Writ. Dennis Groh. Preface by Giovanni Becatti. Evanston IL: Northwestern University Press, 1967.

Malina, Bruce. *The New Testament World: Insights from Cultural Anthropology*. Atlanta: John Knox Press, 1981.

Meeks, Wayne A. "'And Rose up to Play': Midrash and Paranesis in 1 Corinthians 10:1-22." *Journal for the Study of the New Testament* 16 (1982): 64-78.

_____. *The First Urban Christians: The Social World of the Apostle Paul*. New Haven: Yale University Press. 1983.

Morrison, Clinton D. *The Powers That Be: Earthly Rulers and Demonic Powers in Romans 1.1-7*. Studies in Biblical Theology 29. London: SCM Press. 1960.

Munck, Johannes. *Paul and the Salvation of Mankind*. Trans. Frank Clarke. Richmond VA: John Knox Press, 1959.

Murphy-O'Connor, Jerome. "Corinthian Slogans in 1 Cor 6:12-20." *Catholic Biblical Quarterly* 40 (1980): 91-96.

_____. " 'Baptized for the Dead' (I Cor., XV,29). A Corinthian Slogan?" *Revue biblique* 88 (1981): 52-54.

_____. *St. Paul's Corinth: Texts and Archaeology*. Intro. by John H. Elliott. Good News Studies. Wilmington DE: Michael Glazier, 1983.

Murray, Gilbert. *Five Stages of Greek Religion*. New York: Columbia University Press, 1930; [1]1925.

Orr, William F., with James Arthur Walther. *I Corinthians. A New Translation, Introduction with a Study of the Life of Paul, Notes, and Commentary*. Anchor Bible 32. Garden City NY: Doubleday & Co., 1977; [1]1976.

Reicke, Bo. *Diakonie, Festfreude, und Zelos*. Uppsala: Lundequistska, 1951.

Robinson, John A. T. *The Body: A Study in Pauline Theology*. Studies in Biblical Theology 5. London: SCM Press; Philadelphia: Westminster Press, 1952.

Roop, Eugene. *Genesis*. Believers Church Bible Commentary. Scottdale PA: Herald Press, 1987.

Royce, Josiah. *The Problem of Christianity*. Chicago: University of Chicago Press, rpt. 1968; [1]1918.

Ruef, John. *Paul's First Letter to Corinth.* Westminster Pelican Commentaries. Philadelphia: Westminster Press, 1977; [1]1971.

Schmithals, Walther. *Gnosticism in Corinth: An Investigation of the Letters to the Corinthians.* Trans. John E. Steely. Nashville: Abingdon Press, 1971; [1]1956.

Schweizer, Eduard. *The Church as the Body of Christ.* Richmond VA: John Knox Press, 1964.

Scroggs, Robin. *The Last Adam: A Study in Pauline Anthropology.* Philadelphia: Fortress Press, 1966.

——————. "Paul and the Eschatological Woman." *Journal of the American Academy of Religion* 40 (1972): 28-30.

——————. "Paul and the Eschatological Woman: Revisted." *Journal of the American Academy of Religion* 42 (1974): 52-57.

——————. *The New Testament and Homosexuality: Contextual Background for Contemporary Debate.* Philadelphia: Fortress Press, 1983.

Snyder, Graydon F. "The Tobspruch in the New Testament." *New Testament Studies* 2 (1976): 117-20.

——————. *Ante Pacem: Archaeological Evidence of Church Life Before Constantine.* Macon GA: Mercer University Press, 1985; pbk. rpt. 1991.

Theissen, Gerd. *The Social Setting of Pauline Christianity: Essays on Corinth.* Trans. and ed. John H. Schütz. Philadelphia: Fortress, 1982.

Thrall, Margaret E. *I and II Corinthians.* The Cambridge Commentary on the New English Bible. Cambridge: Cambridge University Press, 1965.

Tocqueville, Alexis de. *Democracy in America.* Rev. ed. 2 vols. Ed. Francis Bowen and Phillips Bradley. New York: Vintage, 1956; [1]1941.

Tracy, David. *The Analogical Imagination: Christian Theology and the Culture of Pluralism.* New York: Crossroads, 1981.

Troeltsch, Ernst. *The Social Teaching of the Christian Churches.* 2 vols. Trans. Olive Wyon. Intro. by Charles Gore. Halley Stewart Publications 1. London: George Allen & Unwin, 1950; [1]1931.

Turner, Victor. *The Ritual Process: Structure and Antistructure.* Symbol, Myth, and Ritual Series. Ithaca NY: Cornell University Press, 1969.

Wimbush, Vincent L. *Paul, the Worldly Ascetic: Response to the World and Self-understanding According to 1 Corinthians 7.* Macon GA: Mercer University Press, 1987.

Wink, Walter. *Naming the Powers: The Language of Power in the New Testament.* Philadelphia: Fortress Press, 1984.

TOPICAL INDEX